# Next Generation Datacenters in Financial Services

# Complete Technology Guides for Financial Services Series

## Series Editors

Ayesha Khanna

Jürgen Kaljuvee

## Series Description

Industry pressures to shorten trading cycles and provide information-on-demand are forcing firms to re-evaluate and re-engineer all operations. Shortened trading cycles will put additional emphasis on improving risk management through front-, middle-, and back-office operations. Both business and IT managers need to effectively translate these requirements into systems using the latest technologies and the best frameworks.

The books in the **Complete Technology Guides for Financial Services Series** outline the way to create and judge technology solutions that meet business requirements through a robust decision-making process. Whether your focus is technical or operational, internal or external, front, middle, or back office, or buy vs. build, these books provide the framework for designing a cutting-edge technology solution to fit your needs.

We welcome proposals for books for the series. Readers interested in learning more about the series and Elsevier books in finance, including how to submit proposals for books in the series, can go to: http://www.books.elsevier.com/finance

## Other Titles in the Series

*Introduction to Financial Technology* by Roy S. Freedman
*Electronic and Algorithmic Trading Technology* by Kendall Kim
*Straight Through Processing for Financial Services* by Ayesha Khanna

# Next Generation Datacenters in Financial Services

## Driving Extreme Efficiency and Effective Cost Savings

*Tony Bishop*

AMSTERDAM • BOSTON • HEIDELBERG • LONDON • NEW YORK • OXFORD
PARIS • SAN DIEGO • SAN FRANCISCO • SINGAPORE • SYDNEY • TOKYO

ELSEVIER

30 Corporate Drive, Suite 400, Burlington, MA 01803, USA
525 B Street, Suite 1900, San Diego, California 92101-4495, USA
84 Theobald's Road, London WC1X 8RR, UK

**Library of Congress Cataloging-in-Publication Data**
Application submitted.

**British Library Cataloguing-in-Publication Data**
A catalogue record for this book is available from the British Library.

ISBN: 978-0-12-374956-7

For information on all Elsevier publications
visit our Web site at www.elsevierdirect.com

Typeset by Macmillan Publishing Solutions,
www.macmillansolutions.com

Printed in the United States of America

09  10  11  12    9  8  7  6  5  4  3  2  1

Working together to grow
libraries in developing countries

www.elsevier.com | www.bookaid.org | www.sabre.org

ELSEVIER    BOOK AID
            International    Sabre Foundation

# Contents

The companion website containing an image collection of all the figures in the text can be found at: www.elsevierdirect.com/companions/9780123749567

# Series editors' preface

We are extremely pleased to have Tony Bishop's excellent, timely, and highly relevant book on datacenters as part of our 2009 list of publications in the **Complete Technology Guides for Financial Services Series**. Five trends in particular make the reinvention and streamlining of datacenters particularly relevant: (1) the credit crisis rippling across the globe has put a downward pressure on IT budgets; (2) the crisis has resulted in calls for more transparency and regulations that are embedded in IT controls; (3) energy efficiency has come to occupy top priority in the minds of governments, exemplified most strongly by President Obama's emphasis on it during his campaign and fiscal stimulus package; (4) even as the world economy slowly and painfully recovers from recession, the forces of globalization remain as strong as ever and continue to increase market competitiveness; and (5) the explosion in data continues unabated, and firms continue to struggle over how to make cost-effective, agile, and efficient use of this crucial data asset. All the aforementioned trends point to the dire need for better-managed datacenters—"the digital backbone of the organization"—which makes Bishop's book one of the leaders in the literature on this subject.

The book begins with a very persuasive argument on why today's datacenters are ill-designed and poorly equipped to respond to the challenges companies face. The traditional IT model has been a passive or reactive one, which responds to changes in business slowly, shackled both by its legacy architecture and its siloed delivery model. The new, far more successful IT model is one in which IT is more strongly partnered and aligned with the business, leverages the IT platform across departments, and dynamically reacts to the changing needs of the business in real time. This is known as the Real Time Enterprise (RTE).

So how does an organization adopt the RTE model? Bishop believes that the only way to achieve it is to align the demand and supply of IT via the Next Generation Datacenter (NGDC)—an abstract layer that provides access to all of the parts of the business platform, IT infrastructure, and operating model. The key to the success of the NGDC is that it employs a top-down approach to align business and IT—in other words, business demand drives the features, functionality, and operations of IT supply. The traditional way has been the other way around, which meant that business was constantly constrained in adapting to fluctuating market conditions by the static nature of IT services, and IT could never live up to its modern role of being a full partner to the corporation's strategic ambitions.

Not only does Bishop explain exactly how to implement this top-down approach, but he also provides useful metrics by which to measure the efficacy of this approach, such as Quality of Experience. Complete with extensive templates, checklists, and proven approaches, the book is invaluable to anyone who wants a step-by-step guide in how to set up modern datacenters. Bishop moves easily between key concepts in architecture and implementation, and planning, management and governance, linking them continually to business demand and requirements, providing a holistic approach that is often missing from such books. His rigorous approach to measuring the effects and root causes of IT performance, or lack thereof—the forensic methodology, ensures IT accountability and transparency.

The creation of the Next Generation Datacenter (NGDC), a new approach that is a vital step toward enhanced competitiveness and operational efficiency, is described clearly by Bishop in this book. His approach is as relevant to financial services institutions as it is to all government, telecom, education, media, and manufacturing sectors, to name just a few. By providing a detailed framework with concrete recommendations on how business and IT can align their strategic objectives to result in a dynamically responsive datacenter, Bishop's book is unprecedented in its completeness and unique in that it provides valuable insights into this complex area in a manner that is clear and action-oriented.

Ayesha Khanna
New York
Jürgen Kaljuvee
London

*Series Editors, Complete Technology Guides for*
*Financial Services Series*

# Preface

## A call to action

Each of us has had at least one absurd work situation, be it an impossible deadline that sets up a team for failure, a pennywise–pound foolish decision, or some seemingly crazy business mandate. Poor decision-making processes sometimes appear more like the rule than the exception. Why do we find ourselves in these situations more frequently than we care to admit? More important, what can we do to avoid them?

Talk with any senior manager in IT about the state of their union, and they'll be quick to point out that IT cannot continue as it has for the past two decades. No longer just back-office operations, IT now comprises a significant portion of *what the business is*. With the largest IT budgets surpassing $1 billion per year, businesses can no longer afford to allow IT to fumble about in the dark.

During the writing of this book, the full scope of the 2008 economic downturn is being felt. Organizations that were challenged by IT budgets have suddenly begun hemorrhaging. While sound fiscal policy is always prudent, history shows us it's difficult to save one's way to success. Savvy organizations know this is the best time to position and maneuver their organizations for future growth opportunities as the competition is hunkered down.

While traditional approaches to belt-tightening through smaller budgets and layoffs are sure to follow, they will have limited success and meet great resistance with controlling datacenter costs. The challenge is that the nature of datacenter operations makes it a very human-centric operation. Cut back too far, and production changes will slow to a crawl at the very moment when radical changes are needed to survive.

Prior to the economic downturn, organizations were slowly adopting a Real Time Enterprise operating model. As the fight for survival heats up, organizations will ramp up real-time abilities to react to the radical swings in the marketplace. Those who do not will be at the mercy of the marketplace, which has not been kind to the unprepared. IT must be prepared for the coming change to how business takes place, and IT must lead the charge.

In the process of helping bring control to an organization's fate, IT has the opportunity to transform how it goes about its job. The CIOs and CTOs of organizations have been reactive far too long, but they now have an opportunity to leverage today's business pressures to create new value.

This work is not another academic analysis about how we can all get along. Rather, it is a practical how-to handbook derived from volumes of trial and error. When fortune led me to the role of chief architect[1] in Wachovia's Corporate Investment Bank, I made one of the best decisions of my career: assemble a top-notch team of architects and engineers from a diverse background of companies. (Sadly, but fortunately for me, finding lots of talent frustrated with the status quo wasn't difficult.) The result was an explosion of ideas that led to a radical and successful transformation of the technology-delivery platform within Wachovia[2,3] and ultimately led to Adaptivity, a consulting firm that helps many companies transform their IT operations.

Working to change a paradigm is a calling and not for the faint of heart. I'm exceedingly grateful to have worked with individuals (far too numerous to individually name) who have shown the courage and boldness to make our collective efforts successful. May this guide help you and your organization along on your transformation journey.

Tony Bishop
Tony.Bishop@Adaptivity.com
Charlotte, NC
March 2009

---

[1]King J. 40 Under 40: 40 Innovative IT people to watch, under the age of 40—profile: Tony Bishop. *Computer World*. <http://ww.computerworld.com/action/article.do?command=viewArticleTOC&articleId=9025239&specialReportId=9000362&intsrc=article_sp_report_bot>. Accessed 09.07.2007.
[2]Bort J. The '06 Enterprise ALL-STAR issue: honoring 40 companies and their outstanding technology projects. *Network World*. <http://www.networkworld.com/allstar/2006/092506-grid-computing-personnel.html>. Accessed 25.09.2006.
[3]Babcock C. Information week 400: wachovia puts stock in a service-oriented architecture. *Information Week*. <http://www.informationweek.com/news/software/soa/showArticle.jhtml?articleID=201806191&pgno=1>. Accessed 18.09.2007.

# About the author

Tony Bishop is CEO of Adaptivity and an innovative IT executive with an excellent track record in strategy, design, and the implementation of business-aligned enterprise technology platforms across large organizations. Most recently, he served as SVP and chief architect of Wachovia's Corporate Investment Banking Technology Group, where his team designed, built, and implemented a leading-edge service-oriented architecture and Next Generation Datacenter utility-computing infrastructure.

Tony and his team have been recognized by the industry with awards from *InfoWorld, ComputerWorld, NetworkWorld, Waters,* and *Wall Street & Technology* for their efforts in building world-class technology to differentiate their business.

Tony has 20 years of experience working as a user and a supplier in various design, strategy, and architecture roles across multiple industries. He is the recipient of awards as the Top 40 Under 40: Most Innovative IT Leaders and Premier 100 IT Leaders, as selected by *ComputerWorld* in 2007, and a member of *Wall Street Gold Book 2007*. Tony has been an *InfoWorld* CTO advisory board member since 2006 and provides continuous thought leadership blogs for *InfoWorld (Real Time Enterprise Blog)* and *NetworkWorld (Intelligent Network Computing Blog)*.

# Book conventions

This book has numerous references to the creation of complex tables, where categories are projected onto an $x$-axis and $y$-axis. For each resulting cell, a question (or set of questions) is considered. By systematically asking this question(s) for each combination, a holistic view of the environment can be built in various contexts. Generally Mircosoft's Excel application is good at depicting matrix models as a spreadsheet.

For the sake of clarity, a shorthand notation has been developed to make it easier to communicate these large matrices. For example, the following shorthand would be used to depict a QoE Matrix.

---

**How to Create: Quality of Experience Matrix**

$x$-axis: BVC Category {BVC Subcategory}
         Research {Research}
         Sales and Trading {AES, Equities, Fixed Income, Foreign Exchange}
         Risk {Market, Credit, Counter Party, Trader}
         Back Office {Reporting, Settlement}

$y$-axis: Category {BVC Capability}
         Demand {Service Requirements, Processing Requirements}
         Supply {Implementation Patterns, Resource Consumption, Infrastructure Components, Infrastructure QoE Measurements}

$x$-$y$ **Cell Question(s):** What are the QoE characteristic expectations?

---

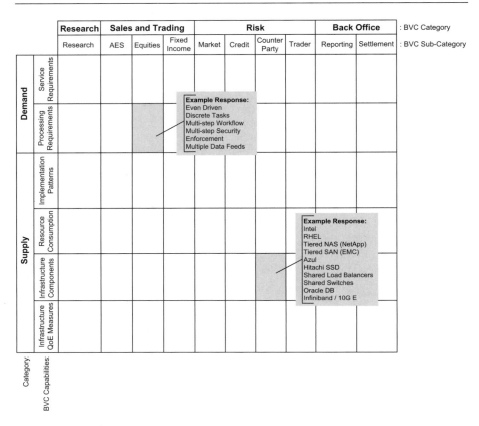

**Figure 1** Example QoE matrix.

This matrix would be depicted as shown in Figure 1.

Other examples of the matrix are those that include a hierarchy along one or both of the axes, depicted by indentions in the shorthand, like the following.

---

**How to Create: Hierarchical Matrix**

*x*-axis: BVC Category
  Research
  Sales and Trading
  Risk
  Back Office

*y*-axis: Category {Secondary Category}
  Level 1a {Level2a, Level2b, ... , Level2x}
  Level 1b {Level2a, Level2b, ... , Level2x}
  ...
  Level 1x {Level2a, Level2b, ... , Level2x}

*x*-*y* Cell Question(s): What are the characteristic expectations?

---

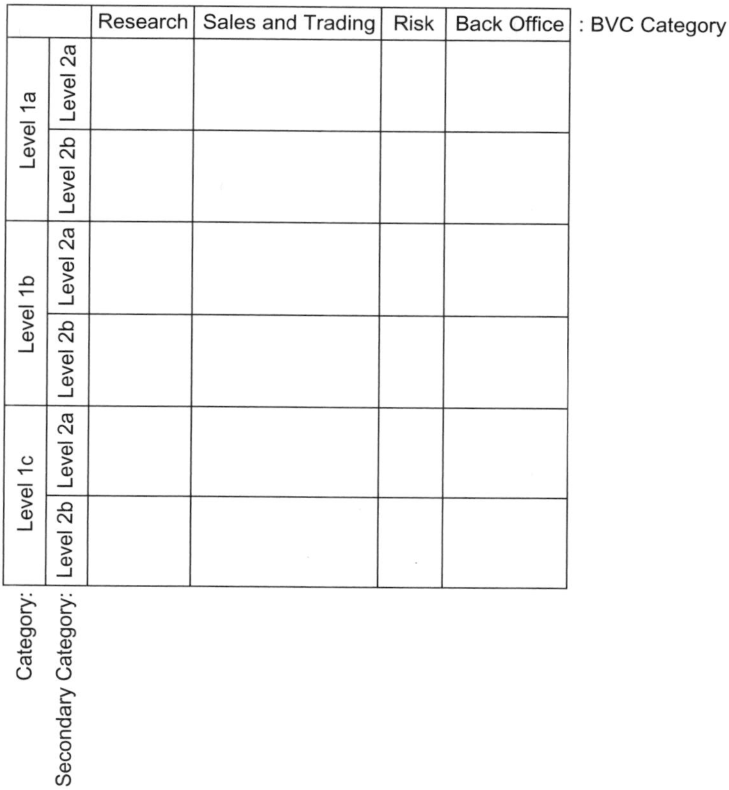

|  |  | Research | Sales and Trading | Risk | Back Office | : BVC Category |
|---|---|---|---|---|---|---|
| Level 1a | Level 2a |  |  |  |  | |
|  | Level 2b |  |  |  |  | |
| Level 1b | Level 2a |  |  |  |  | |
|  | Level 2b |  |  |  |  | |
| Level 1c | Level 2a |  |  |  |  | |
|  | Level 2b |  |  |  |  | |

Category:  
Secondary Category:

**Figure 2** Example hierarchical matrix.

This matrix would be depicted as shown in Figure 2.

Note how the secondary category repeats for each main category entry. It's possible for the hierarchy to be multiple levels deep and also to be hierarchical on the $x$-axis.

# 1 The accelerating demand for datacenters

*It is not necessary to change; survival is not mandatory.*
—*Dr. W. Edwards Deming*

## Key Points

The demand for datacenter space continues to grow, but the business isn't able to support that growth rate using traditional means.

Current legacy infrastructure environments pose a threat to growth and survival for financial services firms in the post-2008 mortgage crisis climate. The time is right to consider ways to deploy more efficient and flexible datacenters.

Today's business climate places greater demand on IT organizations. They face a dual challenge of "keeping the lights on" while providing new services at unprecedented rates with reduced investment support from the business. At the same time, the very business model of IT is changing; how applications, content, information, and infrastructure are delivered. Organizations have come to rely on datacenter services for their external facing customer experience, corporate branding, and internal operational systems. Disruptions in this service can induce significant financial losses or even paralyze an organization completely.

One of the biggest barriers to business execution and innovation today is datacenter complexity. As a result, the major part of IT investment expenses (87 percent of the IT budget)[1] is earmarked for keeping operations running and containing infrastructure sprawl.

Approximately 83 percent of CEOs expect substantial change in the next three years, but only 39 percent did not feel their organizations were ready for that change.[2] The enterprise's inability to devote a majority of its time and investment dollars on innovating and differentiating business through IT results in missed expectations and disappointment within the business user community.

---

[1]Smith M, et al. *IT Spending and Staffing Report, 2008. Gartner*, Id#G00154809; February 20, 2008.
[2]Korsten P, et al. *The Enterprise of the Future*. IBM; 2008.

doi: 10.1016/B978-0-12-374956-7.00001-2

# 1.1   State of the datacenter today

During the last decade, organizations have become increasingly dependent on their datacenter environments, which effectively house the digital backbone of the organization. The pressure to technologically keep up with the competition has created a proliferation of datacenters full of massive amounts of technology resources. This pressure particularly affected the banking and financial services sectors.

The February 2008 *Gartner IT Budget Survey* showed that banking and financial services firms led the way in IT spending at about 7 percent of total revenue (12.6 percent of all operating expenses).[3] This growth was sustained by the highest operating margin of any other industry (about 35 percent). The result was technological innovations in delivering financial services that were generating tremendous returns. In the process, datacenters with thousands of servers and other resources proliferated.

Several factors have come together to create the perfect storm:

1.   The economic downturn of 2008 and expected increase in regulatory requirements
2.   The increasing rate of change to the business model and its implementation in the infrastructure
3.   The growth of IT spending versus revenue generation
4.   The diminishing returns of additional optimizations
5.   The exponential growth of data
6.   The overall lack of efficiency from existing datacenters.

All of these factors will cause a change of behavior of IT and datacenters utilization in financial services organizations.

The end result is that the business must take a very hard look at all of its IT expenditures. Careers will be made and broken in the process. There's a general sense that IT is spending too much for too little. Controlling the rate of spending just to keep existing datacenters operational will be a challenge for some organizations. Altogether, the current trends in datacenter growth do not bode well for the future of IT and businesses.

## 1.1.1   *Credit crisis and regulatory requirements*

The credit crisis and the economic climate of 2008 have radically altered the banking and financial services landscape.[4] In short, the securitization of debt—the engine that has driven the financial industry for the past twenty years—is now out of favor. This, combined with the resulting government bailout, will impact financial institutions for years to come. Transactions and their related

---

[3]Smith M, et al. *IT Spending and Staffing Report, 2008. Gartner*, Id#G00154809; February 20, 2008.
[4]Tabb L. *Lehman, Merrill and Bear—Oh My*. TABB Group; September 14, 2008.

fees are depressed and entire business models in structured products no longer function. As a result, revenue is down significantly, and the banking industry will be preoccupied with reinventing its business model for the foreseeable future.

IT budgets will be negatively affected by the poor performance of the organization. This comes at a time when funds will be needed to drive business innovation as the organization not only reinvents itself but meets the increased regulatory requirements the government will undoubtedly impose. IT will be challenged in meeting these two objectives, but it must be done if it is to survive. Reusing existing assets and repurposing those assets from defunct businesses will be critical to success (see Chapter 3).

### 1.1.2   Trends in real-time enterprise transformation

One recent trend in business is to become more reactive to real-time events. The traditional organization is slow to react to events as they take place and tends to sporadically adjust its activities. In contrast, the *real-time enterprise* works continuously to remove lag in response to events. By being more responsive, it's possible to rapidly change direction and affect the outcome of events. The current datacenter model is poorly prepared to support a real-time enterprise. Changes in the environment often take weeks or months, which is much too long. The business may be aware of events as they occur, but without the proper support mechanisms in place, it is unable to respond appropriately. Then IT is seen as an impediment rather than a solution. As this trend grows, pressure will mount for IT to get out of the way or get on board (see Chapter 3).

### 1.1.3   IT spending versus revenue growth

Traditionally, when a datacenter reached capacity, IT made a business case for building a new facility. But with a modern datacenter costing hundreds of millions of dollars, preparing the facility for the first server is costly indeed. When the economy was humming along, the business was content to feed funds into IT to continue the growth of the datacenter. Now that the economy is on the rocks, the business will have difficulty investing funds into datacenters, never mind building entire new ones. If the organization is short on any capacity, it's unlikely that IT will get any support for building yet another multimillion-dollar facility.

To avoid these challenges, IT must begin to track directly with business growth. Initiatives like *utility computing* have made headway, but they aren't enough. The challenge is that while the business operates in terms of transactions, applications, and services, IT operates silos of resources like servers, network, and SAN. Being aligned will require IT to define its services as directly mapped with business activities (see Chapter 3).

### 1.1.4   Diminishing returns of further optimization

The last decade saw IT devote a lot of attention to optimizing the process of deploying resources into the datacenter and operating the applications running on them. This improvement process is at a point of diminishing returns that can no longer keep up with the accelerating business demand. IT groups are very thinly sliced in their capabilities such that in large organizations it takes the coordination of many disparate groups to effect a change. As the business continues pushing to increase the rate of change to be able to respond to business events, IT will need to figure out how to meet these goals. Provisioning servers and other resources is only a small part of the overall challenge of making rapid changes and increasing utilization. As will be discussed in depth in Chapter 4, virtualization is part of the solution, but it is not the solution in and of itself.

Technology alone can provide moments of competitive advantage, but they are not sustainable in isolation. The competition also has access to the latest technology and will catch up sooner or later (usually sooner). The creation of *sustainable competitive advantages* has long been promised by IT, though few organizations can actually claim they've accomplished this goal. The creation of tailored IT services in direct alignment with business operations can create the desired sustainable competitive advantage (see Chapter 3).

### 1.1.5   Exponential data growth

Markets are witnessing an unprecedented explosion in the availability of data, and firms are eager to leverage this information to increase their profits and expand their opportunities in a global world. Firms are capturing more data than ever before. Not only is the number of transactions increasing due to volatility, but the velocity of transactions is increasing as well. In some industries, such as capital markets, the volume of trades has increased by as much as 100 percent. In addition, there is increasing regulatory pressure from governments to store information for accounting and reporting purposes. With data also comes a new breed of experts who are helping firms crunch and mine this data to make analytical forecasts and use this information to enter new markets and float new products. These analytical tools and methods in turn create additional data to process and utilize.

The amount of data that firms must store today is unprecedented. Chris Anderson, author of *The Long Tail*, calls this the Petabyte[5] Age (a petabyte is a unit of information or computer storage equal to one quadrillion bytes, or 1000 terabytes). In such an environment, the CIO needs the ability to lead an effective data strategy to capture, process, and connect data to all the relevant lines of business (see Chapter 4).

---

[5]Anderson C. The end of theory: the data deluge makes the scientific method obsolete. *Wired Magazine*. June 23, 2008.

### *1.1.6  Lack of efficiency*

In order to keep up with demand, firms have been rushing to invest in datacenters, but they are finding that just throwing technology at the problem is not good enough. Datacenter facility utilization is less than 50 percent, leading to huge inefficiencies and costs, not to mention the increasing carbon footprint that every firm is keen to reduce. The prominent cause of poor efficiency is the inability to match demand to capacity planning dynamically. Companies aggressively pursued new technologies, servers, and datacenters, but they did not focus on the effective use of these facilities.

The resulting sprawl has also led to space, power, and cooling capacity problems. The advent of the high-density blade chassis helped resolve the space problems, but it didn't solve the systemic problem; rather, it just moved it to power and cooling. In a 2007 Gartner survey, 74 percent of respondents identified power and cooling as the primary issues with their datacenter facilities.[6] (This is up from 46 percent in 2004.) A more holistic strategy is needed that will optimize the utilization of all aspects of the datacenter resources (see Chapter 4).

## 1.2   The next-generation datacenter

The next few years will require savvy strategies from IT. More than ever, the business needs IT as a partner to drive business innovation. The challenges are many and are difficult, but there is hope. In the chapters that follow, a full examination of the challenges of today's datacenter will be analyzed, and proven solutions will be presented. The next-generation datacenter must meet all of today's challenges, while being much more cost effective and in tune with business (see Chapter 3).

The basic premise is that by understanding the Business Value Chain (BVC) and how the business generates value, a Digital Supply Chain (DSC) can be tailored to meet those demands. This is accomplished through the design of packaged infrastructure ensembles that implement a platform specifically tailored to the needs of applications and services that run within that portion of the BVC. The collection of ensembles that make up a stage of the BVC are physically grouped together in a Process Execution Destination (PED). The resulting PEDs logically subdivide the datacenter by BVC stages. This has a number of primary effects:

1.  An application/service's computer infrastructure is situated with the other applications/services that it is most likely to communicate with, reducing contention.
2.  The computing resources are no longer generic and are now tuned to the type of workload running.

---

[6]McGuckin P. *2007 Datacenter Conference Poll Results for Power and Cooling Issues. Gartner,* Id# G00155355; March 18, 2008.

3.  This switches IT's focus from delivery of isolated silos of technology resources to high-level services aligned with the business.
4.  This grouping helps mitigate technology risk by providing a clear view of what's required to restore business capabilities in a disaster recovery scenario.

These new services must be supported by a real-time infrastructure (RTI) that can move resources in and out of the prepackaged ensembles as needed dynamically. This requires a much more encompassing infrastructure strategy; including aspects of making sure resources fit the need (Fit-for-Purpose), virtualization, and utility computing (see Chapters 4 and 5).

The result is that IT services provide platform-level computing resources aligned with the way the business is operating and valued. This tailored approach to managing IT has the added benefit of creating operations that are exceedingly difficult to duplicate and thus can create a significant sustainable competitive advantage.

All of the underlying complexity of how these resources are configured and managed still exists, but the way they are consumed is abstracted away from the business. Note that this isn't a free pass to allow a veneer on top of existing IT services; the change needs to be holistic from top to bottom (see Chapter 4).

By starting with small projects and putting in the first building blocks of the new operating model (Chapter 5), followed by the comprehensive development of playbook strategies to implement change (Chapter 6), and finally large comprehensive transformation programs (Chapter 7), it is possible to realize this next-generation datacenter.

In the end, a next-generation datacenter changes the deployment model of how resources are consumed (Chapter 8), valued, and measured (Chapter 9). Adopting this model will also make it easier to farm out aspects of the datacenter, which until now were considered too complex to consider. At a time when datacenter expenditures are coming under heavy fire, it's a significant advantage for the CTO and CIO to have a comprehensive strategy that puts all of the options on the table.

# 2 Challenges in legacy architecture

*"But O the truth, the truth. The many eyes that look on it! The diverse things they see."*

—George Meredith, English novelist & poet (1828–1909)

## Key Points

IT and the business are not aligned in their goals. Because partnerships are strained and common ground for communication can be broken, one of the most important and expansive enterprise investments, the datacenter, impedes growth, has runaway unpredictable costs, and does not support business agility.

The past decade has witnessed unprecedented growth in Financial Services IT due to the Y2K, Internet, new regulations in light of dotcom scandals, new antiterrorism measures, and rapidly growing global and mortgage securities markets. IT has been overwhelmed on many fronts.

Most datacenters work fine now, but what is not obvious is that they work only as long as expenditures can be supported. Since there is not a linear relationship between cost and growth, the moment growth is slowed, the apparent differences become pronounced, and the datacenter becomes a cost liability, especially since 2008.

Change is the most consistent and pervasive business driver for large financial services enterprises. All enterprises are affected by changes in market conditions, the dynamic interconnections of the global economy, new regulations, and continuously evolving customer demands. The pace of this global change has become a force of its own; it is the impetus for greater change. The economic crisis of 2008, precipitated by the mortgage crisis in the United States, illustrated how interconnected all aspects of financial services truly are. As a result, business will pursue diverse change in oversight, risk assessment, and comprehensive decision making, yet the pressure to drive revenue and efficiency will not abate.

Large-scale enterprises are not the only victims of change; senior business executives encourage and champion change and use it to fuel growth. Change is perceived as both an asset and a liability for any financial services firm because the firm's *value chain* (e.g., services and products) drives and fuels revenue. Services are utilized to process requests that include new and existing products, all designed to generate revenue while defraying risk, which is even more salient after the 2008 crisis.

doi: 10.1016/B978-0-12-374956-7.00002-4

The fast-paced world of financial services not only includes capital markets but wealth management, investment banking, and commercial and retail banking, combined with the growing base of international banking. The manifestation of these products is often digitally delivered, which brings the technology to deliver them to the forefront of any financial services business.

As regulatory environments continuously expand and evolve, and executive pressure to discover or create new revenue opportunities increases, it's clear that change will continue to dominate the financial services IT environment for the foreseeable future. It's also clear that investment into IT infrastructure can't be funded at previous levels, when the mindset that ruled was "I don't care what it costs. Just get it done." IT departments at financial services organizations must work smarter, not harder.

This may be a fine sentiment, but it is somewhat intangible. In order to deliver more with less, financial institutions must take an introspective look at their IT practices and make some tough choices. The typical knee-jerk reaction to this type of environment is to downsize staff and execute the same processes with fewer individuals. While this tactic may work over the short term, the depth of the needed cuts, combined with the increased demand for changes to IT systems, will make it impractical over the long term. If driven too hard for too long without adequate rewards, talent will flee the industry, leaving those with inadequate skill sets to carry the load. A more effective solution is needed that doesn't cannibalize the future of the financial services industry's ability to execute.

Identifying a target for significant improvement isn't difficult. For most organizations, the datacenter and the supporting infrastructure and personnel are the largest cost centers, which, when measured objectively, are both very capital intensive and resource wasteful. The question becomes how to improve the efficiency of the datacenter. Hundreds, if not thousands, of incremental improvements have been experimented with over the course of the past decade to raise datacenter efficiency. Progress has been made, but underlying fundamental problems have not been resolved. Achieving any measurable improvement will require a different approach, not just more of the same, only faster. The development of a go-forward strategy requires a definitive understanding of the past and how it affects the future.

## 2.1   IT's dilemma: remodeling the plane while it's in flight

Although change is a key driver for any financial services firm, enormous amounts of information must be accessible both quickly and reliably. The fiduciary responsibility of having accurate records for clients, executives, and regulators is paramount. Accuracy and reliability are so important that every datacenter executive in this industry understands reliability as *the* top priority. Operational stability is a requirement to achieve reliability, and in the face of the accelerated changes in the global economy from 1998 through 2008, that has been very difficult to achieve.

An analogy often heard among senior IT executives is that they are being asked to remodel the plane while it is in flight. (You can just imagine trying to rebuild the wings and work on the engines!) The need for large-scale change and reliability combined with a year-after-year doubling of information processing is difficult at best. To better ready ourselves for future disruption, it's helpful to analyze past events.

### 2.1.1   The predictions

A datacenter is a very expensive investment. It takes many years to plan, build, and then move everything. Most financial services datacenters were built before the effects of the Internet were fully realized. They were built based on the best-practice assumptions of the time. A brief history of the following assumptions that have *not* become reality demonstrates how fluid the IT environment is:

- Technology evolution would be limited to incremental improvements of SMP servers and mainframes. (Inaccurate: Distributed systems became replacements to legacy infrastructure.)
- The thick client desktop as the predominant e-workforce interface. (Inaccurate: Thin client computing dominates today.)
- The preeminence of extensive call centers as the primary mode of interaction with clients via phone. (Inaccurate: Electronic communications have taken over a large chunk of customer interactions.)
- A static regulatory environment on what records were to be kept and how disaster recovery was to be addressed. (Inaccurate: Malfeasance and terror attacks prompted new, stricter regulations.)
- The continued linear growth rate of transactions. (Inaccurate: The rate of transactions has grown exponentially.)
- The nature of the user demographics being serviced would remain unchanged. (Inaccurate: User demographics have changed from primarily internal/expert users to external/novice users.)

### 2.1.2   A multitude of disruptions

No single event made these predictions to be inaccurate. Unpredictable disruptive events that occurred to the global economy over the last decade dictated the course of change.

#### General business environment changes

- The use of the Internet went from brochure-ware to transaction-oriented, and its subsequent growth was unpredictable. A robust Internet presence was a minimal entry for any financial services firm. Every firm promoted an e-commerce executive to champion an Internet-facing strategy, taking any shortcut necessary to get every department to the web, irrespective of the cost, duplication, and general waste it caused.
- End-user access speeds evolved from 9.6 kbs dial-up connections to 6 Mbs cable modems, leading to more stress on client-facing sites.

- With the founding of E-Trade® and its competitors, circa 1996, individuals became personally involved in their finances in a way never seen before.
- At the onset of the 21st century, the dot-com crash caused unprecedented volumes; the subsequent scandals from Enron, Tyco, and WorldCom ushered in a new wave of regulations (e.g., Sarbanes Oxley) that included more complex reporting and data retention (e.g., e-mail, voice mail).
- The terrorist attacks of September 11, 2001, made the entire industry reconsider disaster recovery. Disaster recovery sites had to be located farther away from their traditional counterparts. Most firms discovered that their DR sites were not regularly updated—rendering them almost useless.
- New laws around client background and anti–money laundering analytics were incorporated in the process.
- Investment in IT was dramatically cut after 2001, forcing IT executives to find ways to meet business demand.
  - Outsourcing became very popular because it looked like a quick way to cut expensive programmer costs. While programming costs were radically reduced in some cases, more money had to be spent on project management because of time zone differences, cultural and language issues, and the uncomfortable truth that documentation practices were chronically poor. The result was that organizations got more programmers for their dollar, but application quality often suffered.
  - The move to commodity hardware was viewed as a cost savings because big SMP machines were expensive to upgrade, and the associated licensing and maintenance costs were difficult to justify in an economic downturn. The proliferation of cheap blades looked to be a real cost saver until the complexity grew, power consumption increased radically, and cooling became a major problem because these blades ran much hotter. The floor space saved by the commodity blades were taken up by new cooling systems.
  - The use of open source seemed to be a major cost savings, but the proliferation of open source in a large global financial institution presented potential legal liabilities and created a proliferation of operating stacks that added to complexity, causing more support personnel to be hired.
- In 2008, the era of cheap capital went the way of the dinosaur as the credit markets reacted to a global recession.

## Global financial services market changes

While IT investment was reduced after the crash and the terrorist attacks, key changes in technology and financial services became pervasive by 2004 and accelerated through 2008:

- New financial instruments began their ascent; many of them were over-the-counter (OTC) derivatives that had no established market value, but instead their value was derived in real time as a function of risk factors.
- Layoffs and offshore outsourcing became a key strategic cost-cutting practice that reduced the in-house skill base, even as the pace of growth began to accelerate again.

- Globally low interest rates fueled a frenzy to figure out how financial services companies could generate adequate revenue to feed growth. All aspects of financial services felt this because those with modest incomes wanted to see their retirement funds grow, just as much as those with discretionary wealth did. They also wanted some reasonable insurance against a risky downturn. As a result, all kinds of financial institutions such as fund managers were interested in making money for their clients in more diverse ways that did not just include the stock markets.
- Time-to-market pressures increased for the development and introduction of boutique financial instruments. The interconnected global economy was looking for revenue growth answers, and these new instruments appeared to strike a balance of reward and risk. It was vital to conceive, develop, and disseminate new products in 60 days or less, because once available to the consumer (other financial institutions), the exclusivity of the concept would not last long. These novel instruments would transform from boutique (high-margin, low-volume) to commodity (low-margin, high-volume) in just a few months.
- The new regulatory environment had provisions to hold senior business executives accountable so they could not hide behind corporate anonymity if their books proved to be false. This shifted the responsibility. Regulation had to be taken seriously.
- Valuing new instruments, assessing risk comprehensively, and providing timely regulatory and management reporting forced a new paradigm of more complex and in-depth decision making in all financial services firms, driving more sophisticated mathematical computation. The result was an increase in the amount of effort expended calculating the state of their books. More calculations were required even as the amount of transactions doubled year over year.[1]
- Cost-cutting measures were taken very seriously, and consumer self-service became a key strategy, cutting down investments in call centers, using Integrated Voice Response (IVR) to guide consumers through menus and drive self-service through the Internet. Individual consumers and institutional clients were both channeled through Internet-facing applications.
- Supporting a mobile workforce became critical in the increasingly fast-paced interconnect of the financial services world, presenting challenges to support adequate response to mobile devices, while providing very high security and high integrity.
- Collaboration became critical as cross-product and cross-business service offerings became strategic imperatives for growth. This collaboration went beyond simple documents passing through e-mail but instead included real-time screen sharing, internal chat channels, coordinated document sharing, and integrated video capability through web cams employing video over the Internet. The face-to-face collaboration was augmented with digital telepresence for efficiency and cost containment.
- Mergers and acquisitions occurred very often for some institutions, so integration and assimilation needed to be accomplished in a few quarters, not years, especially with the new regulatory environment.
- The economic crisis of 2008 will surely have further disruptive changes and, at a minimum, will lead to significant further regulatory compliance.

---

[1]Miller R. Massive data streams flow from Wall Street. DataCenterKnowledge.com. <http://www.datacenterknowledge.com/archives/2008/02/07/massive-data-streams-flow-from-wall-street/>; 2008, February 7.

## Technological changes

Technology advancement was not idle during this period of time:

- The Internet became the driving force for how technology was delivered. This technology transformed message sizes to grow by as much as tenfold due to the use of XML. The Internet altered the communication mechanism between enterprises, providing the means to use a public network instead of dedicated point-to-point solutions for every enterprise. This ability came with all of the challenges of security, speed, and reliability that needed to be resolved.
- Fast Internet access through cable TV and DSL links became pervasive; access to information was demanded by the consumer.
- Commodity servers could be bought and placed into racks that had expansion capabilities. They appeared to be cheaper than conventional scale-up SMP machines from the traditional vendors such as Sun, IBM, and Hewlett-Packard. Together these innovations gave IT executives the opportunity to increase vital compute and storage resources at a fraction of the conventional vendor costs.
- The success of the commodity server drove a proliferation of space consumption in the datacenter. The industry responded with the advent of the blade computer, which in turn created its own power, heat, and weight challenges.
- The open source community expanded its scope beyond the operating system, giving development teams the opportunity to expand capabilities, making it less likely that a standard vendor system offering like databases, data caching, and application servers would be used. Proliferation of configurations became the norm across financial services firms, because time to market was still a factor and budgets were tight.
- Security became a prominent issue as it became clear that the Internet had serious flaws that could be exploited and place banks and consumers at risk. Channeling institutional investors to the Internet meant that third-party authentication needed to be addressed so there were clear lines of responsibility when an institutional investor authorized its client to access a financial services firm.
- Around 2005 it became apparent that without ready resources to continue to feed the power and space hungry datacenters, practical limitations on scale and operations of datacenters began to appear.[2]
- Advances in nanotechnology (Intel, AMD, IBM, and Sony) were driving simultaneous increases in performance and size reductions.
- The grid computing paradigm changed the way compute-intensive processing was managed. By being able to execute discrete workloads across many low-cost server resources, capital investment was diverted from very expensive SMP systems but caused a proliferation of these smaller servers.

### 2.1.3   Lessons learned

Of course, with hindsight it's easy to see that many predictions were wrong. While datacenters have been able to adapt, many design decisions would have

---

[2]Tatum R. Power, cooling and other trends in datacenter design. FacilitiesNet.com. <http://www.facilitiesnet.com/powercommunication/article/Power-Cooling-and-Other-Trends-in-Data-Center-Design--2431>; January 2005.

been made differently if foresight was available to predict even a portion of these disruptive events. It's obviously impossible to predict the specific changes the future holds, but it's not difficult to predict that future events will cause changes to the fundamental assumptions and beliefs held today.

Any future design needs to be malleable enough that the core design doesn't fall apart when the inevitable changes take place. Flexibility is key!

## 2.2   A legacy of challenges

IT executives had to handle the radical changes and their consequences as they kept essential services operating. As the changes mounted, datacenter personnel had to manage a set of incremental legacies. Before the Internet boom, there was a massive increase in application and database creation during the early to mid-1990s. That era addressed the proliferation of spreadsheets throughout all financial services firms, which had discovered that traditional MIS had been circumvented as the use of PCs spread like a virus. Vital corporate data was developed on PCs, especially spreadsheets. Cleaning up that proliferation was a major effort that was gaining momentum before the Internet revolution. Most datacenters were built or revised in anticipation of handling this growth, and some reasonable designs were created to manage this new state of information processing.

Once the Internet's true potential and threat emerged, business teams gave developers license to do whatever it took to get an adequate presence on line. Much like a land grab race during the pioneer days, being first at all costs was considered paramount. Databases were cloned; applications were prototyped and sent out. In many cases strategic design was dropped because the Internet was so disruptive, and money was so readily available that a mentality of survival took over. In addition, much of the technology that fueled the Internet boom was immature, barely tested, and, in some cases, pure vaporware.

- New paradigms were introduced, such as web content, document management systems, and promotional e-mails.
- The growing need for information lifecycle management in financial services became apparent quite suddenly. New regulations forced longer data-retention cycles—a minimum of seven years in most cases. Searching for data became critical for these enterprises, especially since users could not understand how they could go to Google and search for anything and get a response in less than one second, while searching for documents they wrote within their own firm could take one hour.
- Back-end fulfillment of credit debit card purchases accelerated, changing the landscape of interbank communication and increasing traffic by orders of magnitude.
- Complete client self-service, including money transfers, online payments, and electronic statements, increased the demand of traditional back-end servers that were never designed to process such a load.
- Few knew how to program, deploy, test, or maintain applications in these new environments. Java, which became a prominent language and operating environment during the boom, had many flaws that were rectified by individually crafted solutions.

- Those running datacenters just tried to keep up without getting trampled. Moreover, proven IT processes such as change control were ignored because the Internet was different, and they no longer applied.
- And then the rush was over, and the layoffs came with a massive reduction in spending and a shrinking knowledge base.

Once the Internet boom was over, scandals emerged, and the terrorist attacks occurred, there was a significant retrenchment. In that environment, senior IT professionals took stock of the boom's legacy and saw the following:

- Massive duplication of data stores with no clear indication of how to converge the data.
- Proliferation of applications and front ends that used the mainframes as back ends.
- A whole new expectation of client interaction that must be supported.
- Layoffs and cost reductions, and loss of knowledge about how to operate the systems.
- Loss of executive credibility/confidence in IT.

As the changes from 2001 through 2008 came about, IT executives tried to come to grips with the cost factors:

- Embracing open source to cut licensing costs and promote agility.
- Acquiring commodity hardware to offset the expense of conventional SMP machines.
- Finding ways to process the changing demand that was evolving.
- Establishing approaches to consolidate an unmanageable legacy of heterogeneous platforms that exhibited no plan.

## 2.3  How different executives view the datacenter

The technology, architecture/development, and middle/front office executives understood their drivers during 1998–2008 and responded to the changing landscape based on their understanding of the business need.

**Technology (CTO Organization):** The datacenter staff did what they could to accommodate the changes in demand: They struck deals to get lower prices on volume discounts and arranged the datacenter layout in a way everybody could understand and that would simplify management. The datacenter is the center of their world.

**Architecture/Development (CIO Organization):** Architecture/development functions were focused on accelerating the release of specific functionality and increasing reliability on an individual application basis. The datacenter is often considered an invisible resource to be used as needed. Its large size and the lack of visibility often gave the impression that the datacenter would be effectively able to scale whatever size was needed.

**Middle/Front Office:** As long as the business was moving forward and capturing market share, the inefficiency of expenditures was viewed as a function of the speed of unconstrained growth. If the business waited for the architecture and technology teams to figure things out, the opportunity would be missed. The datacenter is tolerated and seen as a necessary evil.

### 2.3.1   CTO organization POV

Datacenter executives viewed their role as having two primary drivers: maintain reliability and contain costs. These executives were not usually brought to the table for strategic discussions about where the firm was going. Rather, they were told what to do—cut costs or get out of the way of progress during the boom times. Datacenter professionals attempted to contain costs and maintain reliability.

- They attempted this by driving hard deals with enterprise vendors to make the supply of standardized platforms available with deep discounts. These platforms had very similar configurations to ease operational complexity. Unfortunately, many applications have unique requirements that require nonstandard equipment.
- Picking only a few large vendors so finger pointing was reduced when problems occurred. Relying on these vendors to offer their solutions in hardware and software ensured that a manageable maintenance strategy could be followed. Often this goal is compromised to support the requirements of the business's preferred third-party application providers' requirements.
- Organizing by functions that datacenter professionals understand, specifically arranging for pools of resources grouped by technical function (e.g., network, SAN, database, application server, web server, messaging server, etc.). This makes it easier (from their perspective) to inventory, cycle out old models, and manage cable maintenance, while attempting to stay ahead of the demand curve by procuring enough infrastructure resources in advance so they are ready to be allocated. While it's easier to manage the groups this way, it often makes the supply of resources very lumpy (e.g., adding an additional 50 GB of SAN may require the purchase of a whole new SAN array at a cost of $1 million).
- Optimizing maintenance by grouping similar technologies together so that technicians can perform maintenance, problem determination, and problem resolution more efficiently, thereby enhancing reliability. While it's easier to manage the individual groups this way, it makes the groups focus on their specific element of ownership and creates unhealthy competition to divert blame for a problem.
- Approving commodity hardware for use, to drive costs down, and facilitate the procurement process (e.g., it's possible to buy another few blades for a project as its need grows). However, making it easier to purchase incrementally has had the unintended consequence of contributing to server sprawl and low server utilization statistics.

The CTO organization is farthest removed from the front lines, which limits its ability to affect the situation. It is continuously asked to justify its existence and expenditures, while simultaneously being pressed to grow resource (CPU, Network, SAN, etc.) capacity. Correlating resource growth to business value is a complex and difficult undertaking, compounded by exponential growth in and changes to configurations. As physical capacity, space constraints, power, and cooling limits are reached in datacenters, growth of core resources is no longer incremental. Since these physical limitations are poorly understood by those with the pursestrings, these costs are hidden by distributing them throughout the chargeback model, which makes expenditures even more difficult to explain. The typical CTO is happy to share ideas with anyone willing to listen:

> *Everyone wants speed of deployment and new hardware delivery, but everyone refuses to understand the cost of reliability until something breaks down. Trying to maintain reliability by reducing the number of configurations in production while the development teams keep adding more configurations is challenging. The word standard has lost its meaning.*
>
> *Server utilization reports indicate average usage is less than 25 percent, but we get an influx of new requests for specific hardware configurations from the CIO organization. I am having trouble justifying new expenditures given these utilization rates. When I try to press the point, the business unit that needs the new hardware overrides my efforts. This is especially true with the numerous grids emerging/expanding all over the enterprise and the resulting amount of data being accessed, causing hot spots. Worse yet, each grid has unique configuration and operating characteristics, so I cannot leverage my grid team across those implementations.*
>
> *This sprawl makes our datacenter capacity problem worse. Over the past few years, we've realized we have some physical constraints that no one predicted. Floor space is less of an issue, but we cannot supply enough power to run and cool the machines due to the density increases in today's equipment. For example, we cannot put in any more cooling units because the floors cannot handle the load, especially near the trading floors (not to mention that power costs 45 percent more than it did five years ago, and we need more of it). When I explain the challenges, I get a response as if I should just magically make these problems disappear.*

## 2.3.2   CIO organization POV

IT executives in charge of application and services development view their role as having a number of key drivers: innovate to keep up with the changing needs of the business, accelerate development time to get features out faster, and find ways to improve performance. Architects and developers do the following to handle these challenges:

*   Buy new tools to rapidly facilitate the delivery of new functionality to the business (such as content management, messaging software, and, more recently, collaboration). The general consensus is that buying and fixing are more productive than building from scratch. However, these products are not mature in many cases, and it takes considerable internal CTO and CIO team effort to make them work reliably.
*   Use open source operating tools for operating systems, application servers, data caching, and so on. Not only do these solutions offer attractive licensing cost models, the turnaround time to fix problems is often faster (typically days as opposed

to months) than waiting for features and/or fixes from the traditional platform providers. Challenges with this approach include rapid releases, validating the security of the products, weighing the maturity of the solutions/management tools themselves, and increasing the number of platforms supported.

- Rapidly release features and functions out for use, because in many cases the end users (whether internal or external) cannot articulate what exactly is needed to solve a business problem—especially with some of the new paradigms. While production prototypes often make business sense, they further compound the rate and the number of changes required in the environment.
- Promote standardization through frameworks. Factoring out common functionality and promoting reuse make sense. Unfortunately, the need for speed to market often overrides these longer-term goals for short-term gains. Without a clear measure of value that is understood by the business, framework teams are often the first to receive the axe during tough times, which acts as a disincentive for the best and the brightest.

The CIO organization finds itself sandwiched between doing the right thing for the business and grappling with the physical challenges of the datacenter environment through its CTO teams. While somewhat sympathetic to the challenges the CTO organizations face, the general attitude is that it's their job to figure out how to manage the technology. With the time to market pressures the business puts on the CIO teams, it isn't surprising that each delay is met with a request to expedite, which introduces additional chaos to already overburdened processes. The CIO teams are all too ready to share the apparent ineptness of the CTO teams with the business to absolve themselves of blame for delays. Challenge a CIO on this, and you might get a response like this:

*The business has made revenue growth a clear driver, and while my teams are doing all they can to support that, I feel their progress is considerably slowed when it comes to getting new features into production. It takes months to get new equipment in for new applications or application enhancement. My teams are constantly being held back from final deployment due to backlogs and inadequate operational training. The business expects a six-week turnaround for new revisions, which I can meet. However, once it enters the datacenter, I have no control over deployment time; it often takes weeks. I have difficulty explaining the reasons for delay to the business; it doesn't seem that complicated. Plus, when my team identifies innovative ways to solve business problems, they get considerable resistance about deploying the new technology from the datacenter staff.*

*My senior staff spends considerable time troubleshooting problems to critical applications because no one will admit his piece is at fault. Triage is incredibly difficult, and this is compounded by some of the virtualization technologies we have put in place to drive efficiencies. The datacenter teams (e.g., database, messaging) each claims their portion works; meanwhile, average recovery for critical applications exceeds an hour. Furthermore, there is no guarantee that once the problem is isolated, it can be fixed quickly and problems often recur.*

### 2.3.3   Middle/front office organizations POV

Business executives are in charge of daily business operations and are consumers of datacenter applications and services to execute activities such as position tracking, risk assessment, sales activities, and a multitude of others. They drive most the application and service requirements, since they have the practical firsthand knowledge of using the systems and have the most insight into industry trends. The following are some of the drivers:

- Revenue generation is the highest priority; it drives the need for the rapid development and deployment of products to create an edge on the competition. As sole provider, a premium can be charged; much of the revenue generated by a new product occurs when it is first introduced. A new product's lifecycle is very short, so time to market is critical. The intense competition between firms causes boutique products to turn into commodity products within months. This competition is what creates the time-to-market driver.
- It takes dozens of product releases to find a big winner, which makes it difficult to invest in a large infrastructure for each one. However, when a winner is determined, the infrastructure must be immediately scaled to meet the demand. The fortune of a product reflects the willingness of the business to invest into resources for it; however, IT systems aren't structured to recognize this beyond a Recovery Time Objective (RTO) level and some sense of user interaction/traffic.

The outside IT view of the datacenter is entirely different. As the consumers of the end applications and services, the datacenter is an abstract concept and often the source of excuses for delays from IT: "There isn't enough capacity. We need to purchase more." "The servers will take ten weeks to deploy." "The SAN is misconfigured." "The cabling was executed incorrectly." If a senior businessperson were pressed to summarize her view of the IT, she would have to use a very broad brush:

> *The datacenter and development teams fail to adequately meet our business needs. Despite having thousands of servers, we don't have ready capacity for new business opportunities. New applications and features seem to take an excessive amount of time to enable. There is too much complexity, waste, poor performance, and cost inefficiencies. This is especially apparent when my staff has to notify IT that our systems are down. IT seems unable to understand our competitive landscape or rapidly react to business events when they happen. This reduces the organization's agility in responding to market variability, makes my job more difficult, and ultimately results in decreased shareholder value.*

### 2.3.4   Reconciling differences

These three points of view are clearly in conflict. Each perspective is correct, but each deals with only a fraction of the whole challenge. Each of these groups has taken incremental steps to try to improve its respective situation.

However, since the core challenges are larger than any single group, results have been limited. These differing points of view also explain why trivial issues between them are often escalated to the top tier of the organization. The larger the organization, the more apparent these conflicts become.

Note that this problem is larger in scope than datacenter operations and encompasses IT delivery on the whole. The datacenter plays a central role, especially with respect to the nonobvious constraints that are imposed. The complexity of implementing, applying, and consuming the resources within a datacenter is so large that it isn't completely understood by any party, nor are they incentivized to do so. Even with the best of intentions of each person involved, competing priorities and performance metrics quickly make a mess of things.

There's a tendency for each group to lay claim to the most important role, but a business is a team effort, and it takes a diverse set of roles and skills to deliver to the customer. A halt should be brought to continual and unproductive finger pointing. Striving to align and beginning the process of moving these parties in the same general direction can significantly reduce the conflict. In a perfect world we'd be able to eliminate these conflicts by aligning business and support groups through incentives. Incentives are generally a tricky subject, with whole books devoted to the topic. The key point for our purposes is to remember that *you get what you measure*. If the CTO organization's primary measure is cost reduction, you can expect costs to go down, but response time won't improve. If the CIO organization is measured on its performance to deliver on a few mission-critical applications, then more likely the others will suffer from a lack of attention. The measurements taken to gauge group performance are reflective.

A well-thought-out Service Level Agreement (SLA) plan that measures expected behaviors can go a long way in improving team focus. In addition, when incentives are not aligned in large organizations, actions like cost cutting for the CTO tend to drive costs up for the CIO groups, resulting in a net spending increase and defeating corporate goals.

A word of caution: Speeding up a broken process will only cause the process to break faster and more spectacularly; if the underlying infrastructure isn't properly designed to deliver to an SLA, individuals will attempt to compensate until they can't (and then boom!). A successful process will be relatively easy to execute because the proper support and infrastructure are in place to make it happen. Not just any SLA is sufficient. It must be structured to meet the business goals, such as time to market, performance objectives, and so on. It's necessary to create a line of business view of the business value chain and create an analogous digital supply chain that represents the technological infrastructure in support of it. Each step along the digital supply chain will have significant differences in the type of infrastructure characteristics needed, which in turn influences the solution selection. Aligning the support teams to deliver to these requirements and measuring their success to it can close the gap between business expectations and delivery.

## 2.4   Entrenched legacy infrastructure

Allowing the driving forces of the CIO and CTO organizations to remain unaligned with the overall business goals has led to some high-impact limitations to growth and agility. As a consequence, legacy infrastructure that is unable to meet business needs has become entrenched and is a significant barrier to progress.

An example of entrenchment is an urban expressway that was built without input from a city plan as to *how* the city would grow. It was built to handle three times the current traffic flow in anticipation of city growth. Once that expressway was built, all the supporting infrastructure for it would dictate how the city would grow. For instance, the land near exit and entry ramps would be fought over by retail developers, but it would detract from residential development. The placement and growth of the government center and various municipal services such as hospitals would be affected by placement of the expressway.

Suppose the city then grew in totally unexpected ways, such as the creation of more blue-collar jobs, requiring more factories and delivery routes. How would the entrenched expressway affect the unexpected growth of such industries and its support functions? As a result of the change in growth, the expressway may need to be widened or additional exit ramps added. Think of the amount of disruption due to detours that would occur. In a sufficiently busy urban area, this transformation could take decades.

This problem of an entrenched legacy infrastructure cannot be underestimated. Not only does a separately evolved infrastructure limit how growth can be accommodated, but it actually could dictate the path that growth will take and at what rate. Anyone who has ever had to endure the crawling delays due to perpetual highway construction knows how frustrating this can be. The business is equally dependent on the datacenter infrastructure as the arterial systems of its business functions. When it is told it cannot grow at the rate it needs to, it feels the analogous traffic jam frustration.

## 2.5   Moving forward

Despite the best efforts of all involved, the expenses of operational costs are growing significantly faster than revenue growth. With the economic downturn of 2008 and the subsequent decrease in revenue, this situation can no longer be tolerated. Business direction must have a heavier influence on the direction of IT. Cost structures must be brought into alignment with revenue. This can be accomplished by aligning business demand as defined by the business value chain and with a digital supply chain that enables a more appropriate infrastructure supply. Only from this top-down approach can operational costs be guaranteed to remain in tight alignment with business revenue.

The organization has created a set of rules that define accepted behavior; the resulting products and customer services are a direct result of those rules. The datacenter itself is a microcosm of similar emergent behaviors (manifested as products and customer services), which are driven by the organization's culture and its rules. The very rules that allow an organization to operate are themselves at the center of challenges that must be addressed to bring all the different groups into alignment.

Change just for the sake of change is not very productive. "How can we change?" becomes the important question. In an ideal world, technological changes would be instantaneous. Unlimited resources with infinite flexibility would win the day. As each business event took place, it would be anticipated, so the revenue generators would be able to pounce and capitalize on it. The front/middle office teams wouldn't have a single complaint, and their revenue-generating capacity would only be constrained by the business environment and their ideas.

While reaching this ideal will never happen in the real world, it's an admirable goal to reach for. The closer IT comes, the more capable the business is to reach its goals and the less likely IT acts as a constraint. In fact, the enterprise has coined a phase for this: "The Real Time Enterprise."

# 3 Real Time Enterprise

*"It's all knowing what to start with. If you start in the right place and follow all the steps, you will get to the right end."*

—Elizabeth Moon

## Key Points

Change is becoming baked into the operating model of the business. IT must be prepared for this radically different business model.

*Sustainable business advantage* cannot be provided by technical resources alone. However, it is possible by closely aligning IT with business operations.

Unlike most species, humans are found across the four corners of the earth. From the humid tropics and arid deserts to the freezing tundra, traversing the seven seas or mastering the highest mountain, humans thrive. It's our adaptability to environmental diversity that allows us to adjust to dynamic eventualities. It is not due only to our biology, which adapts to environmental conditions, but also our ingenuity—as simple as canteen and shade, as complex as space exploration.

For organizations today, it takes similar characteristics to thrive. As business conditions change, organizations must rapidly adapt to varied requirements. In fact, business positions can fluctuate more rapidly than environmental conditions. A well-placed advertising campaign can drive spikes of interest in your company; if you're not ready for the surge, there likely won't be a second chance at those customers. Disruption of service can literally induce significant financial loss or completely paralyze an organization. Financial services organizations are notorious for rapid product commoditization; rolling to market weeks ahead of the competition translates into considerable financial gain. Oftentimes, entire business models are reinvented overnight (ask those who have recently worked in structured products). The cold, harsh reality of the business world is adapt or fail—survival of the fittest.

With this as the backdrop, the business comes to IT to request new feature functionality. It isn't that every bell and whistle are needed but rather, it's about being able to rapidly adapt to changing business conditions. IT has a core responsibility to not only assist in a company's adaptability but to also be a major source of innovation and drive it. The success of a business is proportional to its ability to adapt to circumstances and meet demand.

doi: 10.1016/B978-0-12-374956-7.00003-6

## 3.1  The real time enterprise

In an effort to become more responsive to business events, organizations have evolved into Real Time Enterprises (RTE), where real-time information is used to adjust operations on the fly. Gartner defines a Real Time Enterprise as follows:

> The RTE monitors, captures, and analyzes root-cause and overt events that are critical to its success the instant those events occur, to identify new opportunities, avoid mishaps, and minimize delays in core business processes. The RTE will then exploit that information to progressively remove delays in the management and execution of its critical business processes.[1]

Traditionally organizations were forced to be passive or reactive to business events. Reporting on operations was traditionally executed on a weekly, monthly, and quarterly schedule. By the time management learned about events that had taken place, the opportunity to change the outcome had long passed. In the late 1990s, it began to be practical to start the practice of tapping real-time feeds of information on operations, which provided greater insight, allowing the organization to react faster. The Real Time Enterprise is the logical progression of continuous improvement of timely information to become proactive in responding to marketplace events.

Organizations that have adopted this model have shown significant competitive advantage. A prime example is Wal-Mart, which uses a real-time flow from cash register sales to dynamically control its inventory reorder. The benefits of having this up-to-date information readily available have been proven many times over. In financial services, real-time information has also been used to great advantage. Organizations that calculate their *statutory liquidity ratio* (SLR) on a daily basis have been able to significantly reduce their *cash reserve ratio* (CRR) when compared with competitors that complete calculations monthly (thereby overestimating the reserve needed). Since the CRR for a large bank can be anywhere from $10 mm–$100 mm or up, a more accurate reserve can free significant amounts of daily capital.

Another example includes organizations that have automated feed processes. Traditionally, all middle office trading desks had manual postday operations that needed to be completed before their data were ready for batch consumption. The automation of these tasks and automatic serving up of the underlying data has significantly reduced the likelihood that the batch process gets a late start because of human error or delay. This has saved many financial services firms from being assessed with costly SEC fines that result from not meeting sensitive reporting requirements.

[1]McGee K. *Gartner Updates Its Definition of Real-Time Enterprise*. ID: DF-222-2973; March 25, 2004.

### 3.1.1  Continuous improvement

In his book *Building the Real-Time Enterprise*, Michael Hugos introduced the concept of the OODA Loop—Observe, Orient, Decide, and Act—as a way to structure how an organization can take advantage of real-time information:

> There are four steps in the OODA Loop. The first step is to observe. This is the process of collecting and communicating information about the environment. The next step is to orient. This is the most important activity because it is where information is turned into an understanding of the situation upon which the next two steps will depend. In this step, the environment is described, the positions of the different players in the environment are defined, and the relevant trends, threats, and opportunities are identified. In the decide step, different responses and plans for implementing them are created and evaluated. The most appropriate response is chosen, and that leads to the final step–act. In the act step, action is taken and results occur that are favorable, not favorable, or indeterminate. These results are picked up in the observe step and the loop continues.[2]

During the decide step, if the decision is made to *act*, then there are two possibilities: improve an existing system and/or process or create a new process and/or system. The business accelerated its ability to recognize opportunity provided by this insight, and IT has become more adept at supplying the real-time information needed to detect the opportunity. If the resulting action is within the current capabilities of the process or systems, then a fast reaction is possible. However if the resulting action requires a change to the systems, a rapid response is doubtful. The typical time to upgrade an application is 30 weeks.[3] IT is only just beginning to learn how to implement the resulting decision—to act fast enough to be relevant. Enabling business to internalize and respond to business events requires that IT become exceedingly flexible.

A typical request within an RTE may include the doubling of resources associated to an intraday risk calculation engine during highly volatile markets. Most organizations would find it impossible to react fast enough to make the change. Their standard response to this scenario is to purchase additional capacity to handle the peak load, which would sit idle until the next time volatility spikes. An RTE organization's response would be radically different. Capacity would be dynamically drawn from lower-priority systems and reserve pools to continuously supply adequate resources. In the former case, response time can be measured in weeks, and in the latter, it happens in real time.

[2]Hugos M. *Building the Real-Time Enterprise An Executive Briefing*, Wiley; 2004;77.
[3]Gillen A, et al. *Measuring the Business Value of Server Virtualization: Understanding the Impact of Guest Management*. IDC Whitepaper, June 2008, Figure 2, p. 11.

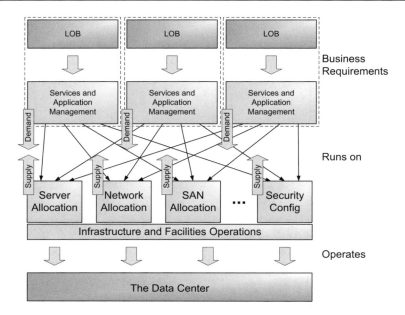

**Figure 3.1** Typical siloed supply rat's nest.

At first, the idea of IT being so agile seems impossible. Given today's standard deployment and allocation models, this is understandable. After all, accelerating a broken process only makes it break even faster.

### 3.1.2   IT in a real time enterprise

The major problem with today's delivery model is its siloed organization. The services and application teams spend an inordinate amount of time interfacing with the infrastructure and facilities operations team. Significant coordination between several teams is required to effect any change to a service or application (Figure 3.1). Notice how service and application management are organized around a line of business, whereas the resources are organized by physical type (often with even more granularity than shown). This impedes the effectiveness of the infrastructure as it takes a significant amount of effort to have resources assigned during deployment and makes dynamic allocation of resources based on load problematic, if not impossible.

For every service or application that comes online, a number of resource requests are required. If any one group errs in its configuration, the entire deployment process is delayed. If performance is lacking or an error occurs, then it takes all the supply teams to debug the process. At initial deployment, services and application teams tend to overrequest resources due to the complexity (and in many cases, the futility) of increasing capacity later. Some organizations have tried adding an overlay group for technology delivery, but rather than solving the underlying problems, it glosses them over by relocating where the complexity occurs while introducing yet another layer of bureaucracy.

In short, the process of force-fitting services and applications onto generic and siloed resources is a flawed practice that is ripe with complexity. Virtualization and automation without changing the delivery model is more of the same in a smaller footprint, only a bit faster.

To fully meet real-time business expectations, IT is entering a new phase where organizations must orient delivery of services across the entire IT supply chain to behave and operate in a real-time manner. Those organizations that don't embark on this transformational journey will not deliver the desired business growth and maximized shareholder value that is the fiduciary responsibilities of IT executives in support of their businesses. The problem is more complex than just speeding up current operations. Fundamentals will have to change to meet the order of magnitude difference in expectations.

By way of analogy, consider a successful home construction firm. The founder of the firm built a log cabin with his grandfather while in his teens and found his passion. As a young man he began developing one-off small custom homes. Along the way he makes business connections and establishes a sophisticated organization that successfully develops a few subdivisions across the southern region of the United States. Ultimately the company branches out to mixed-use housing communities integrated with trendy shops and restaurants. Each logical growth step along the growth path for this organization is incremental; the skills of building one type of building directly translated to the next type.

If this firm suddenly undertook an opportunity to build a mixed-use residential skyscraper, there is a distinct likelihood of failure of both the project and the firm. Why? The organizational model doesn't scale to the opportunity. Neither the traditional home materials and methods of construction nor the supplier and subcontractor relationships are suitable when applied to the construction of a skyscraper. Even simple things can become difficult, such as working within an active infrastructure (electrical, subway, gas, phone, roads) of a city center, as opposed to an empty field. To become a construction company able to build this new type of structure would require a focus and energy to change the underlying fundamentals about how construction is approached. The resulting organization would not resemble the original.

Today's applications/services and IT organizations are faced with a similarly daunting challenge in trying to properly support an RTE. Consider the differences between the traditional and emerging trends as depicted in Figure 3.2. An organization based on the principles of the *reactive enterprise* is not scalable into an RTE. If an RTE is desired, a transformation process must occur to make the necessary changes that affect the IT organization as a whole.

The notifications enabled by RTE alone aren't enough to make a meaningful difference to the outcome. The organization must be able to follow through with being able to actually react to the event. If any one of the layers depicted in Figure 3.2 remains in reactive mode, then there's going to be a gap in seamless execution. The RTE model is in its infancy, and as it matures it's going to become more and more demanding of the supporting IT elements of the organization. As the rate of change in business accelerates, if IT is having trouble keeping up now, the future is indeed going to be bleak for IT if it doesn't evolve.

**Delivery Model:** The general success of the siloed model of delivery IT services has had a cascading influence on the whole IT stack. Before silos were

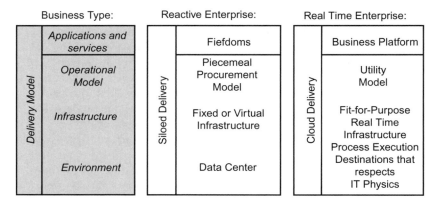

**Figure 3.2** IT as the foundation of the business.

---

**Reactive Enterprise vs. Real Time Enterprise Response**

Consider the following two scenarios on how a business event may be handled by a reactive enterprise vs. a real time enterprise. The reactive enterprise scenario:

*While reviewing the monthly reports, we noticed a shift from variable interest mortgage products to fixed ones due to the collapsing interest rates. We devised a promotion model that the engineering team in support of sales was able to deploy to our site three weeks after its conception. We anticipated a spike in traffic, so I assigned my best project manager and approved the required escalation to get a new pair of servers and 50GB of additional SAN purchased and configured within the datacenter in time for the launch.*

The real time enterprise scenario:

*We were alerted by sales that there is an emerging trend away from variable interest mortgage to fixed ones due to Monday's drop in the interest rate. I approved a new promotional model that was configured into our sales platform this afternoon. The branch office response has been tremendous; they've been reaching out to customers who have been on the fence about refinancing with great success. In fact, as the traffic began spiking, the infrastructure auto provisioned two new servers and 10 GB of additional SAN from our third-party infrastructure partner. The configuration and application deployment were seamlessly executed.*

Which organization would you rather invest in?

used to break down complex tasks, highly skilled engineering teams were needed to deliver end-to-end solutions. Silos attempted to reduce complexity at each step of deployment, which in turn allowed dedicated staff to focus and become experts on and at the limited scope of their respective roles. While this model enjoyed varying degrees of success in the past, it is now showing strain. The segmentation of tasks has become very fine-grained, creating an explosion of subcategories of expertise with few who understand the end-to-end deployment process. The resulting organization has turned into a bureaucratic morass. It doesn't affect simply the delivery of resources but the entire delivery process, including the provisioning of applications and services.

To simplify the consumption of IT services, what's needed is a more holistic delivery of aggregated functionality. In the context of an RTE organization, this translates into a logical delivery model that abstracts away the complexity of applications/services, operating model, infrastructure, and environment: a cloud,[4] if you will (Figure 3.3). The jump from a siloed to cloud delivery model for IT services isn't an incremental change; rather it's a paradigm shift. As such, transforming from a siloed model to a cloud model requires a transformation

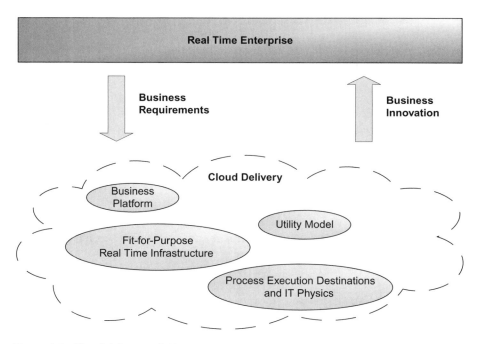

**Figure 3.3** Cloud delivery of IT services.

[4]As it's still emerging, the industry is still arguing over what the exact definition and scope of *cloud* should be. If history is any indicator, this debate will rage on for a decade or more before people get tired of it. The more practical among us will concentrate on "what's needed" and let the result settle the debate.

of how the whole organization operates. New technologies and practices have surfaced that decompose the overly complex siloed approach of delivering IT services. Chapter 8 discusses the cloud as a delivery model and the technology that makes this new model viable.

**Applications/Services:** The boundaries between applications/services of the different lines of business have grown too strong and are impeding the organization from developing a holistic business platform. Web services are limited to the scope of a single application or a small core of applications, making them of little more use than components. Big pieces of overlapping functionality (e.g., multiple flavors of risk calculation engines) are commonplace, and the organizational structure is overwhelmed with fiefdoms. There is limited understanding of how specific applications and services map against business value.

To succeed, an RTE needs a fine-tuned *business platform* oriented around providing adequate configuration options rather than hundreds or thousands of loosely coupled individual applications. As the *business platform* becomes better aligned with business goals, it will be able to more readily and rapidly respond to business events.

**Operational Model:** Traditional operating model policy allowed for the incremental purchase of generic resources that were distributed via an internal fee structure as they were consumed. A lack of transparency related to business outcomes and IT utilization exists with this model, which complicates spending justifications. This dilemma is exacerbated additionally by overprovisioning, which is rampant because it's difficult to procure additional resources, especially in terms of funding (e.g., go to the well once).

A *utility*-based operational model solves these challenges. A utility's incremental purchasing ability makes it easy to relate the actual use of resources with the costs associated with running the service. This, in combination with the means to dynamically adjust provisioning to the "right size" (not too big; not too small) the environment based on demand, makes the need for overprovisioning a moot issue. A business platform view of the application and services brings better clarity to the costs of running a system, which can now be fully considered within the context of business value generation.

**Infrastructure:** However sophisticated today's siloed models of supply have become at delivering/provisioning resources, consuming them takes the coordination of several teams and slows the overall rate of execution. Virtualized resources are more efficient to allocate, but they do not change the underlying challenges. They make it easier to allocate resources poorly if inadequate policies are in place. Incrementally more agile and faster isn't nearly enough; a new scale of agile and fast is needed. The core issue is that a supply model organized around siloed resource types is misaligned with the way applications and services consume resources.

An RTE needs infrastructure that is holistic, can be tailored to the type of processes that need to be executed, and dynamically adjusts to the load applied: a Fit-for-Purpose Real Time Infrastructure (RTI). A Fit-for-Purpose

RTI (discussed more in Chapter 4) creates the fundamental agility required for an RTE to rapidly respond to events.

**Environment:** Traditionally, the focus of the environment is the physical datacenter. The siloed deployment of generalized infrastructure resources, which don't respect the physics of the deployments (e.g., the application data placed on one side of the datacenter and the application servers on the other), is not effective or efficient.

Resources that are local to other frequently accessed resources will significantly outperform a generically allocated system spread throughout a datacenter. Through the creation of Processing Execution Destinations (PEDs; see Chapter 4), it's possible to dramatically improve the performance and manageability of one of the organization's most expensive assets: the datacenter. The key enabling concept for the environment is respecting the IT physics of the environment; the reality of the physical needs of the resources must be respected.

Generally, IT has been fairly successful in breaking down layers to make each one more manageable. However, as we break down these layers, it's important that business context be kept from top to bottom—for example, there's been the recent development of datacenter power and efficiency measurements, such as PUE and DCiE.[5] It's unfortunate that these metrics don't account for how effectively resources are being applied to the business. A datacenter may be very efficient in its PUE, but if 50 percent of the servers are underutilized, about half of the power being used at the facility is wasted, which isn't efficient at all. You get exactly what you measure, so be careful about what's measured. The cautionary tale here is that all layers must be considered as a whole, not just in parts.

As we consider the creation of a new IT model for better alignment, we must consider the whole. If the concept of the cloud delivery is limited to IT resources, the bigger RTE opportunity will be missed. If the LOBs don't think in terms of a *business platform*, the bigger RTE opportunity will be missed. Figure 3.4 shows how all of these elements come together to better align the supply of infrastructure to the demands of the business. Notice that the silos are no longer present. The *cloud delivery* acts as an abstraction layer to how IT services manifest themselves, but it also integrates the business platform, IT infrastructure, and operating model so they are considered holistically.

There's a subtle but important point that shouldn't be missed about the difference between the Reactive and Real Time Enterprises. Reactive enterprises tend to map IT elements in the context of their physical manifestation, whereas RTEs think about these IT elements logically. Logical elements are easier to mold to the constantly changing needs of the business than their physical counterparts. In the fight for survival, it can mean the difference between thriving and fading.

---

[5]Belady C, et al. Green grid data center power efficiency metrics: PUE and DCIE. *The Green Grid*. 2008;4.

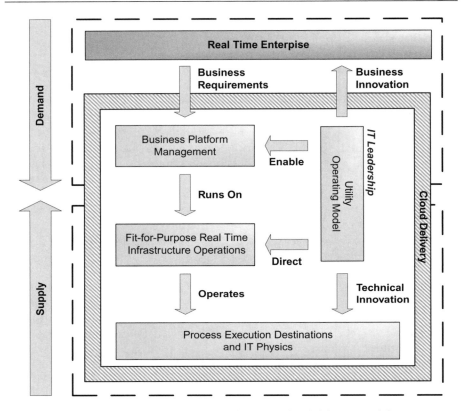

**Figure 3.4** Aligned demand and supply enabled via a cloud delivery model.

### 3.1.3 The new IT environment

Leading firms have already accepted that technology platforms need to evolve to support RTE operations. Many are already in the process of transforming to improve the long-term competitive position of business. The ability to deliver information and processing power anytime, anywhere, as the business needs it is critical to this strategy. This logical platform to clearly define capabilities of service agility, optimize transaction IT unit costs and dynamic execution control is needed to lead the way. This platform can be conceptually described with the following attributes:

- Coalesce cross-client experience, decision support, and just-in-time fulfillment with real-time execution and information availability.
- Deliver "service when needed, as needed," based on the business's explicit service requirements.
- The ability to implement new, unique products or differentiated capabilities in a timely manner for purposes of competitive advantage and operational control.

- Leverage and reuse common component services (both business and infrastructure) for productivity, efficiency, and competitive advantage.
- Provide the necessary plumbing—rich user experience, dynamic execution environment, intelligent mediation platforms, real-time data frameworks, optimal system footprints, dynamic network coordination, and automated orchestration and tooling to enable autonomic management, monitoring, and reporting.

When the platform design is right, the organization will be able to clearly address the following:

- How to become more flexible and responsive to the dynamic needs of the business.
- How to simplify and reduce the complexity of the IT environment.
- How to get more value out of project and operational IT spending—both systems and people.
- How to reduce costs while delivering improved service.
- How to eliminate dedicated silos of data, systems, and infrastructure as they currently exist.
- How to reduce the time it takes to build and deploy new business services.
- How to implement and sustain predictable qualities of service.

To do this, organizations must create a platform strategy and supporting IT operating environment that is completely driven by an organization's business priorities. It is these priorities that establish the drivers from which an application, system, and network infrastructure strategy can be created. Many organizations talk about "the needs of the business" but do little to actually understand the underlying realities beyond a very superficial grasp. This stance will not advance the development of an RTE.

## 3.2   Alignment as a strategy

If the company deploys faster servers, it'll only be a few months before the competition does the same. When the company deploys bigger disk arrays, the competition will do the same soon enough. While it's tempting to focus organizational improvements around tangible metrics, there's a hazard there, too. Operational effectiveness is still necessary, but not sufficient.[6] Single-purpose implementation of commodity components or even novel configurations will only provide brief advantages until they are imitated or surpassed. They have no business context.

In attempting to *optimize, optimize, optimize,* IT has severed itself from the business. Consider this racing team: a Formula One vehicle is the pinnacle of high-tech racing. No expense is spared, and few rule limitations impede the development of the highly tuned race car. Optimization after optimization is applied to the car to eke out every bit of performance from the vehicle. Despite

---

[6]Porter M. What is strategy? *Harvard Business Review.* November–December 1996;61 (Reprint 96608).

all these optimizations, all is lost if the car is entered into the Baja 1000. IT is often building the Formula One vehicle when an off-road buggy is really what's needed. The entire strategy is totally dependent on the context of the goals.

Beyond the obvious communication disconnects between what the business is trying to accomplish versus the implementation, IT has lost its edge in being able to create sustainable competitive advantage. Momentary competitive advantage is periodically created, but it's difficult to maintain because generic improvements are easily replicated.

Creating a sustainable competitive IT strategy requires that the IT organization be structured to provide services that are uniquely qualified in meeting business needs. Making strategic tradeoffs to design an entire system of IT services with the associated skills, competencies, and resources cannot be decoupled from business strategy, which makes it exceedingly difficult to replicate.[7] Chapter 5 provides a detailed guide for developing these types of IT services.

If the primary source of competitive advantage lies with the combination of what the business is doing and how it is accomplished, the relationship between the two will have to be strengthened to take advantage of it. The transformation to an RTE organization is an ideal vehicle to forge a new bond between the two—one that is not only stronger but much more difficult to replicate.

### 3.2.1 IT as the analog of the business

The 1980s introduced two very important business modeling tools: *value chains* and *supply chains*. The value chain begins at the *subjective* value a customer places on goods or services and works backward from there to define activities that incrementally form that value.[8] The *supply chain* begins with raw goods and maps out the sequence of activities needed to transform them into a finished good or service. Traditionally, these two different views of the world have competed with each other. Indeed, we're seeing the analogous argument in organizations today between the business, which is focused on a *value chain*, and IT, which views the world as a *supply chain*.

More recent work in this research area observes that the value chain and supply chain each have their worth and can work together to gain a more holistic view of the operation.[9] For the business to thrive, the customer has to perceive value, which is described by the value chain and delivered via the supply chain. In a financial institution, generally the business focuses on defining the value chain (or *Business Value Chain—BVC*), while the application, services, and IT teams define the supply chain (or *Digital Supply Chain—DSC*; Figure 3.5) with an aligned BVC and DSC working together.

---

[7]Porter M. What is strategy? *Harvard Business Review.* November–December 1996;61 (Reprint 96608).

[8]Porter M. *Competitive Advantage, Creating and Sustaining Superior Performance.* New York: The Free Press; 1985.

[9]Feller A, et al. Value chains versus supply chains. *BP Trends.* March, 2006.

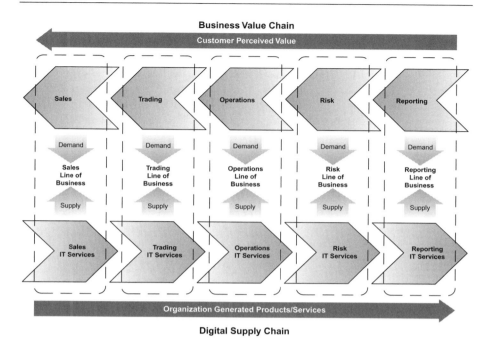

**Figure 3.5** An aligned BVC and DSC working together.

Mapping out the BVC (which is unique to each organization) is a way to understand how the business functions and perceives value. IT can use this information to design services that really help the business perform (and not just keep the lights on). The DSC is the analog to the business, which is how the products and services are realized. Clearly, if the BVC and DSC are out of alignment, the organization is not maximizing its potential, and changes to the BVC can cause large perturbations to the DSC. When the BVC and DSC are aligned, it's difficult to tell one from the other; effectively they become one.

In an RTE, the problem of keeping these aligned is more difficult. By definition an RTE will rapidly adjust based on business events. This implies that the DSC must be able to rapidly adjust, too. This means that the alignment process is not a point in time but must instead be fluid. A rigid DSC implementation will inevitably generate friction between the different portions of the organization, as were discussed in Chapter 2. When the business forces an unprepared DSC to comply, the typical result is decreased reliability. The BVC and DSC must change in lock step—the business and IT acting as a sort of yin and yang.

With this lens it's obvious that a DSC that implements the siloed model of raw resources (servers, SAN, etc.) is not at all aligned with a BVC. The challenge is overcoming the desire to optimize the BVC and DSC apart from each other. Generally customers experience the business and technology as one, but almost every organization does not treat them as one. As the differences between BVC and DSC mount, the organization compensates via people, processes, and technology patchworks, which adds additional layers of inefficiency that are difficult to remove later. A more effective model, which is able to create a truly sustainable competitive advantage, is to get IT to fully align its DSC to the BVC needs and keep them aligned. Sustaining this alignment requires a radically altered view on how IT services are delivered, what they are comprised of, and the supporting infrastructure used to realize them. Chapter 4 details the implications of using the BVC to determine what the DSC should look like. Chapters 5–7 walk through the process of transformation from the existing environment to a Next Generation Datacenter that enables an RTE.

The compelling drivers of globalization and increasing importance of IT as the Digital Supply Chain of the business positions IT executives and their organizations to be more strategic and critical than ever before. To succeed, IT organizations must transform from a "lights-on" culture to one able to drive sustainable strategic differentiation.

# 4 Design from the top-down

## Key Points

The traditional bottom-up datacenter model, complete with generic resources organized into silos of operations to meet business needs, results in missed business opportunities and is at the root of datacenter sprawl.

A top-down model oriented around the business value chain that defines business demand in real time and drives the dynamic allocation of virtual resources from tailored fit-for-purpose physical resources leads to an effective business solution and resource efficient Next Generation Datacenter.

A traditional datacenter model operates in a bottom-up supply mindset: "Just build it because they're coming!" This approach does make each siloed resource offered (server, SAN, network, etc.) easier to manage. However, it creates localized optimization around the supply of each of the resources provided while ignoring the relationships among the resources that interconnect and complicates the configuration and deployment process by involving so many different teams. It's been well proven that you get what you measure. In the case of deploying a new application, SLAs of individual deployment groups (e.g., engineering an application server or database server) will be the driving factor that dictates the time necessary to effect new deployments and configuration updates. Unfortunately, the fact that business opportunities will be missed doesn't factor into deployment calculus.

In contrast, a top-down approach considers business demand first and then determines how to build and supply datacenter resources. This way, operations are optimized and tied to business priorities. In a datacenter, this means being able to rapidly deploy and modify application infrastructure on demand for new applications in real time as a response to varied business events for existing applications. Measurements, and therefore datacenter operational performance, revolve around the time required to deploy and modify infrastructure/applications.

Becoming top-down business-demand focused requires a more nimble infrastructure design and a radically different management model. The primary goal of a top-down design is to be responsive to real-time business events (e.g., shifting resources dynamically to right size environments to current load). This is in stark contrast to typical IT responsiveness, which is often measured in weeks and months. In order to take this step forward, a review of the current bottom-up approach is warranted.

doi: 10.1016/B978-0-12-374956-7.00004-8

## 4.1   Bottom up: past design decisions influence today's operations

It is essential to understand that past design choices limit datacenter services and their ability to maximize business return. Design choices in the datacenter have typically been made in isolation. Each aspect of technology brings its own experts; the result is the bottom-up approach to datacenter design. Table 4.1 shows the ways the challenges with this approach can manifest themselves.

Despite having made many optimizations to the silo model, these problems persist, and the organization is still unsatisfied with the overall results. Revisiting these design choices can uncover opportunities to minimize complexity and reduce waste, eliminate performance barriers, and restructure costs. A complete understanding of what is done and what could be done is the foundation to aligning the datacenter with an organization's priorities. The following are the challenges of the bottom-up approach.

*Silo Operational Models:* Typically, datacenter lifecycle management is a collection of disparate processes. This is a result of two primary factors: reactive planning for datacenter infrastructure management and bottom-up silo design and evolution of new components. This creates disconnected management and processes that fail to meet the expectations of the business.

*One-Size-Fits-All:* Datacenter infrastructure and vendor strategies are usually built around a perceived standardized footprint. This is typically designed bottom-up with little or no correlation to workflows, workloads, information, content, or connectivity requirements. Such disconnects result in poor performance, unnecessary costs, across-the-board waste, and agility issues for the business and IT.

*Supply-Driven Management:* With a majority of datacenter infrastructure managed from the bottom-up by design, the typical approach is to standardize, partition, allocate, and implement a "vanilla" solution that is attached to the network based on the topology of the datacenter floor. Provisioning is then designed for and around peak workloads, which typically leads to overprovisioning due to the difficulty of changing the environment later, further exacerbating the problem of server sprawl. The business workload and service requirements that incorporate performance, price, or efficiency factors are not incorporated, resulting in inconsistent service delivery and a misalignment of needs.

*Spaghetti Transaction Flow:* Transaction flow across traditional datacenter infrastructure is not designed to consider or utilize the proximity of various devices that comprise a service unit as additional capacity is required. This results in significant performance

Table 4.1  Characteristics of the bottom-up approach

| One-size-fits-all | Physical datacenter layout |
|---|---|
| Supply-driven management | Silo operational models |
| Spaghetti transaction flow | Legacy skill sets |
| Lack of proximity of devices | |

hits, where compute, memory, I/O fabric, disk, storage, and connectivity to external feeds to service a single application are provided in terms of layout, not of service delivery. This approach affects performance and creates waste with unnecessary network traffic and bandwidth usage—all causing return on equity (ROE) to suffer.

*Proximity of Devices:* Traditional datacenter infrastructure design does not consider proximity of the various devices comprising a service unit that deliver processing to users. This inhibits performance (user experience of the business suffers) in that compute, memory, I/O fabric, disk, storage, and connectivity to external feeds are provided in terms of layout, not in terms of service delivery. Performance can be impacted by 30 times due to this approach. Moreover, this creates waste in terms of unnecessary network traffic congestion and bandwidth usage (ROE suffers).

*Physical Datacenter Layout:* The typical datacenter layout incorporates homogeneous pooling of various classes of resources. Servers by multiple classes (e.g., database servers, application servers) are typically in multiple pools; storages by file or by block are in different pools in their own area of the datacenter; network load-balancers, network switches, and network routers are pooled/deployed seemingly randomly throughout the datacenter. This approach appears sound in terms of physical floor organization, but it is not designed for optimal workload throughput or time to provision. The problems multiply when space allocations estimates are off from the actual usage, which either force large equipment moves or further randomly divides the infrastructure. The average provisioning and initial configuration cycle in datacenters with this type of layout is measured in weeks or months versus the minutes or days needed to provision, troubleshoot, or perform to meet the needs of the business.[1]

*Legacy Skill Sets:* Most organizations' talent planning is also implemented in silos. Specifically, personnel are trained for a finite role without any consideration of the corresponding impact of the role/skills on end-to-end service delivery (i.e., how the application operates). This creates a barrier to change that must be addressed when optimizing datacenter infrastructure, as well as a lack of sensitivity to business needs.

The challenges are daunting and have been contended with since the datacenter's inception. Incremental approaches have had limited success in improving the situation. In the interim, datacenters have become overwhelmed with server sprawl, which has caused power, cooling, and space requirements to explode. To make matters worse, large portions of compute power sit idle and can't be taken advantage of by systems that are resource constrained.

As business events create change in the environment, it becomes more important to be able to quickly adjust to changing requirements. In some cases, the business model itself may depend on being able to execute changes rapidly. For years the financial industry has been repurposing trading platform systems into risk calculation engines for nightly operations.[2] Even in cases such as this, the business is demanding more. The more volatile the environment, the more likely opportunities will be missed if reaction time isn't fast enough.

---

[1]Gillen A, et al. *Measuring the Business Value of Server Virtualization: Understanding the Impact of Guest Management*. IDC Whitepaper, June 2008, Figure 2, p. 11.

[2]Margulius D, Dawn of the Real-Time Enterprise. *InfoWorld*. Accessed 17.01.2003. <http://www.infoworld.com/article/02/01/17/020121fetca_1.html>.

The traditional siloed model of infrastructure deployment is too brittle and slow to react to these demands. These deployments are fine for their original static purposes, but they are not suited for rapid configuration changes. The support staff is ready to deploy cookie-cutter copies of core services and manually install software and/or modify configuration. The end result has dramatically curtailed an organization's ability to alter infrastructure configuration in response to changing business events.

Many who have recognized this problem but are unable to identify a holistic solution have turned to technologies in search of a solution. Technologies such as virtualization that coarsely divide physical resources into multiple virtual ones have improved the situation somewhat. However, there is overhead for running in this mode, and the boundary of operations is limited to predefined clusters that limit the growth of resources available to an application. Some workloads, such as CPU and IO intensive tasks, don't work well if virtualized. Furthermore, virtualized resources in and of themselves don't react to business events or dramatically increase the deployment or repurposing of new infrastructure. So while this does improve the situation in the short term, industry observers see this as a stop-gap measure until more complete solutions can be brought to bear.[3] Compacting servers without changing the underlying way they are utilized only delays the inevitable. Also, since deploying logical servers is "easy" compared to physical ones, without proper controls in place for when new servers are warranted, the original improvement goals may be lost to unnecessary deployments.

Fundamentally this bottom-up siloed approach underscores to the business the narrow rules of the datacenter. While the business accepts that there are fundamental components that comprise the organization's infrastructure, they don't really want or need to know about them. This approach is like a homebuilder who entertains a possible homebuyer with piles of bricks, uncut wood, and tools. The homebuyer doesn't much care; she just wants to see the finished product: her house.

## 4.2  Top-down: aligning supply to demand

A change of approach is needed to meet the demands of the business, which can be found by changing the lens through which the datacenter design is considered. Switching from the bottom-up supply-driven viewpoint to a top-down demand-driven viewpoint is the key to unlocking the true potential of the datacenter environment. This deceptively simple concept has dramatic implications to the design and implementation approach of the datacenter environment.

In a top-down demand-driven viewpoint, the business value chain (the demand) drives the features, functionality, and operational characteristics of the infrastructure (the supply). If the datacenter enables the characteristics

[3]Lass, Julie, "Virtualization Itself is Not the End-GAME – Making Enterprise Software Easier to Deploy, Manage, and Support Is", "AMD:The Virtualization Blog," Mar 30, 2009.

needed by the business value chain, then it is truly in service to the business and not the unhealthy alternative.

From economic theory we know that the most efficient way to get demand and supply in balance is through the creation of a marketplace. In this context, the marketplace is the datacenter itself. Note that IT cannot, nor should, control the demand (business value chain), but it only can influence the supply (infrastructure).

One might be tempted to claim that this is exactly what the siloed infrastructure groups are designed to do, but as we noted earlier, this is not the case. The isolated and rigid nature of resource supply is much too lumpy to smoothly meet and react to demand requirements. IT's challenge is meeting this supply in fine-grained increments.

Traditionally, application/service teams are required to understand the portion of the business value chain they support, but each team's understanding is typically isolated to minimize complexity. The technology organization focuses its attention on meeting the needs of these application/service teams and treats them as the customer (rather than the business users themselves). The proposal of adopting a top-down design implies that this will no longer be sufficient. Rather, the application/service and technology organizations must both have a base understanding of the full business value chain and how technology at each stage along the value chain is applied to align with the business goals.

Even with only a high-level overview of the business value chain, it becomes clear that each stage of the value chain has different drivers that define the needed technological characteristics. This has profound implications on how the infrastructure supply needs to be designed (Figure 4.1).

The first observation is that the demand on the infrastructure has an ebb and flow to it. Sales and trading peak during the daytime, while risk and reporting peak after normal business hours. Trading volume varies hourly depending on market conditions, while the operations and reporting load picks up during the end of month and spikes at the end of the year. The traditional implementation of infrastructure binds resources to specific groups, teams, and/or applications. However, the organizational demand varies hour by hour and minute by minute. To be efficient and effective, IT needs the flexibility to supply infrastructure as dictated by this demand, not the artificial ownership boundaries of the organization's structure. These artificial boundaries introduce productivity inefficiencies into the datacenter marketplace.

A second observation is that the approach of creating isolated pools of generalized resources is not the most effective method for supplying infrastructure. For example, the microsecond latency requirements of trading systems differ from data throughput requirements of risk systems. Generalized resources in support of these systems can only partially fulfill requirements, and, therefore, each system makes performance compromises. With two sets of resources, one for low latency and one for high throughput, each can be optimized, such that neither stage's performance is compromised. The end result is an environment characterized by higher utilization and less overall resources. The adoption of

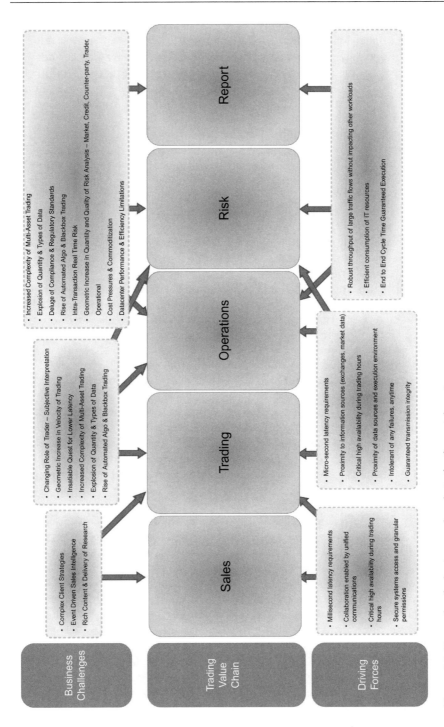

**Figure 4.1** Example of a business value chain for financial services.

specialized resources for task types allows each resource to be more efficient and effective, further improving the productivity of the datacenter marketplace. These two radical observations stem from taking the top-down demand-driven view and can be summarized as follows.

*Observation #1—Fluctuating Demand:* Scheduled and unscheduled business events dramatically affect demands on infrastructure, which must be flexible enough to rapidly react to apply supply dynamically, on demand, and in real time.

*Observation #2—Tailored Supply:* Resources optimized for the task at hand are consistently more effective than many generalized and nonoptimized resources.

From this we can define the core tenant of the top-down demand-driven design: *Fluctuating demand must be aligned with tailored supply.*

## 4.3   The impact of fluctuating demand on rigid supply

As demand becomes more volatile, supply must become more dynamic to meet it. Figure 4.2 shows this interaction between supply and demand. As business demands increase (volatility), opportunities are missed if the environment doesn't react fast enough. As infrastructure supply becomes more flexible, more resources are available. The performance zone is achieved when infrastructure supply is balanced with an organization's business demands.

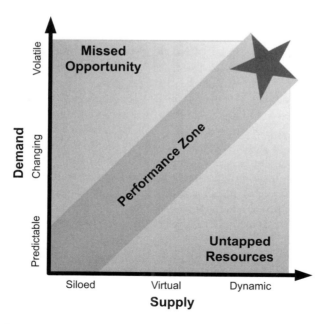

**Figure 4.2** Balancing supply and demand.

Consider those business events that must be incorporated during normal execution. If they're predicable and static, then managing infrastructure is easy. Once working, it can largely be left alone to operate, which is how today's datacenters were meant to function.

As technological solutions became more integral to organizations, virtualization technologies were introduced to help ease the supply crunch. This added flexibility helped bring coarse resources to bear. Instead of services being directly tied to their respective infrastructure, the services became tightly bound with the virtual resources. While this is a step in the right direction, optimizations tend to be localized to a few applications and hamstrung by limited ability to keep in sync with real-time business events.

Today the scale of IT operations has grown to such size that they are threatening to collapse under their own weight despite all earlier optimization efforts. Datacenter sprawl has become so pervasive that football fields of infrastructure have been deployed, and yet the business is missing opportunities for lack of resources. Significant portions of this infrastructure are running at low utilization or are reserved solely for disaster recovery. Embracing these opportunities can mean the difference between thriving and not surviving.

To understand why datacenter troubles persist, consider today's bottom-up siloed operations. There are organizational silos to handle facilities, such as power and cooling, equipment procurement, rack and stack, and those that manage various higher-level services, such as SAN, networking switches/routers, firewalls, file servers, database servers, application servers, OS management, and so on. Usually it falls to the application team or an overlay coordination team to marshal all the resources necessary to execute tasks the business requires (e.g., deploy a new risk-calculation system).

The end result is a rigid process that takes weeks, or more commonly months, to accomplish the business's goals. Indeed, application development time can often take less time than the deployment process. Expediting this deployment process only exacerbates the problems. Not only does it disrupt other in-flight activities, but when steps are short-circuited, errors occur that require troubleshooting expertise by more senior staff, which in turn introduce additional delays.

The traditional response to such disruptive events is to push back on those that are requesting the process to be expedited under the guise that there is not adequate time to complete the request. This causes an unhealthy environment in several ways: the implementers are always under the gun to complete the next impossible task; managers and their teams spend precious resources arguing what's reasonable and what's not; and the business remains unsatisfied despite the efforts of everyone involved.

Many initiatives have tried to smooth this process: SLAs from various groups on turnaround time, outright refusal to expedite requests, the introduction of workflow systems, and the accumulation of additional staff to manage the deployment processes, to name just a few. At best, incremental improvement is seen, but the underlying issues compounded by contention and strife remain. And all this just to execute one application rollout! Add to this the complexity of dozens of application teams clamoring for priority, and it is not a pretty situation. This process doesn't come close to coping with the fluctuating demands of business events in days, never mind in real time.

Typical problems found in rigid solution implementations, include the following.

- *Flexibility:* Both providers and consumers of IT infrastructure are frustrated by the complex and time-consuming process of deploying infrastructure. Once resources are in place, it is difficult to implement changes to them by their very nature.
- *Coordination:* The traditional approach of designing, procurement, deployment, and management activities is not holistic; instead, the tasks are separated into silos of control, making coordination difficult.
- *Resource Provisioning:* The amount of resources needed to supply a service is not fixed but rather demand characteristics vary over time. This means the service spends a large majority of its existence either over- or underprovisioned due to the difficulty of adjusting the scaling resources to meet demand.
- *Virtualization Scope:* The introduction of solutions utilizing virtualization and varied dynamic technologies are treated in the context of a single (or few) application(s); therefore, only a portion of their value is captured.
- *Peak Load Capacity:* The team usually designs the hardware to process two to five times the current anticipated peak load, leaving the resources significantly under-utilized at most times. But because of inherently fixed configurations, no other application or service can share that unused capacity.
- *Local Optimization:* Deployment and management fall under the control of operations and/or engineering where configurations and physical placement are arranged by hardware asset type (e.g., database servers have a section of the datacenter, application servers are placed in a different section).
- *Dispersed Resources:* Application growth may force new dedicated servers to be dispersed across the datacenter, which also slows response times and introduces additional latency.
- *Collaboration:* Highly collaborative applications and application tiers are rarely placed in close enough proximity, which increases latency, affecting response times and overall performance.
- *Physical Movement:* Movement of hardware resources around datacenters is currently unacceptable due to a lack of instrumentation to gauge and report on impacts, not to mention the potential for interruptions of service.
- *Managing Peaks:* Applying needed resources to mitigate processing peaks is difficult, time-consuming, and requires new asset procurement.
- *Workflow:* Existing processes and procedure are manual and do not consider management/administration of new technologies; workflow automation is nonexistent, which is key to productivity improvements.
- *Staff Overhead:* Design and procurement are based on individual application need and are typically marshaled through an organization by the application team.
- *Tools:* Metrics and monitoring tools are rarely robust enough to report, anticipate, or react to change; therefore, the consequences of spikes in demand are rarely correlated across the entire application.

While each compromise in and of itself doesn't appear significant, the result is a datacenter full of services that are overprovisioned on infrastructure that is randomly disbursed. This creates a maze of physical and logical interdependencies, destroying value due to losses of efficiency and agility. Here are some examples:

- Server growth is uncontained, but utilization on a 24-hour scale is typically less than 30 percent.
- Power, real estate, and personnel costs continue to grow unabated.
- The growth in servers and other infrastructure does not guarantee meeting SLAs for critical applications. Additional infrastructure often adds to response time and latency issues due to sprawl.
- Rapid growth of a datacenter increases complexity and cost, while often degrading performance, availability, and productivity—three key measures of user experience. Rapid and random infrastructure additions that are complicated by space constraints and/or limited planning make problem determination harder and make failure scenarios more obscure.
- All measures of Quality of Experience (QoE—user experience, cost, and efficiency) are subject to failure on a regular basis; balancing them becomes a full-time job in futility.

The business is no longer asking but *demanding* that its investments into technology be used toward the creation of significant competitive advantage. Keeping the lights on is no longer sufficient, and ramping up existing rigid processes has proven futile. To meet this goal, a fundamental shift needs to occur in how datacenters are implemented and operated.

---

### A Warning about Rigid Solutions

In the late 1800s, it was common to construct buildings with materials that were considered the sturdiest. From the foundation to the roof, builders of the day each picked the materials they each perceived best. The end result was the sturdiest and most rigid structures they could design. The 1906 San Francisco earthquake and its tragic consequences showed the fallacy of these efforts (Figure 4.3).

While a sturdy structure bears the weight of a building well, any lateral movement can lead to material failures with catastrophic effect. Significant effort has since been expended to understand the dynamics of how the earth moves and its effect on structures. This research has determined that the more rigid the structure, the more likely a catastrophic failure can occur.

Fundamental to the failures of late-19th-century architects was the bottom-up approach to material selection. Rather than thinking about a building's integrity as a whole, they were inclined to think of it in its constituent parts. The paradigm shift necessary was to consider the building as a whole and design from the top down—a building that achieves a distinguished look and is able to survive all the elements Mother Nature has in her bag of tricks.

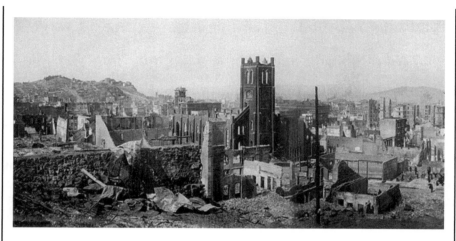

**Figure 4.3** The aftermath of the 1906 San Francisco earthquake.

Much like how the architects of the 20th century changed their designs to avoid catastrophic failures by considering the building and its environment as a whole, today's datacenter architects must consider the business goals of why the datacenter exists (e.g., to serve the business) and not just the sturdiest materials (e.g., what brand of firewall to buy). All of the various elements of the datacenter must mesh to create an agile solution to meet the rapidly changing and evolving demands of the business.

## 4.4  The tailored and dynamic environment

The creation of a dynamic environment requires fine-grained control over all the resources in the environment. In the traditional application server deployment model, an operating system is installed onto a dedicated physical server, and an application is installed onto that operating system. This process chains together the application, the OS, and the physical resource. Any meaningful change to this configuration is usually accomplished by wiping the physical server and restarting. Most operations are manual (or manual with a tool assist) and slow to take place (Figure 4.4).

The more tightly bound an application is to its underlying platform, the less capital efficiencies are realized. The IT waste associated with underutilized hardware resources has been clearly demonstrated,[4] which in turn has

[4]Gillen A, et al. *Measuring the Business Value of Server Virtualization: Understanding the Impact of Guest Management.* IDC Whitepaper, June 2008.

spawned the creation of datacenter consolidation programs that devise ways to more tightly compress the application infrastructure footprint onto existing hardware resources.

The industry has gravitated to virtualization technologies that enable a physical server to run multiple virtual server instances, effectively expanding the number of available servers in a hosting environment. Fundamentally, virtualization enabled a new degree of freedom with respect to how servers are provisioned and deployed (see middle of Figure 4.4). However, OS virtualization only separates one link of the platform stack that binds an application to its underlying platform. Specifically, an application is still tightly bound to the virtual server it runs within, and the OS virtualization technology itself is still tightly coupled to the physical server it is running. Also, virtualization clusters are limited in their physical scale, so multiple clusters are needed in large

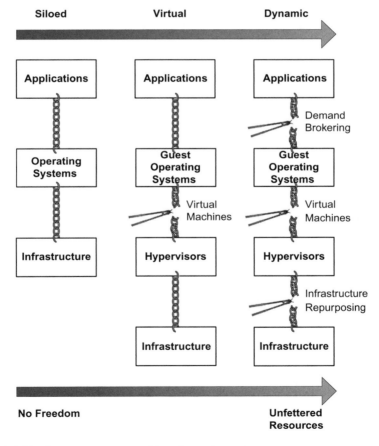

**Figure 4.4** Freeing resources to enable a dynamic environment.

environments. These constraints limit the scope of its value to accomplish the consolidation of services into a smaller footprint.

Breaking the remaining bonds will free resources so they can dynamically adapt to business needs in real time (see Figure 4.4). This facilitates additional application footprint consolidation and frees resources for other purposes. IT capital is more efficiently utilized, and the additional flexibility these measures produce enables significant responsiveness to business drivers.

### 4.4.1   Proposed solution: a Fit-for-Purpose Real Time Infrastructure (RTI)

A Fit-for-Purpose RTI represents a shift in thinking about how total IT supply is designed, purchased, deployed, managed, and utilized, which facilitates the elimination of silos of operation and the management of the environment holistically and dynamically in real time—solutions to the primary challenges of the traditional approach.

This logical model is comprised of two fundamental concepts: Fit-for-Purpose and RTI. While each concept does not require the other to operate, together their synergy creates significant business value: a dynamic and real-time service-oriented infrastructure based on business demand that allocates optimized resources from infrastructure supply to that demand as needed/when needed. Let's explore these concepts further.

### 4.4.2   What is Fit-for-Purpose?

For a moment, instead of resources in the datacenter, consider personal transportation, such as sports cars, SUVs, pickup trucks, and U-Haul trucks. With little thought, you'd be able to choose the appropriate vehicle for almost any situation. You would probably want to use the sports car for a weekend getaway trip. If you have to drive the kids to soccer practice, the SUV would probably be most appropriate. If you are helping a friend to move, you'd probably want the U-Haul. The point is that picking the right vehicle category for the trip can make life easy or difficult. Fit-for-Purpose is about avoiding ending up with landscaping stones and mulch in the trunk of your sports car.

Resources in a datacenter are often deployed in isolation—focused on a single application or transaction requirement—without consideration of the overall collaborative work characteristic at hand. The demands of work can vary significantly and can be broadly categorized as low latency, complex transactions, numerical processing, and information integration. Rather than force-fitting work onto generic hardware, it's important to consider the total needs of each work category and how to optimize supply to them. For example, the creation of a Java Optimized execution environment with a Java Appliance Accelerator is a significantly more effective solution than each application deploying another application server to run Java.

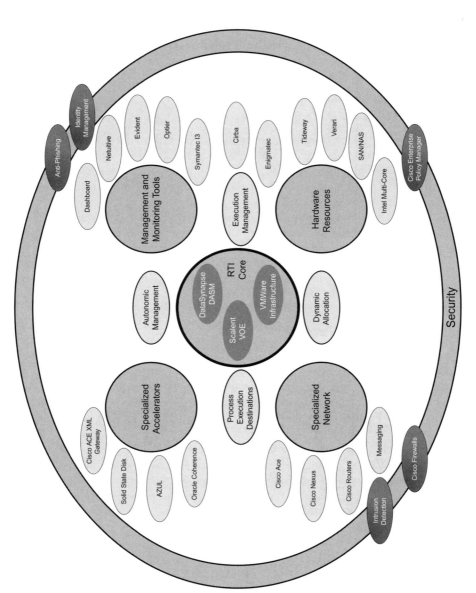

**Figure 4.5** RTI core elements and technologies.

### 4.4.3 What is Real Time Infrastructure (RTI)?

The purpose of RTI is to implement fluidity of resources to meet demand in real time while enhancing the quality of experience,[5] enabling transparency of processing so latency can be understood for every component of an application and facilitating faster deployment time, providing a better competitive edge. This requires autonomic management capabilities that predict problems, enable self-healing in case of failure of a system, a global dashboard view that relates business transactions to its effect on infrastructure supply, and guaranteed execution of designated transactions based on business policy. Figure 4.5 shows some of the different types of technologies and products employed in an RTI solution.

### 4.4.4 Operating characteristics of a Fit-for-Purpose RTI

Putting these two concepts together dramatically improves on their individual value. RTI is designed to make IT as agile and responsive as the business needs. While RTI alone does yield agility, there is a limit to its ability to generate efficiency. The addition of Fit-for-Purpose acknowledges that each resource and element of work has different capabilities and characteristics. A Fit-for-Purpose infrastructure matches resource capabilities with work characteristics for more efficient and effective execution. Together, the concepts of RTI and Fit-for-Purpose work in concert to create multiple pools of heterogeneous resources that can be dynamically brought to bear for the various types of work the organization is challenged to execute, which facilitates comprehensive operational control of the environment.

These characteristics make it well suited to align fluctuating demand to tailored supply, the core tenant of our top-down demand-driven design. The key operating characteristics of Fit-for-Purpose RTI are as follows:

- Dynamic allocation of IT supply to real-time demand based on service contract requirements, including guaranteed execution response, throughput volume, work characteristics, and time constraints or cost/margin rules. Dynamic allocation is further augmented through workflow automation that extends the capability of policy-based alignment of resources.
- Real-time transaction work management that synchronizes work characteristics (demand) with resource capabilities (supply) to meet execution management service contract requirements.
- Self-healing attributes, such that failures are seamlessly repaired without human intervention.
- Efficient execution of work on infrastructure that is tailored to the type of processing needed.

---

[5]Quality of Experience (QoE). A maturity model premised on the belief that cost efficiency and service quality must be balanced in order for any technology approach to be sustainable, and have continued business buy-in.

# 4.5   Realizing a Fit-for-Purpose RTI design (design principles for RTI)

Realizing a Fit-for-Purpose RTI design requires a significant understanding of the needs of the environment. Here are the five key areas that need to be addressed to realize the design, which will be elucidated in subsequent sections of the document:

*Drivers:* The business and IT drivers that define the goals of the design.

*Artifacts:* The quantification of business consumption demand and platform infrastructure supply that describe the usage of the environment.

*Core Competences:* To take advantage of the understanding formed from the artifacts, there are a number of core competences that need to be developed.

*Technologies:* With the preceding understanding and competences, technologies must be deployed to realize the vision. The artifacts are used to influence the selection from the various available technologies to choose those that best meet the Fit-for-Purpose design principles.

*Governance:* The policies and procedures used to manage the IT environment.

## 4.5.1   Drivers

Additional benefits beyond solving the traditional challenges are enabled by this type of design. To realize its full value, we need to consider the entire spectrum of business and IT drivers. Note that there are two sets of goals: those of the business consuming the infrastructure (demand) and those of the IT Infrastructure team (supply). Both must be considered in developing the design.

### Business goals and drivers

*Reduced Time to Market:* IT becomes agile enough to add new services and products, reducing lead time from months or weeks to days.

*Business Capacity:* IT can increase its processing capability as the business grows, handling unexpected spikes in transactional demand in real time.

*Budget Predictability:* IT can show that its costs are predictable and proportional to business growth.

*Competitive Advantage:* When fully realized, RTI represents a significant step toward IT becoming a strategic asset for the business instead of just another cost center. IT becomes a strategic enabler for the business (see Appendix B).

*Business Assurance:* IT can demonstrate SLA performance guarantees through consistent availability of resources, regardless of business demands.

### IT goals and drivers

*Supply Efficiency:* RTI mandates a fluid set of infrastructure services that make resources available to meet oncoming demand at the level that is needed, when it is needed.

*Utilization Efficiency:* RTI assumes demand fluctuates for different applications at different times.

*Demand-Driven Utilization:* RTI utilizes a Fit-for-Purpose analysis approach that promotes a top-down demand-driven design approach that can be configured bottom-up for specific application needs.

*Reuse:* RTI respects and incorporates physical limitations into the fit-for-purpose analysis, where the operational characteristics of performance, security, and availability are compared across the constituent patterns of applications to determine similarity.

*Performance through Localization:* RTI principles include consideration for proximity when assembling an execution environment for collaborating applications (i.e., taking latency and response time into account).

*Performance through Optimization:* RTI designates four fundamental operating environments (infrastructure patterns) that facilitate specific operational behaviors. Once analyzed, any application/service will be able to operate in one of those four environments.

*Quality of Service:* RTI provides a tactical capability to utilize resources based on business polices that balance: user experience, efficiency, and cost.

*Improved Processes:* RTI tactics affect how systems and infrastructure are designed, managed, serviced, and utilized.

*Organizational Roles:* RTI tactics positively affect how IT organizations are structured in terms of roles and responsibilities, providing more agile responses to new needs and problem resolution and determination.

## 4.5.2   Artifacts

Once the drivers are well understood, a number of artifacts are developed to characterize how the environment should be utilized. The purpose of these artifacts is to quantify the environment in terms of business consumption demand and platform infrastructure supply, which facilitates a healthy and holistic grasp of the complexity of the problem being solved from the two primary perspectives of the business consumers and the infrastructure supply team. The following descriptions are of artifacts that are generally created in the process of developing, deploying, and using a Fit-for-Purpose RTI environment.

### Business consumption demand

*Business Value Chain:* The creation of a value chain depicting how business execution correlates to IT infrastructure implementation of underlying capabilities.

*Forensic Analysis:* A process whereby the existing business platform and supporting infrastructure are identified and documented. These details are usually left to local system managers, so organizations frequently have a lackluster overall view of existing systems, their purpose, and how they interact. This information is critical in planning a future state business platform.

*Current State Alignment Map:* A number of views used to describe how the Business Value Chain maps to products and promotes the desired Qualities of Experience (QoE), including latency, throughput, resiliency, and cost. Once available, infrastructure gaps and duplicate systems in the value chain become apparent. Their elimination makes the organization more efficient and effective with its IT budget.

*Product and Portfolio Management:* Coalescing business and technical priorities in continuous capability adoption to ensure sustainment and differentiation of your business through IT.

*Economic Model:* Define the business and IT linkage of demand and supply. Orient analysis and model output around the interactive dynamics of consumption of IT resources by the business and the fulfillment behavior of processing by IT. This needs to be correlated with the value chain function and the corresponding products or services that are differentiated by business type (liquidity, risk transference, advice), business importance (margin, labor, flow), and cost to transact.

*Dynamic Economic Model:* A defined business and IT linkage of demand and supply. The model must be created around the interactive dynamics of IT resources by the business and the fulfillment behavior of processing by IT.

## Platform infrastructure supply

*Demand Mapping:* In natural language terms (no geek-speak!), define and capture the "day in the life of the business," what it expects, and where the problems are. Be sure to understand sensitivities to cost, bottlenecks, and timing constraints, as well—specifically, quality attributes and operational requirements of the business in terms of calendar events (e.g., different usage at end of month), demographics (i.e., user types, business lines, and geographic spread), and competitive benchmarking across the straight-through-processing (STP) value chain.

*Future State Design Map:* Infrastructure gaps, missing characteristics, and duplicate systems are identified from the Current State Alignment Map. The Future State Design Map depicts the resulting business platform once those issues are resolved. This results in additional efficiency and more effective monetary allocation to IT.

*Fit-for-Purpose Operational Footprints:* The categorization of operational qualities based on demand facilitates the realignment of processes, thereby optimizing infrastructure resources to required characteristics. Tailored and coordinated operational footprints are organized in tightly coupled physical environments called Processing Execution Destinations (PEDs).

*Abstraction as a Fundamental Design Principle:* The design of each infrastructure component and layer needs sufficient abstraction so operational details are hidden from all collaborating components and layers. This maximizes the opportunity to create a virtualized infrastructure, which facilitates rapid deployment and simplicity of operation.

*Service and Change Management:* Dynamic models of operation require processes and procedures of service, delivery, and change management to accommodate the "on-the-fly" and "as needed, when needed" operations of IT.

## 4.5.3 Core competencies

Having drivers and artifacts are not enough to develop the full understanding required for designing and efficiently utilizing the environment. A number of core competencies are needed from those involved, including a solid sense for and ability to perform:

*Business and IT Alignment:* to understand high-impact areas, biggest pain points, and future state vision.

*Dependency Mapping:* to gain insight into the interrelationship of applications, content, and services.

*Rigorous Measurements Discipline:* to discover supply-and-demand characteristics.

*Fit-for-Purpose Design:* to create optimal platforms based on the real-time assessment of business demand.

RTI *Implementations:* to pilot, verify, validate, and educate.
RTI *Operations:* to ensure consistent resilience and efficiency.
RTI *Sustainable Model:* to create and maintain a strategic asset for the business.

### 4.5.4 Technologies

In the context of business and IT drivers, with the understanding of the business consumption demand and platform infrastructure supply artifacts, and by the abilities of the core competencies a Fit-for-Purpose RTI technology design can be created/implemented that meets the business needs and yet is manageable by IT. The following list contains a number of the technologies commonly used and their primary value, followed by an example of how they have been brought together in a financial services environment.

*Grid Brokers:* Dynamically allocate workloads to resources with appropriate processing and memory characteristics.
*Service Brokers:* Dynamically allocate work in real time to available compute resources based on business policy (Figure 4.6).
*Provisioning Tools:* Prepare application "personas" that create virtualized infrastructure resources (Figure 4.7 and see Figure 4.6).

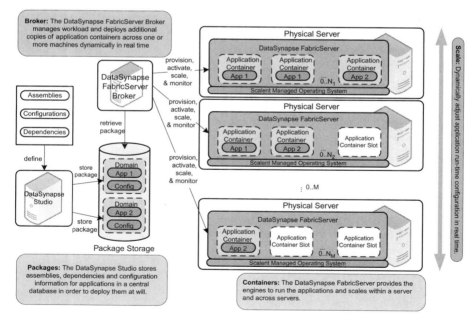

**Figure 4.6** Scalent VOE™ and DataSynapse FabricServer™.
Manage current and new resource infrastructure dynamically. VOE provisions bare metal, and FabricServer enables the ability to define, package, provision, activate, scale, and monitor applications, dynamically adjusting where and the number of instances of an application based on demand, seamlessly and in real time.

*Network Attached Appliances:* Offload intensive processing from servers, enhancing
   throughput while significantly lowering power consumption and datacenter footprint utilization.

*Network Accelerator Devices:* Advance protocol switching, streamline authorization,
   and format translation at wire speed, enabling faster, less complex integration.

*Solid State Disks:* Provide large data set access at memory access speed.

*Transactional Caching and Data Federation Facilities:* Enhance performance (response time
   and throughput), reduce data movement, and facilitate transparent multisource data
   access.

*Instrumentation Technologies:* Measure latency across all hops a transaction takes correlated measurement of an application across all tiers, comprehensive utilization
   dashboards, and predictive analysis tools.

*Optimized Processing Containers:* Reduce power consumption and floor space by utilizing unique vertically cooled processor racks (Figure 4.8).

*Multicore CPUs:* Accelerate multithreaded applications and consolidate processing of
   single threaded applications (see Figure 4.8 for an example).

*Specialized CPUs:* Application logic burned into a chip (field programmable array) that
   runs many times faster than conventional software.

*Dependency Mapping Facility:* Presents facts about how applications and services are
   related in production.

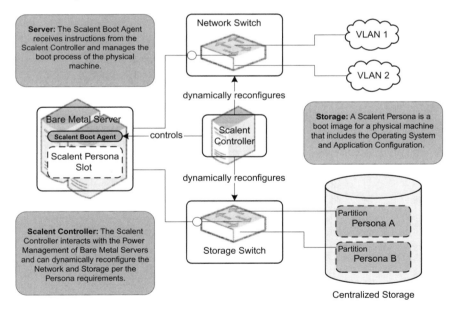

**Figure 4.7** Scalent's Virtual Operating Environment (VOE).

Scalent's Virtual Operating Environment technologies enable a bare-metal server to boot
up any Scalent managed operating system instance, which is referred to as a Persona. At
boot time, the Scalent controller decides which Persona to load by configuring the storage
switch to redirect to the proper partition. If needed, Scalent can also configure ports on the
network switch to make sure the device connects to the right VLAN. This lets a processing
resource dramatically change its function (e.g., an application server can be turned into a
database server).

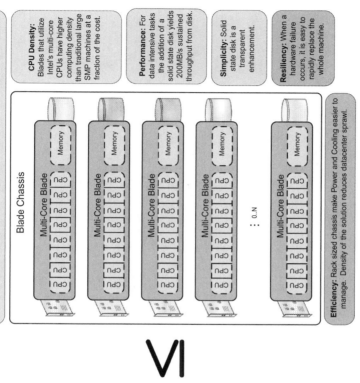

**Performance:** Intel multi-cores accelerate performance of applications that are multi-threaded and provides a more efficient use of resources for a wider range of applications.

**CPU Density:** Blades that utilize Intel's multi-core CPUs have higher computing density than traditional large SMP machines at a fraction of the cost.

**Performance:** For data intensive tasks the addition of a solid state disk yields 200MB/s sustained throughput from disk.

**Simplicity:** Solid state disk is a transparent enhancement.

**Resiliency:** When a hardware failure occurs, it is easy to rapidly replace the whole machine.

Blade Chassis

Multi-Core Blade — CPU CPU CPU CPU CPU CPU — Memory

Multi-Core Blade — CPU CPU CPU CPU CPU CPU — Memory

Multi-Core Blade — CPU CPU CPU CPU CPU CPU — Memory

Multi-Core Blade — CPU CPU CPU CPU CPU CPU — Memory

: : 0..N

Multi-Core Blade — CPU CPU CPU CPU CPU CPU — Memory

**Efficiency:** Rack sized chassis make Power and Cooling easier to manage. Density of the solution reduces datacenter sprawl.

Large Scale SMP Machine

SMP Module — Memory CPU Memory / Bus / Memory CPU Memory

SMP Module — Memory CPU Memory / Bus / Memory CPU Memory

SMP Module — Memory CPU Memory / Bus / Memory CPU Memory

SMP Module — Memory CPU Memory / Bus / Memory CPU Memory

Bus

**Reduce Resource Costs:** Cap legacy investment; Employ lower cost yet more efficient resources (e.g. Multi-core blades instead of a large SMP machines).

**Figure 4.8** Multicore CPUs with solid state disk.

Cap legacy investment; employ lower-cost yet more efficient resources. Blades that utilize Intel's multicore CPUs have higher compute density at a fraction of the cost. Additionally, a blade solution has more flexibility on how it is deployed than traditional large SMP systems.

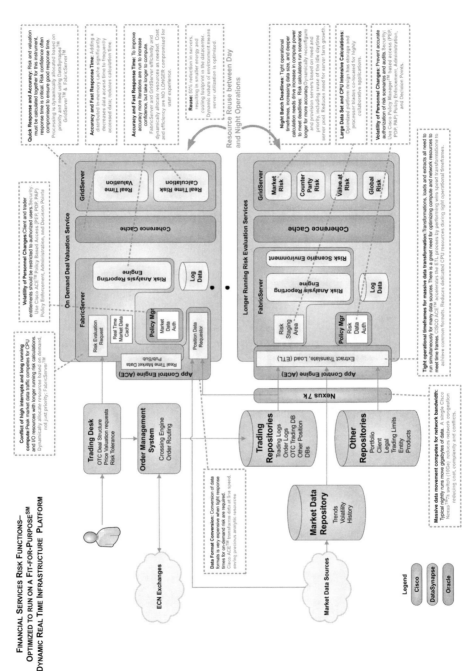

Figure 4.9 Financial Services Risk Functions optimized to run on a Fit-for-Purpose RTI platform.

Figure 4.9 shows an example of pulling all these technologies together for Financial Services Risk Functions.

### 4.5.5  Governance: the key to sustaining RTI value

The introduction of Fit-for-Purpose RTI as an approach for IT to become more agile is not just about buying particular sets of technology. It is about a shift in IT thinking that will give IT the grounding required to become a strategic enabler of business goals as opposed to being just a cost center. IT and businesses must work together and think of IT as an investment. This requires a shift in process, people skills, and technology usage. This shift needs to have an underlying theme about investment discipline, which requires IT governance.

IT governance has been a controversial topic for some time, because while everyone agrees that governance is critical to the long-term success of Enterprise IT, there is rarely a consensus about how it should be done. During the boom years of 1996–2000, any kind of rationalization was ignored because the Internet was so disruptive that reaction to service was the key strategy. After the crash of 2000, the result of this nondirected proliferation of applications became evident as the number of customers facing applications and product databases routinely tripled across large enterprises. Suddenly, governance was established to essentially stop proliferation, but it did not address renationalization, as budgets were tight and the focus was on critical applications that kept the business running. The movement away from large SMP machines to commoditized blade racks after the crash was prompted by the belief that significant cost reductions would ensue, but this movement caused a different set of proliferation issues, including excess complexity and server sprawl, which has been covered in this book.

In neither case were the issues of proliferation or rationalization addressed, and with the resurgence in the economy occurring in 2004, the consequences of not having a coherent governance strategy began to emerge in terms of runaway costs, unnecessary complexity, and reduced agility.

IT governance cannot be a passive rubber stamp, nor can it be a stifling, irrelevant ivory tower exercise. IT governance is about incorporating the discipline of IT portfolio management, along with a set of sustainment processes for product management, incentive alignment, skills augmentation, and the creation of an internal IT marketplace that both reuses and produces IT assets. This marketplace requires the currency of trust as its catalyst, and trust can only occur when accurate and timely information is readily available at the appropriate level of detail for each stakeholder group.

*Portfolio management*

Portfolio management is about making sure that investments are guided as they relate to business goals. The guiding principle for IT portfolio management is that every dollar spent on IT is an investment. IT competes for investment dollars in an organization with every other department (sales, marketing, and client services). When a business makes an investment in IT, the business expects some or all of the following:

- Better ability at revenue generation, better efficiency, or risk reduction.
- Greater agility so the business can respond to market and regulatory pressures faster.
- Insight into the alignment of IT and the achievement of business goals.
- Can IT show alignment and support to business goals?
- Can impact be measured; is value traceable across stakeholders?

## Portfolio management vision

Investment in IT can be managed as a portfolio of assets that have cost and value over time. Portfolio management, which includes governance, must put the assets into aligned context with the business goals. Business and IT must take an investment management view of these assets so the collective senior leadership understands, guides, realizes, and governs the portfolio. In this new paradigm IT is about showing its relevance. The components of the vision include the following:

- Aligned business and IT that improves business strategy results.
- Communication between business and IT is significantly improved.
- Business values of delivered assets are measurable and tangible.
- Other intangibles can be viewed as well: customer satisfaction, efficiency, and regulatory compliance.
- Risks in technology can be measured in terms of skills, product maturity, and so on. The risk of doing nothing can also be measured.
- Strategic cost avoidance can be practiced because there is structured analysis of duplicate efforts.
- Investment discipline is exercised so that low-value efforts are identified early and stopped.
- There is portfolio focus so uncoordinated funding is reduced, emphasizing shared services where possible.
- Investment leverage is encouraged.
- Cross-LOB sharing is measured and tracked as a key to rationalization and efficiency.
- Contribution to IT assets and compliance to standards are rewarded according to value.
- Optimization and agility is fostered through the use of standard best practices.
- The results can be shown to leverage investments in the RTI environment.

## Managing RTI through portfolio management

Migrating to RTI efficiently requires governance of existing services and assets and a clear understanding of future requirements. IT executives not only require an inventory but also an integrated view of the information that explains those assets. A repository is required to house all of the portfolio management information, which in turn is collected from numerous sources in a large enterprise, including CMDBs, various inventories, performance statistics repositories, and so on. The IT assets have many levels of detail, but executives think of IT assets in terms of services, applications, and infrastructure. Executives must be able to access knowledge that enables them to understand their asset base so that they can provide directives for change and then have architects, project managers, developers, and operations all be able to have a tangible connection to those targeted assets, while accessing greater levels of detail to make the changes.

## The key management principles for IT governance

Business and IT executive buy-in is crucial with IT as investment as the guiding principle. Without this, the initiatives that are so transformative will have no grounding. Executives must actively guide the investments; grounded in business capability, risk tolerance, and the need for agility.

Organizational and incentive structure alignment is critical to success. Executive management must be paid based on an ability to hit RTI goals that include supporting specific IT governance goals. The problems of domain of control need to be addressed. Most executives feel very uncomfortable if they do not own all of the assets that their applications run on. Shared services, frameworks, and shared infrastructure break that domain of control, so organizational structure, processes, and incentives must be created that accommodate this new paradigm.

Dynamic governance is critical. This requires that applications and infrastructure in transition must be accounted for. Typically infrastructure, procedures, and applications become more complex during transition before they are simplified. Exceptions need to be considered and accounted for. Change needs to be embraced, and that includes changes to applications that are not necessarily strategic but are required to run the business. It is during this time of change that a new set of shared values about how to use and operate a Fit-for-Purpose RTI need to be defined and promoted.

Fit-for-Purpose RTI must be supported as if it were a utility with processes to create and review SLAs and create tangible chargeback models. Feedback must be part of this process, which includes performance and availability measurement, goals compliance, and operational efficiency. Executives must have transparent access to information so they can make informed decisions. Training must be targeted to make the change to a dynamic RTI and a dynamic management process. It must be thought of as a maturity process requiring levels of training for all stakeholders.

An IT marketplace should be established so asset designs, working products, asset reviews, and hard performance data can all be viewed as part of the IT portfolio management repository. This repository will enable marketplace dynamics that can effectively leverage the Fit-for-Purpose RTI platform, fostering agility, transparency, and cost effectiveness. The goal of these management principles is to enable the organization to be agile so it can effectively take advantage of the resources and better meet the goals of the organization.

## 4.6  Processing Execution Destinations (PEDs)

To physically realize the Fit-for-Purpose RTI logical model, the top-down approach must be employed to map business processing demands (BVC) with tailored processing resources (DSC). These mapped relationships can then be correlated against infrastructure qualities to capture, visualize, and isolate how to optimize datacenter infrastructure to meet the goals of performance, availability, cost, and efficiency.

This is accomplished through the design of packaged infrastructure ensembles that implement a platform that is specifically tailored to the needs of applications and services that run within that portion of the BVC. The collection of ensembles that make up a stage of the BVC are physically grouped together in a Process Execution Destination (PED). The resulting PEDs effectively subdivide the datacenter by BVC stages.

The ensemble design concept is the physical manifestation of the fit-for-purpose logical architecture. The approach emphasizes that the service consumer is provided predictable, satisfying response times while balancing cost and efficiency of the operating platform within the larger environment. Core to this design is the development of a physical footprint of infrastructure (network, storage, compute, memory, disk, I/O, housing container, power, cabling, etc.) that is tailored to the workload. This footprint concept has to be thought of as a composition of service delivery units that can be consumed in a variable manner-on-demand consumption and real-time reconfiguration (like a utility).

As mentioned earlier, the processing demands of work can vary significantly and can be broadly categorized into the categories *low latency, complex transactions, numerical processing,* and *information integration,* which is how the suggested ensembles are organized. Figures 4.10–4.14 show the different ensemble types.

A PED is implemented as a pool of integrated and validated ensembles of technology solutions to support the needed BVC operating characteristics. This is not a siloed pool of resources, but rather it contains everything required to execute its targeted work type, as a platform. Note that PEDs may hold more than one ensemble to meet the multiple operating characteristics needed by that segment of the BVC (e.g., the use of a low latency ensemble combined with a numerical processing ensemble in support of Front Office Trading).

Provisioned resources from the appropriate PED will meet the needed load characteristics of allocation requests by design, and will be enforced by the allocation manager. In alignment with the Fit-for-Purpose RTI logical model, provisioning should be done dynamically and in real time.

Within a PED, the ensembles are interconnected via a unified networking fabric that offers low latency and high-throughput connectivity and with a variety of common infrastructure services. Some services are ubiquitously available to all ensembles, while others perform specialized functions only required for particular workloads. The architecture is modular, providing for simple scale-up and scale-down capabilities based on business demand.

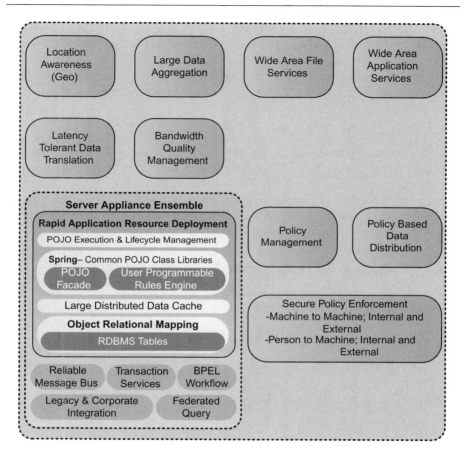

**Figure 4.10** Ensembles in a logical architecture.

Getting the applications and services to operate within this type of model requires that the application development process include the consideration of the packaging and automated deployment as part of production readiness and not as an afterthought. The RTI technologies discussed earlier have tools to facilitate this that largely reduces the work to a one-time setup of configuration information.

Once the applications and services are enabled to provision at need, it becomes a matter of policy on how resources are supplied to meet business demand. Furthermore, the RTI infrastructure supports switching workloads with SLAs measured in minutes or seconds, depending on the physical resource type. It's possible to react to business events dynamically in real time and in an efficient manner.

As an added benefit, once business functionality is organized into PEDs, disaster recovery can be streamlined. Instead of the traditional application by application approach to DR, a more holistic strategy can be employed. The PED encompasses a segment of the BVC and its related DSC. When the PED is recovered it will also restore the encompassed business functionality. Contrast this to the traditional approach of bottom-up recovery, where the attention is first on the resources and/ or data and little consideration is given to whether something useful to the business is operating. By managing the recovery at a PED level, much of the complexity of individual application recovery can be dramatically simplified.

### 4.6.1   Low latency ensemble

In critical customer-facing supply chain environments, there are mission-critical workloads that are sensitive to millisecond-level latency delays. In such an environment, data must be delivered to systems with no queuing or buffering, there must be extremely high system resilience during trading hours, and data translation must be done at wire speed. Figure 4.11 shows a simple representation of the key elements for a low latency ensemble.

### 4.6.2   Complex transaction ensemble

Transaction processing functions of sophisticated business supply chains require interaction with numerous internal and external systems to complete a single

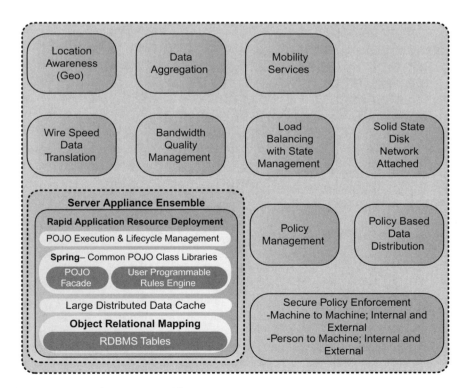

**Figure 4.11** Low latency ensemble.

transaction. This type of workload execution requires an ensemble that has continuous availability, coordinates movement of the transactions through the system, and maintains high levels of security throughout the transaction lifecycle. Figure 4.12 shows the key elements of this type of processing ensemble.

### 4.6.3 Numerical processing ensemble

The ability to model and analyze potential events and outcomes is critical to any organization's survivability. Therefore, an ensemble optimized for numerical processing that enables massive calculations and enormous data read/write in the least amount of time is a business differentiator. Figure 4.13 depicts the key elements required for such an ensemble.

### 4.6.4 Information integration ensemble

The final ensemble type deals with the integration of data from many typically disparate sources to provide a unified view of the information. This capability

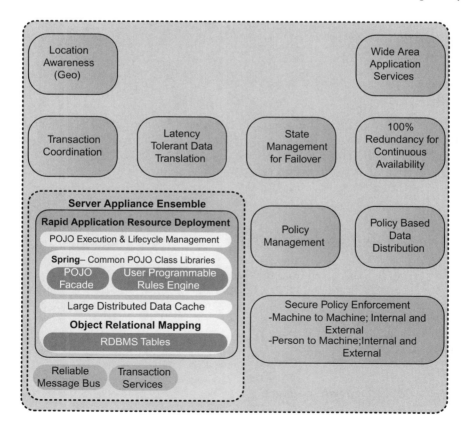

**Figure 4.12** Complex transaction ensemble.

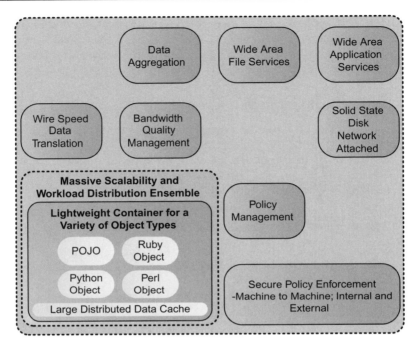

**Figure 4.13** Numerical processing ensemble.

is vital for internal functions such as client relationship management and is mandatory for external functions like client statements and regulatory reporting. As shown in Figure 4.14, this type of ensemble requires key elements like high security, data aggregation/translation/distribution and high throughput (but not necessarily low latency).

## 4.7    The Next Generation Datacenter (NGDC) design

Thus far we've discussed taking a top-down demand-driven viewpoint, a Fit-for-Purpose RTI logical model, and a PED physical model. Together these concepts make the foundation of the Next Generation Datacenter design. The NGDC design itself (Figure 4.15) is organized around two architectural views into the infrastructure: the Deployment Architecture (Demand) and the Platform Architecture (Supply).

### 4.7.1    Deployment architecture

Traditionally ignored in a datacenter design, the Deployment Architecture is where the top-down view of the Business Value Chain meets the Fit-for-Purpose

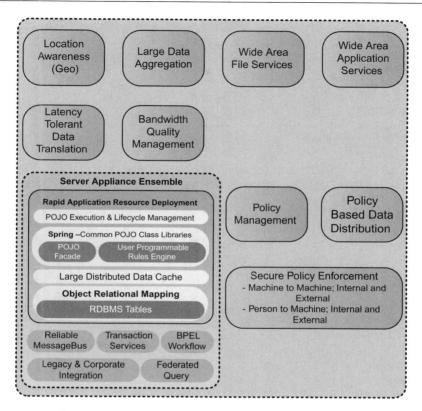

**Figure 4.14** Information integration ensemble.

RTI environment and therefore the PEDs. The Deployment Architecture takes into account the physical location of resources such that services that interact with each other are co-located as much as possible. Key design attributes of the Deployment Architecture include the following:

- *Business-Driven Execution Design:* Applications and services grouped by value chain function and processing type, eliminating spaghetti transactions that cause negative business performance impacts.
- *Fit-for-Purpose Datacenter Design:* Tailored functional ensembles of components and services within the datacenter footprint that are engineered in a demand-based manner to meet the needs of the business value chain function and drive optimal performance, cost, and efficiency.
- *Business Demand* is driven by business goals, operational qualities (events, transactions, and reports), and workload descriptions (performance, availability, cost, and efficiency).

On the left side of Figure 4.15, two PEDs are shown that have been architected top down but engineered to be tailored bottom up to fit a particular

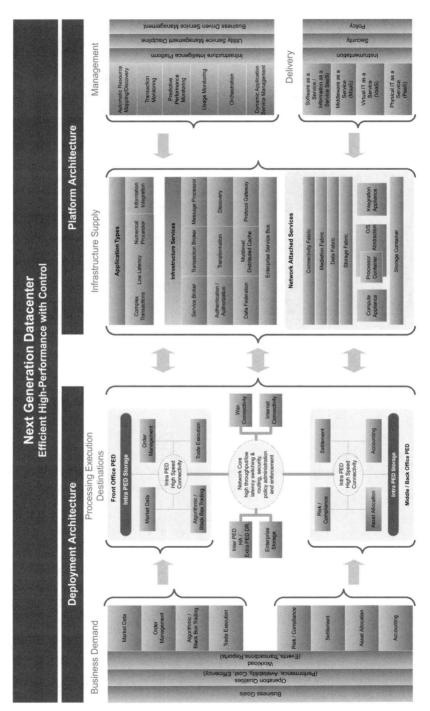

**Figure 4.15** Next Generation Datacenter.

suite of business functions that collaborate heavily and also demonstrate similar operating characteristics.

A Front Office PED and a Middle/Back Office PED are depicted. Each PED provides fast, cohesive interconnectivity for business functions that must collaborate heavily with high-performance requirements. There is intra-PED storage that provides shared access to commonly used data. This data may be on spinning or solid state disks, depending on the operational qualities of the business functions.

In particular, the Front Office PED would need to process large, unthrottled amounts of incoming data, but it would also need very high availability, so a dynamic caching facility would be needed to satisfy both of those requirements. While this PED depicts capital markets business functions, these can easily be replaced by a business-to-commerce (B2C) function set, including rich media streaming, or a large real-time point-of-sale aggregator for a retail chain.

The Middle/Back Office PED depicts the fulfillment side of capital markets, but it could also facilitate business-to-business (B2B) fulfillment as a result of a large B2C Front Office PED. The operating characteristics of middle/back office functions are an aggregation of large data sets where latency is less of an issue, but large calculation processes that iterate to achieve certain accuracy are emphasized, as are complex data transformations. Intra-PED storage would be used heavily as staging areas for the various phases of data manipulation that these functions perform.

The functions residing in the Front Office and Middle/Back Office PEDs need to communicate using larger data movements. The interaction is infrequent, but the volumes transmitted would be very large.

The critical nature of the functions running in these two PEDs would require an investment in disaster recovery and intraday high availability/recovery. The combination of high-speed interconnections through the network core would ensure seamless changes in operations. These two PEDs contain critical functions that affect an organization's revenue stream and would likely need to obtain and send information to other applications in an enterprise (some not in PEDs); therefore, access to enterprise storage is shown.

### 4.7.2   Platform architecture

Platform Architecture is comprised of traditional IT assets deployed within the datacenter, with a focus on logically grouping infrastructure supply and its management and deployment. In the NGDC, these assets are not fixed but are instead dynamic.

Key design attributes of the Platform Architecture include the following.

*Dynamic Application Service Management (DASM):* A unified management fabric providing dynamic and automated provisioning, configuration management, real-time metering, and runtime control of business application and infrastructure services across the virtual datacenter footprint.

*Process Unanticipated Peaks:* A datacenter operates as a service utility that reflects a demand-based model where services are used as needed and pools of resources are allocated on demand as required.

*Facilitate and Control Growth:* Simplified engineering combined with dynamic management promotes greater efficiency and enables greater agility in the implementation of new services, while reducing costs, waste, and unnecessary consumption, resulting in sustainable growth efficiency.

The infrastructure supply represents the target platform that will run the applications and infrastructure services and contain network attached services. Applications are characterized by type (complex transaction, numerical processing, rich media, and information integration). Typical infrastructure services are shown. The list can be much longer, while network attached services are shown as a logical depiction of the ensembles mentioned earlier.

Utility services are the key differentiator in the NGDC architecture as they include the facilities to operate the NGDC in a dynamic real-time manner. Business policies are shown as drivers of the dynamic execution management used in the PEDs. Comprehensive utilization reporting and SLA adherence reporting provide guidance on how to optimize the NGDC operational model.

On the right-hand side of the infrastructure supply, the management functionality is described. The focus is on deploying the various means of monitoring the environment (transaction, predictive performance, and usage monitoring) in combination with automatic resourcing mapping and DASM to bring transparency and control to the environment.

Also, on the right-hand side of the infrastructure supply, the delivery is described as an evolving set of service offerings, including software as a service (SaaS), middleware as a service (MaaS), virtual IT as a service (VaaS), and physical IT as a service (PaaS). The distinguishing aspects for the NGDC delivery architecture include the following:

- Comprehensive instrumentation allows both dynamic real-time adjustments in allocation schemes and comprehensive trend analysis that facilitates decision makers to refine polices and a strategy as the datacenter evolves.
- A security model, which once hardened is reused many times.
- Policies for allocation of resources based on demand, not just fixed priority.

The center of the diagram, where the deployment and platform architectures juxtapose, depicts the dividing line where business demand and technology supply meet and must be kept in balance. The dual view of the architectures allows the CIO and CTO organizational viewpoints to coexist and provides a common language between the two parties so that the ultimate business goals can be met.

### 4.7.3  Next Generation Datacenter design principles

The Next Generation Datacenter reference architecture is used to guide the design and construction approaches necessary to build the NGDC. The following are a set of guiding design principles organized around efficient, high performance, and control.

## Efficient

*Customizable Infrastructure Footprints:* In financial market firms the trading lifecycle executing across the digital supply chain experiences fluctuating volumes, frequency and workload types. Firms have to tailor the infrastructure service footprint into an ensemble of components and capabilities that can ensure optimal service delivery and efficiency for variable processing requirements (in areas, including market data collection and delivery, data delivery into the trading process, trade engine execution, trading decision support, and on-demand risk and posttrade processing).

*Unified Fabric:* The unified fabric combines integrated infrastructure service footprints that encapsulate compute, memory, disk, I/O, storage, and various processing appliances into a single footprint while incorporating quality of service, content acceleration, switching, routing and load balancing as needed. This eliminates the design limitations of systems that are not connected in a way that provides the best performance and least amount of infrastructure dynamically. This drives speed, scale, and cost efficiencies.

*Service and Change Management:* Dynamic models of operation require processes and procedures of service, delivery, and change management to accommodate the on-the-fly and as needed, when needed IT operations.

*Abstracted:* The design of each infrastructure component and layer needs to have sufficient abstraction so the operational details are hidden from all other collaborating components and layers. This maximizes the opportunity to create a virtualized infrastructure, which aids in rapid deployment and simplicity of operation.

*Dynamic Provisioning:* To promote organizational agility, the typical delay between application release and deployment must be shortened from weeks to days. Application teams are better positioned to determine how their configurations should be arranged. A facility is required that enables application teams to safely deploy changes to applications eliminating wasteful coordination cycles with datacenter personnel. The datacenter staff spends less time patching and provisioning applications, and less confusion minimizes configuration drift over time.


## High performance

*Economic Model:* Define the business and IT linkage between demand and supply. Orient the analysis and model creations around the interactive dynamics of consumption of IT resources by the business and the fulfillment behavior of processing by IT. This needs to be correlated with value chain functions and the corresponding products or services that are differentiated by business type (liquidity, risk transference, advice), business importance (margin, labor, flow), and cost to transact.

*Demand Mapping:* In natural language terms (no geek-speak!), define and capture the "day in the life of the business"—what it expects and where problems persist. Be sure to understand and incorporate sensitivities to cost, bottlenecks, and timing constraints as well. Quality attributes and business operational requirements (calendar events, demographics, competitive benchmarking across the straight-through-processing (STP) value chain) are critical links in accurately mapping demand.

*Fit-for-Purpose Operational Footprints:* The categorization of demand's operational qualities allows for processes to be correctly directed to optimized infrastructure resources that match the required characteristics. Tailored and coordinated operational footprints are organized in tightly coupled physical environments (PEDs).

*Simplified Engineering:* The utility will only be viewed as a success if it is easy to use, reduces time to deploy, if provisioning is highly reliable, and is responsive to demand. Applying the preceding principles simplifies engineering and meets objectives that will make the utility a success. Simplified engineering promotes greater efficiency, enables the datacenter to migrate to "green" status, enables greater agility in the deployment of new services, and reduces cost, eliminates waste, decreases time to deploy, and provides a better-quality service.

*Product and Portfolio Management:* Coalescing business and technical priorities in continuous capability adoption ensures sustainment and differentiation of your business through IT.

## With control

*Implement Virtual Resources:* Once runtime management, resource management, and instrumentation are in place, only then do you implement "everything virtual." This is a critical lesson that traps most organizations where they start bottom up without the ability to manage and ensure business alignment.

*Virtual Infrastructure Lifecycle Management:* Policy- and event-driven bare-metal provisioning of infrastructure services that supplement dynamic peak transaction loads and near real-time provisioning of additional capacity on demand in a coordinated manner based on business priority.

*Dynamic Runtime Orchestration Management:* Runtime control and execution enforcement—ensuring that the right work gets done at the right time with the right resources. Businesses operate dynamically in real time; your infrastructure needs to as well. Think of it as a composition of service delivery units that can be consumed in a variable manner-on-demand consumption and real-time reconfiguration.

*Consumption Management:* Instrument and capture objective factual data that describes which users, accessing what applications, consume what server(s), network, application, and storage resources and for how long. In particular, ensure that end-to-end delivery is correlated against consumption measures of latency, availability, throughput, data aggregation and persistence, disk swapping, memory volatility and coherence, compute time, event size, and I/O time.

*Real Time:* Infrastructure allocation, reprovisioning, demand monitoring, and resource utilization must react as demand and needs vary, which translates into less manual allocation. Instead, a higher degree of automation is required, driving business rules around allocation priorities in different scenarios to the decision-making policies of the infrastructure, which can then react in sub-seconds to changes in the environment.

*Dynamic Economic Model:* This involves a defined business and IT linkage of demand and supply. The model must be created around the interactive dynamics of IT resources by the business and the fulfillment behavior of processing by IT.

*Business Policy and IT Security Enforcement:* Comprehensive, real-time business and security policy enforcement execution in bare-metal speed timeframes. The ability to implement point-of-policy enforcement and administration that serves business agility requirements with guaranteed, non-repudiated transactions and secure data delivery creates a competitive advantage and significant efficiencies compared with traditional, regulatory-driven entitlement strategies.

### 4.7.4  Next Generation Datacenter business benefits

In summary, these are some of the more readily obtainable benefits of a transformation to a Next Generation Datacenter:

- Become more flexible and responsive to the dynamic needs of the business.
- Simplify and reduce the complexity of the IT environment.
- Get more value out of project and operational IT spending (both systems and people).
- Reduce costs while delivering improved service.
- Eliminate dedicated silos of data, systems, and infrastructure as they exist today.
- Reduce the time it takes to build and deploy new business services.
- Implement and sustain predictable qualities of service.

# 5 Designing the foundation

## Key points

The transformation of the datacenter to meet the Next Generation Datacenter (NGDC) principles is a large-scale change management program. Develop a plan that starts small with some critical applications, builds reputation, and then grows rapidly.

Management of this critical first project will require the organization to think and align differently. Do not underestimate the effect this kind of change will have, both positive and negative. The investment in change must spread across people, process, and technology.

Chapter 4 presented the case for a Next Generation Datacenter (NGDC) design that is fundamentally different from how today's datacenters are designed and operated. As a practical matter, entire datacenters cannot be converted overnight due to both physical and political realities. A bridge strategy is necessary to intersect with the legacy design and infrastructure to begin putting in the core building blocks so the NGDC can be realized.

The focus of this chapter is the analysis and design processes that use business requirements to optimize the creation of services and operating platforms that are aligned to the workload characteristics of business applications. While some aspects of the processes mentioned in this chapter will be familiar to most financial services IT organizations, the degree of business alignment influence described in this chapter is more pronounced and holistic. These processes drive design decisions top-down through the infrastructure.

The business requirements connection to the infrastructure sets these design activities apart, because they address the factors of business demand that affect the supply. This chapter focuses on introducing these processes within the context of a few targeted projects that will matter to the business. The targeted projects must be significant enough for the business to care, yet manageable enough to show results in about 90 days.

The projects should set the stage for large-scale packaging of easy-to-consume NGDC services. The initial goals for these projects should be tangible results that can be measured and shown to senior executives who will determine future investments. Typical success measures are increased performance or better manageability of the target applications, but business drivers do vary, and the goals should match those drivers. Success in these early initiatives will lead to the creation of core building blocks (i.e., processes, technologies, and new

doi: 10.1016/B978-0-12-374956-7.00005-X

skills) that will drive the adaptation process necessary to the migration of an optimal datacenter footprint design.

# 5.1   Change management plan from the start

The scope of building a NGDC is enormous, so a change management strategy mindset for executing this transformation is needed from the start. Realizing this vision is an ambitious plan by any measure and will need all senior leadership as backers, as it will affect every corner of operations. Gaining this consensus, even if you're the CIO or CTO, will require a significant amount of energy.[1]

## 5.1.1   Controlling scope

By limiting the scope of the first implementations to small portions of infrastructure—say, a troubled application suite—a foundation can be laid in the process of solving issues that have been otherwise intractable. This yields a high-impact way to prove the value of the design principles while setting the first building blocks of the NGDC in place. After a few visible short-term project wins, the knowledge gained and confidence created can be leveraged into a large-scale change management program to transform the datacenter. (Chapter 6 will introduce the concept of a playbook to facilitate the large-scale transformation process.)

The pilot project candidates should consist of a few mission-critical applications that face serious technical challenges in their implementation due to their bottom-up design approach. Use the Chapter 4 section "Bottom-Up: Past Design Decisions Influence Today's Operations" to look for problem characteristics that would be more easily managed within a Fit-for-Purpose RTI.

## 5.1.2   Keeping the end game in mind

As the projects are executed, the goal (beyond fixing the troubled service) is to enable portions of a new operating model that put the organization on the path to enable a Real Time Enterprise. These new operating model assets are the building blocks that will be continually leveraged to help the transformation process gain traction through proven successes.

Choosing which should be the first building blocks is company dependent. The criteria for selection should be weighted toward areas that will be perceived as highly relevant to senior management (again this is a time to be brave) and will make significant improvements to the operating model. Chapter 6 will provide additional details into the makeup of these building blocks.

Selecting applications that are of importance to the business early on is important. It's much easier to rally resources to fix these applications, as they're something the business is willing to invest in. Furthermore, when the business sees a dramatic improvement in the performance of a critical application, the

---

[1]*Leading Change* by John P. Kotter is an excellent change management resource that explores common pitfalls of transformation programs and promotes an eight-step process for creating major change.

team will be in a good position to make the larger transformation case. This is always a balancing act, as critical applications are typically revenue generating, and one mistake could prevent the chance to move the transformation forward or could destroy a person's career. The balancing act requires some senior management soul searching. It is not unusual for some of the most critical applications in an organization to have significant problems despite enormous efforts on the part of developer and operations. These applications have often grown too fast and have become complex to operate and keep reliable. The decision is a test of executive resolve.

### 5.1.3  Expect resistance to change

As the change management strategy is brought about, the consequences of the broad impact to the organizational structure must be managed. Many individuals will have a vested interest in the existing order and will not actively cooperate with the change process (some will be actively opposed). Having the pilot wins in place will keep you immunized so you can continue to push for change and, as momentum builds, provide the inertia needed to affect the broad-scale change being promoted. Each success should be documented in its context of the problematic behavioral characteristics that were alleviated. This can be used to show the broad applicability of the solutions and minimize the naysayers who claim their application is exempt because it is different.

### 5.1.4  Communication

Continual communication of the vision is paramount; start with a factual record of the problems and suggested resolution steps based on the NGDC principles of Chapter 4. Advance the message to encompass the overall management/operational process in the context of resolving the challenges of the selected pilot applications. Later, as success becomes apparent and the foundation is laid, a context is formed for the senior leadership that can be engaged with the evolving broader vision of the NGDC.

Given the possibility of tackling a high-profile application and its potential good and bad consequences, the fact-based communication needs to take on a distinct marketing flavor. This transformation is important and will be company altering, so such changes require a marketing perspective because the change agents must convince target audiences with very different viewpoints (as discussed in Chapter 2). The marketing of tailored benefits that will address specific concerns is a strategy that will be needed throughout this transformation.

Successful transformation requires that a core transformation execution team be created that is well versed in change management practices; each team member must be empowered to effect the necessary changes and be led by program manager(s) that understand the long-term vision. It's typical to start with several loosely related projects, which will become more tightly aligned toward the NGDC goal as the building blocks are laid. It's critical that the team understand the end-game strategy and see how the pieces come together.

This team can reside in either the application/services or technology organization, depending on the culture of company. Both organizations have to change to make the transformation take hold. These changes will only come as a result of targeted role definitions and incentive structures to encourage new behavior. The CTO organization will be significantly impacted by the departure from the bottom-up siloed culture and will experience a dramatic change in the day-to-day operations (albeit easier to sustain). The CIO organization will have to change its mindset on how services are consumed. It will no longer be in complete control of the physical infrastructure in support of its solutions. The introduction of virtualization technologies has caused adaptation to take place in some organizations; as a result, operational changes may not be quite so dramatic. Unfortunately, these virtualization strategies are usually undertaken for less critical applications (often third-tier applications like periodic reports), so the operational models have not been extended to critical applications and thus skepticism about any such operational models, viability for revenue generating applications will be strong.

For these reasons, placing the transformation team within the application/services organization, which also has a closer relationship with the business, may make sense. In addition, the transformation team definitely needs to be very sensitive to the delivery of full application services to the business, which the technology organization traditionally hasn't had to manage.

The senior leadership needs to help this team knock down the barriers to change. There are many techniques for this. A particularly effective one is aligning the performance metrics of individuals with the goals of the transformation effort, which will evolve as the maturity of the implementations mature. Senior leadership is also needed to help communicate to the business leadership, which is critical for communicating value generation and securing funding, and generally supporting the efforts of the transformation execution team.

As individual projects conclude and the operating model around the building blocks mature, an assessment of the overall progress of the transformation effort must be mandated where results and lessons learned are clearly documented for the next step. Seek out additional projects that will help further the goals of putting in additional building blocks. The advocates of transformation must be tolerant of the degree of change that the organization can tolerate. The organization may not understand the degree of tolerance for some time, so it is wise to consider projects that will stop noticeable operational pain in reasonable time frames, (e.g., think in three-month periods). At some point in the process the transformation effort builds to critical mass and it's time to press for the organizational changes needed to fully realize the NGDC operations (more on this in Chapter 7).

## 5.2   The beginning

Finding the first pilot application usually is not difficult. It'll be the one that is continually missing SLAs, repeatedly experiencing failures, the one business is screaming the loudest about, and generally the development team is at a loss as to what to do about it. While finding it might be easy, figuring out what to do with it requires systematic discipline to decomposing and resolving its problems.

It's typical to join the troubleshooting bridgeline to find that all the support groups are each reporting green lights on their dashboards but that the holistic application performance is horrendous. The root of this problem can again be traced back to the bottom-up approach of thinking about the application environment. This must be reversed to consider end-to-end application performance.

Leveraging a forensic sciences approach will provide an end-to-end perspective of an application's operating characteristics, which will uncover the true root causes of poor application performance. This approach will help IT to identify and decisively improve IT service delivery and quality of experience.

## 5.2.1 Forensic methodology

For•en•sic[2] (f -r n s k, -z k) *adj.* – Relating to the use of science or technology in the investigation and establishment of facts.

Meth•od•ol•o•gy[3] (m th -d l -j ) *n.* – A body of practices, procedures, and rules used by those who work in a discipline or engage in an inquiry; a set of working methods.

In the context of complex IT systems, *forensic methodology* is the process of systematically investigating a system to understand and document it in terms of its business function.

Complicated IT systems are generally poorly documented or understood because the amount of information needed to describe a system is larger than most can summarize without losing important details. (The classic problem: Can't see the forest for the trees.) Even the system's designer may be at a loss to describe the system in the context of its business function. Because of the complex and unwieldy nature of this information, organizations must create a discipline to rapidly identify relevant factual information about a system and document/communicate it. The three major scenarios where employing forensic methodology makes the most sense are documentation, diagnostics, and prognostics.

### Documentation

Many systems are poorly documented, which causes numerous problems for the operations team that is responsible for upkeep or the development team looking to modify the system. The execution of the forensic methodology can quickly and accurately create a set of living documentation that describes the system. As the system evolves, problems are resolved, or ongoing concerns are tracked, there is a clear and concise way to keep the documentation up to date.

The generated documentation is hierarchically organized so that it is referable to a broad audience, allowing the consumer to delve into the details according to their comfort level. This allows everyone from a business owner to system

---

[2]Source: *American Heritage® Dictionary of the English Language.* 4th ed.
[3]Source: *American Heritage® Dictionary of the English Language.* 4th ed.

architect and developer to work off the same information with a common understanding.

This context of the methodology ideally employs technology that can automatically discover, document, and map application and system component dependencies. Moreover, the tooling must be able to fingerprint the infrastructure and triage any deltas of change to quickly help isolate root cause and return service levels to normal.

## Diagnostics

When a production problem occurs, the infrastructure operation and application support teams must be able to quickly diagnose the problem and take corrective action. The forensic methodology and the documentation generated afford teams the ability to evaluate the system holistically. Its systemic approach helps ensure that the teams aren't myopic in their diagnostic evaluation.

The results of using the forensic methodology for diagnostic purposes is the root cause resolution of performance or service delivery problems and is especially useful when the faults are the combination of a number of technical or process problems.

The diagnostics context of forensic methodology needs to employ technology that tracks user transactions as they occur in real time so rapid problem identification is readily available. The data from the tooling (both visual and in report form) can enable accurate and rapid forensic cause and effect of where performance or service delivery is breaking down.

## Prognostics

Prognostics, an extension of the diagnostic model where predictive algorithms are used to diagnose failures before they occur, are the most undervalued aspect of the diagnostic process. Using the forensic methodology allows one to understand which aspects of a system are important to profile. By watching the growth rates of these targeted areas, one can eliminate many problems before they materialize in the production environment. Trending, the process of watching the usage of the limited resource pieces of a system over time, can predict when a resource constraint will be superseded. Proactive action resolves these issues before they have a production impact.

This context of forensic analysis needs to leverage self-learning technology that can analyze system events in real time and provide intuitive intelligence to proactively control problem and incident management.

### 5.2.2   The forensic model

The forensic model is a systematically generated matrix that facilitates documenting the problem faults that are found in the system. By traversing the services, tiers, and layers that make up the system implementation, all the different elements (technology, process, etc.) that could have an issue are considered individually, which yields a holistic picture of the system and identifies problem areas.

---

**How to Create a Forensic Matrix**

*x*-axis:  System Implementation Layer
Technology
Process
People
End-to-End Support
Workload Profiling
Infrastructure Characteristics
Service Level Agreements

*y*-axis:  Evaluation Category {Evaluation Subcategory}
Client/Desktop {Applications, Coordination, Infrastructure Services, Components, Operating Environment, Connectivity, Hardware, Physical Environment}
Database {Applications, Coordination, Infrastructure Services, Components, Operating Environment, Connectivity, Hardware, Physical Environment}
Server {Applications, Coordination, Infrastructure Services, Components, Operating Environment, Connectivity, Hardware, Physical Environment}
File Server {Applications, Coordination, Infrastructure Services, Components, Operating Environment, Connectivity, Hardware, Physical Environment}
SAN {Applications, Coordination, Infrastructure Services, Components, Operating Environment, Connectivity, Hardware, Physical Environment}
Disk Array {Applications, Coordination, Infrastructure Services, Components, Operating Environment, Connectivity, Hardware, Physical Environment}

*x-y* **Cell Description(s):** Each cell in the matrix is focused on answering one primary question: What is the current status of each Evaluation Subcategory for each System Implementation Layer? The color of each cell (black/dark grey/light grey) reflects the overall state of the System Implementation Layer. Additionally, each cell that designates an issue (black/dark grey) should include a brief description of the underlying problem.

---

A forensic matrix (Figure 5.1) imposes a disciplined approach to finding gaps in the current monitoring tools portfolio. It is likely that the Forensic Matrix will identify short comings in the measurements being made of the system(s).

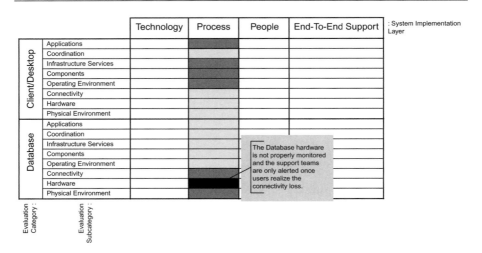

**Figure 5.1** Forensic Matrix sample.

Refer to Chapter 9 for the best approaches to the entire process of measuring, monitoring, and correlating results in a complex operational environment.

### 5.2.3  Leveraging the forensic model

The root causes identified in the forensic model need to be analyzed and prioritized according to several factors, such as the value and the complexity of fixing the problem. When considering the priority of fixes, high-value and easy items should be enacted immediately. The remaining items will require the team's value judgment but should be executed in an order that is most helpful to the business and customers, not the engineering team.

## 5.3  NGDC design artifacts

The creation and packaging of technology as consumable NGDC services is a critical component in building and deploying an NGDC infrastructure. There are ten key artifacts involved in defining and designing the building blocks needed to create an NGDC tailored to your organization's needs. Each of these artifacts hinges on a set of activities that involve design decisions and choices. These decisions are best created with a focused senior group of professionals guided by a CIO mandate that these activities are critical to any transformation process. Each of these activities includes a set of goals and a set of expected outcomes which include design artifacts that articulate what decisions were made and why. These activities and their associated artifacts will be used to guide the right choices for the problems being addressed (Figure 5.2).

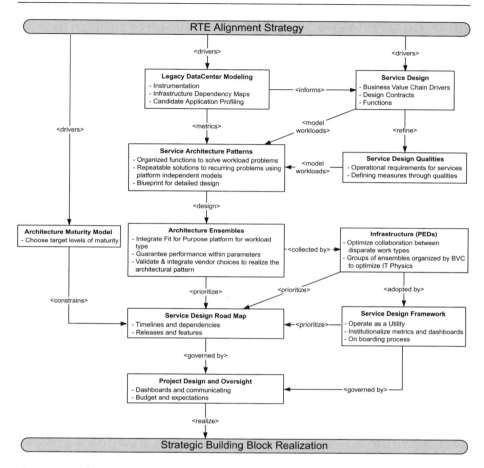

**Figure 5.2** Information flow among artifacts.

*Information flow among artifacts and the relationships among the artifacts.* All of the artifacts are explored in this chapter by stating the objectives of the element, describing the associated activities, providing examples of the artifacts, and explaining the best practices for eliciting and synthesizing the information that produces those artifacts.

These elements are most successfully created during tightly focused collaborative workshops. These workshops should include senior executives in the early stages for most elements to ensure that all stakeholders understand that this initiative is considered strategic and critical. Most of these workshops will include multiple stakeholders (e.g., multiple business lines, multiple roles such as CIO directs, product line architects, analysts, and project managers), as this is critical to meet the transformation goals.

## 5.3.1  *Legacy datacenter modeling*

Legacy Datacenter Modeling is a series of activities structured to gather information about how resources are consumed in the datacenter and the effects that those consumption patterns have on current supply. These activities yield a measurable current state view of the operational environment through the use of measurement tools, infrastructure dependency discovery tools, and application profiling workshops. A set of artifacts is produced that succinctly articulates current state limitations and challenges in the datacenter, which can then be compared with the perceived limitations (by senior business and IT executives).

These activities set the groundwork for instituting a forensic methodology into the organization where there is an approach to investigating problems reactively, and a basis for establishing proactive problem projections. Forensic methodology will be discussed in detail in Chapter 7. The three classes of activity in this element are the following:

*Application Profiling Artifact:* Use a detailed questionnaire to interview the candidate applications that will consume the infrastructure services to understand the business demand they address, to get a sense of what that demand does to the infrastructure, and how the application is designed to handle that demand.

*Infrastructure Dependency Mapping Artifact:* Understand the breadth of infrastructure dependency between candidate applications (especially since it is like datacenter sprawl) and the age of an application will have likely created unnecessary connection hopping between heavily collaborating applications. An automated infrastructure discovery tool will need to be implemented. It is also critical to understand how the infrastructure is managed so that change can be placed into context.

*Application Benchmark Artifact:* Gather baseline performance data for candidate applications and those that support them in terms of all infrastructure resource consumption (e.g., compute, network, storage, middleware, caching engines, etc.). This consumption must be viewed through the daily lifecycle through each application and its supporting services. The data must be correlated with defined SLAs incident reports and problem triage reports. While it may be necessary to introduce modern comprehensive tools, every effort should be made to gather information quickly and use it as a baseline for many other elements described in this chapter, so the default should be to use whatever is on hand but investigate what else to acquire as part of the larger program.

Numerous stakeholders including application teams, datacenter operations teams, the service design teams, and senior executives will guide the NGDC investment. This varied stakeholder group will need different views of the gathered information with audience appropriate detail.

Any undertaking within the NGDC transformation domain will take time and money to execute. It is imperative to focus on the most pressing problems first, and supporting data that backs the anecdotal statements about datacenter limitations is required to set the right urgency and priority for change.

This kind of investment will guarantee significant scrutiny; the only way to ensure that the NGDC program is properly funded is by continually showing success through improvements. Baseline performance data is required to show the "before" state because, as the program proceeds over time, people will forget the limitations they were operating under. Hard facts are a powerful argument for change.

## Objectives and goals

Measurement is the key to controlling the environment, especially if the environment will undergo a series of transformations. The goals of this element are to gather factual data that can be used to ignite change, set the proper priorities, check progress, and make corrections as the business demands change. The ultimate aim of any datacenter modeling activity is to set the standard for how the NGDC will operate as a Real Time Infrastructure (RTI) in the future.

*Business Capacity:* IT can increase its processing capability as the business grows, handling unexpected spikes in transactional demand in real time.

*Supply Efficiency:* RTI mandates a fluid set of infrastructure services that make resources available to meet oncoming demand at the level that is needed, when it is needed.

*Utilization Efficiency:* RTI assumes demand fluctuates for different applications at different times.

*Demand-Driven Utilization:* RTI utilizes a Fit-for-Purpose analysis approach that promotes a top-down demand-driven design approach that can be configured bottom up for specific application needs.

Measurement and modeling is the key to achieving accurate datacenter modeling.

## Execution

Once the drivers are well understood, a number of artifacts are developed to characterize how the environment should be utilized. The purpose of these artifacts is to quantify the environment in terms of business consumption demand and platform infrastructure supply, which facilitates a healthy and holistic grasp of the complexity of the problem being solved from the two primary perspectives of the business consumers and the infrastructure supply team.

## Define success

The legacy modeling exercise is critical in the early transformation stages and remains an integral part of the entire transformation lifecycle. The key success factor is making the legacy modeling effort sustainable by instituting processes that allow profiling, dependency mapping, and instrumentation efforts to become part of regular operating processes. Success occurs when these activities no longer have the tag *legacy* attached to them.

## Inputs

Legacy datacenter modeling does not start in a vacuum. Any global financial services firm will have some base data about the datacenter. It is important to gather the best-understood current state documentation available, even if it is outdated and incorrect. The fact that it might be outdated and incorrect can be a powerful lever for change. These are some of the documents you should gather:

- Current SLAs that are considered enforceable and are tracked by the business.
- Any Operating Level Agreements (OLAs) that have been defined to support the SLAs.
- Incident reports on infrastructure problems and application SLA violations. Trends in incident reports are an important input.
- Current reports from performance tools about the candidate applications and support services.

## Artifacts

The artifacts produced will be used to gauge the complexity of transforming the datacenter, validate the perceived pain points, and provide input to the migration strategies that will be discussed in Chapter 6. The results will also be used by the service design teams as the interdependencies and metrics influence the design tradeoff process in architecture, ensemble, and PED construction.

### The application profiling artifact

The service design team must run a set of profiling workshops focused on the targeted applications. The product line architect should attend for any application in that business. The system manager must also attend to provide the information.

The profile is a structured set of questions designed to elicit business requirements based on a set of measurable qualities. The element in this chapter named "Service Design Qualities" has an in-depth explanation of qualities and their importance. These quality questions are placed into three sections.

- **Understanding Demand:** This section explores specific business factors that the application must address (Table 5.1).
  - The business impacts in terms of major transactions processed and the degree of direct revenue impact the types of business that support it in terms of reporting, decision making, or compliance-related activities.
  - The amount of growth anticipated, in terms of users, transactions, and revenue.
  - User demographics including roles and their impact on revenue or compliance, geographic factors in terms of time zones, and their implications for end-of-day and rolling books. Language differences are worth noting as well, due to the need for special translation processing. National jurisdiction issues are also important, because of data movement restrictions and their effects on how such policies are implemented.
  - Understanding the degree of support expected in terms of hours of operation, escalation, and the impact of required maintenance.
- **Understanding the Consequences of Demand on Supply:** This section explores how business demand affects supply (Table 5.2).
  - Availability: the impact of unscheduled downtime on revenue and the expectation for failure recovery, including operational timeframes and expected recovery times.

**Table 5.1** Example questions for understanding demand

**Application demographic survey—understanding demand**

| Demographic category | Demographic measure | Description | Application answers |
|---|---|---|---|
| Business Impact | Major Transactions | What are the major transactions that the application supports or the reasons the application was created? | |
| User Experience | Simultaneous Usage | Are there any licensing restrictions on the number of simultaneous users this application can support? | |
| Security | National Jurisdiction & Legal Requirement | Does the application have to create a security barrier around national boundaries with regard to data or functions? | |
| Application Support | Normal Support Hours | What are the normal support hours, and what level of support can the users expect? | |

**Table 5.2** Example questions for understanding the consequences of the demand

**Application profile survey—understanding the consequences of the demand**

| Quality category | Quality measure | Quality description | Quality answers |
|---|---|---|---|
| Business Process | Batch Processing Requirement | Is there a business need that specifically requires batch processing (i.e., it is not possible or does not make sense to do the activity in real time)? Typically, this would be for periodic processes that must happen at close of business, month end, and so forth. | |
| Integration | Data Source Integration-Output | What is the number of destinations for information that this application must disseminate? This includes message streams and data files. | |
| Messaging Characteristics | Asynchronous | How much of the messaging is asynchronous? | |
| Performance | Response Time | What is the expected response time range for a task? This implies that there is an entity (human or other application) expecting a response. | |

- Business process support: How flexible must processes be in terms of changing the business process model?
- Degree of integration required to meet business needs: How many other applications or services does this candidate application interact with? How many sources of data? What is the interaction method between all its collaborators, emphasizing the degree of asynchronous and synchronous messaging as opposed to file passing?
- Performance requirements: understanding the extremes of throughput, response time, and latency, along with the extent of peaks.
- Security: understanding the requirements for encryption, data retention, and access.
- **Characterizing the Supply**: Once the demand and the consequences of serving that demand are understood, an analysis of the supply can be undertaken. This section of the profile explores the way candidate applications are designed, built, deployed, and changed. Aspects of application architecture and the change and release process are explored to understand the impact demand has on the lifecycle of an application (Table 5.3).
  - Application architecture including component structure such as the use of commercial software products.
  - The change process associated with this application, including how often releases are expected, how long it takes to deploy, and fall back expectations.
  - System resources survey: what the application currently operates on, including the number of tiers, the extent of connectivity utilized, and all of its collaborating services and applications.

## The application profile heat map matrix artifact

After a number of application profiles are complete, the synthesis of characteristics across these applications should begin. The categories explored should be

Table 5.3 Example questions for characterizing the supply

| Application infrastructure and resources survey—characterizing the supply | | | |
|---|---|---|---|
| Category | Topic | Description | Answers |
| Application Architecture | Component Composition | Is the application or subsystem composed of multiple components? Are they developed by separate groups? Can they be deployed independently? | |
| Change Process | Sign Off Process | How many groups must sign off on a change? | |
| Deployment Model | Introduction of New Release | Is a new release built by the developers? Is it placed in a staging area? Is it load-tested in UAT? How is the load test performed? | |

Note: The artifacts depicted for profiling show sample questions in the categories of Understanding Demand, Understanding the Consequences of Demand, and Characterizing the Supply. They are not inclusive of all the questions that should be asked in a profile. Profiles used by the author have approximately 60 questions, about 20 for each category.

examined for trends so pain points and gaps can be viewed in broader terms. A heat map summarizing pain points across selected applications is a useful tool to be used across many stakeholders (Figure 5.3).

---

**How to Create: Application Profile Heat Map Matrix**

*x*-axis:  Application Metric {Application Metric Subcategory}
   Deliver Business Functionality {Requirements Defined, Application Repository, Functionality Reuse, Representative Testing, Technical Support, Defect Identification}
   Performance {Processing Delays, Network Delays, Disk Delays, Page/Swap Delays}
   Timely Resilience {Measured MTTF, Measured MTTR, HA Recovery, Disaster Recovery}
   Operational Efficiency {Disk Allocation, CMDB, Security}
   Quality Improvement Programs {Trending, Root Cause Analysis, Capacity Planning, Executive Reviews}
   Technology Trends {Disaster Recovery, Skill Sets}

*y*-axis:  Application
   Application 01
   Application 02
   ...
   Application xx

*x-y* **Cell Description(s):** The matrix answers two essential questions: How large is the IT GAP? And what is the complexity of the remediation effort? It is up to the creator of the matrix to determine whether to use color, shape, size or other metric to display the information. In the following sample, the team used color and size to display the two dimensions.

---

One of the most important factors to consider when creating the Heat Map Matrix is the politically sensitive nature of the exercise. The tendency is to be politically correct when displaying the information, which is not a good practice. It is important to depict the actual state of the environment as part of the exercise.

### Infrastructure dependency mapping artifact

The services design team must work with the targeted application teams to map the infrastructure dependencies between those applications (Figure 5.4). There are several automated tools that can be utilized, and the specifics are described in Chapter 8. Initially the tool vendor must provide support while the dependencies are discovered so the internal team can learn to unravel unusual situations. The application team must be consulted to validate and qualify the findings. Generally, the findings have been surprising to most application teams.

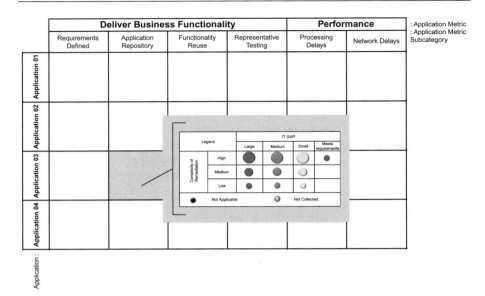

**Figure 5.3** Application profile Heat Map Matrix sample.

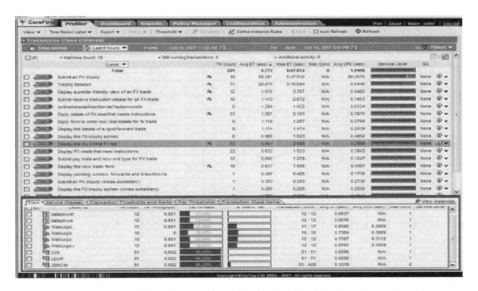

**Figure 5.4** Optier's CoreFirst Transaction Monitoring Tool depicts dependencies.

## Application benchmarks artifact

Part of the dedicated team that will design the services needs to utilize existing tooling to benchmark the key target applications and verify what information will be utilized in the workshops and profiling sessions (Figure 5.5). The system managers of key applications need to participate in these benchmarks, and the product line architect for each business line should also participate in the review of the benchmark findings for any application in their domain.

Benchmarking tools that can show summaries of defined SLAs and their service health are preferred as the long-term tool, but as a start, any measurement that reflects reality is a good start. This artifact shows defined services and their measures.

## Steps

The main legacy datacenter mapping activities can be run in parallel for maximum effectiveness, but any information from the dependency mapping or benchmarking activities would help ground the profiling work. The degree of parallel activity will depend on the size of the initial teams. The broad steps are mentioned here.

- A series of small workshops must be run where key applications from all business lines are profiled for specific quality categories as just mentioned. The detailed profiles elicited from those critical applications will aid in creating architecture, patterns, and ensembles.

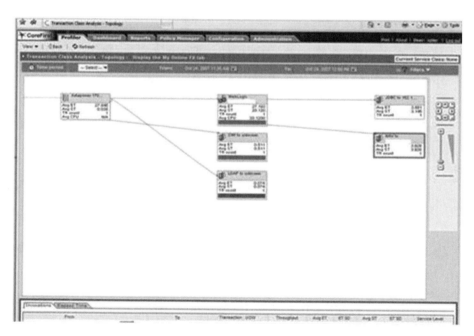

**Figure** 5.5 Optier's CoreFirst Transaction Monitoring Tool used to benchmark performance.

- The application profiles must explore the business demand, the effect of that demand on application design and operation, and the architecture of that application.
  - One of the key consequences to explore is time to market pressures on the application in terms of release cycles and time to deploy once the application is production ready.
  - Other key aspects that must be explored are the number of service level violations and the current approach to scale in the face of growing demand, which are addressed with NGDC tactics of deployment and management.
- A mapping of infrastructure dependencies must be run using automated tools to uncover the true complexity that exists in the infrastructure. This mapping will provide many insights, including the complexity of any transformations. It will be used in creating the service road map element. This infrastructure mapping will show the effects of datacenter sprawl on suites of collaborating applications.
- Baseline performance benchmarks must be run on the current infrastructure to determine how the current application suites run against the infrastructure. The result will be an important measuring stick as the service qualities are defined. It is expected that there will be gaps between the current measurements and the service quality definitions.

## Usage

Legacy datacenter modeling is the foundation for change. You cannot change what you cannot control, and you cannot control what you do not measure.

- Profiling results tie back to business demand. The characteristics found from the profiling trends validate anecdotal stories about operational and developmental pain points.
- Dependency maps show how deeply interconnected applications are. These tools can discover links that are not documented and used only rarely. This dependency map can be used to uncover bottlenecks due to datacenter sprawl or legacy communication paths that have long outlived their usefulness.
- Benchmarking is essential to measure from the organization's starting point. It is a base to show progress as changes are made; it is a factual base that change agents can use to champion transformation progress.

## Do's

- Educate the application teams as any of these activities moves forward; engage them, and show them how the results are for their own benefit.
- Publish all findings and ensure there are executive summaries available for review monthly.
- Remember that visual aids are key; large pictures with colors and call outs about the problems are critical to convey findings to senior level engagement.

## Don'ts

- Don't treat these activities as onetime events. Even though the first application teams to participate in these activities may have enough enthusiasm to be rigorous about these activities, not all teams will want to profile their applications or feel compelled to do so. It is important to learn what works for the organization and institute it in a repeatable manner.

- Don't underestimate the resistance to the profiling efforts. They will be considerable until the value is shown.
- Don't treat profiling or benchmarking reviews as an inquisition—remember the lessons of Chapter 2. This current datacenter condition was a collective effort—moving forward is the only answer. So while very aggressive behavior is not conducive to cooperation, the profile team has to be particularly wary of application teams sugar coating their applications performance. Real performance data is critical to obtain.

## 5.3.2 Service design

Service design is a series of activities focused around iterative workshops that flesh out what kinds of infrastructure services are required as stepping stones toward a NGDC. The activities focus on what the infrastructure services should do; how they will be consumed; and what efficiency targets are required to meet the needs of the business and justify the investment. The outcome of these workshops will be a list of defined services that can be used as a basis for detailed design.

Even though the services will be initially used by a small number of applications, these services should be designed to work across business lines, and therefore represent an investment in shared infrastructure. This investment goes beyond initial development and roll out costs. There must be a commitment to long-term ownership for each service by a group that will be accountable to all stakeholders. That means service ownership cannot reside in a particular line of business. This will be a highly controversial stand in most financial services organizations. This understanding must be conveyed and agreed upon before the workshops, since the service's design and implementation teams must be identified prior to the start of those workshops.

The artifacts produced out of the workshops will utilize pictures and tables to convey the breadth of services defined. Multiple stakeholders will use the artifacts from these design workshops. The service design architects will use the artifacts to create detailed designs of the services. Application architects will use the artifacts as guides when considering their application migrations. The CIO and senior IT management will use the artifacts as part of the investment discussion to fund this work.

Successful design and implementation of infrastructure services will increase the degree of sharing and reuse among different applications, which will reduce datacenter sprawl and increase overall resource efficiency. The proliferation of infrastructure services, each with a custom platform, not only contributes to sprawl, but violates the premise of running IT like a portfolio where investments are looked at from a strategic point of view. Sample service designs can be found in Table 5.4.

**Table 5.4** Example services and design qualities found in a dynamic infrastructure

| Service name | Definition | Service qualities |
|---|---|---|
| Dynamic Application Deployment and Activation | *Packaging:* Policy- and parameter-driven assembly of components, dependencies and configurations (of an application), and constraints. *Deployment:* JIT deployment of the right package to the right destination with the right configuration. *Activation:* JIT automated activation of application services in support of business demand. | *Time to Deploy:* Days to minutes. *Effort to Deploy:* Hours to minutes. *Consistency of Deployment:* Increase predictabilty. *Demand Sensitivity:* Just in time (JIT) responsiveness of business application needs. *Institutionalized Deployment Knowledge:* Providing centralized deployment information and mechanisms. |
| Dynamic Infrastructure Service Provisioning | *Infrastructure Service Lifecycle Management (How):* Deployment, activation, and deactivation of core infrastructure of virtual machines, rules engines, containers, caching services. *On-demand Instantiation (When):* Allocation of infrastructure services to applications based on business demand. | *Demand Sensitivity:* JIT responsiveness. *Control:* Automated management of infrastructure service deployment. *Efficiency:* Maximize asset usage based on supply and demand. *Time to Deploy:* Days to minutes. *Effort to Deploy:* Hours to minutes. |
| Dynamic Runtime Service Orchestration | Real-time matching of demand and supply. Enforcement of service contracts and entitlements to best fulfill demand based on available resources. | *Control:* Guaranteed execution and fulfillment of service based on contract. *Centralized Planning:* Business trending and analysis of work correlated against the service contract. *Dynamic Demand Management:* Optimized management of fluctuating demand and events based on service contracts (event driven, calendar driven). *Sustainment:* The persistence of work execution in continuity situations. *Consolidation:* The real-time aggregation of demand and execution of work on an optimized footprint. |

*(Continued)*

Table 5.4 Continued

| Service name | Definition | Service qualities |
|---|---|---|
| Utility Resource Management | Dynamic assignment of work and allocation of the appropriate combination of resource types (network computer and storage resource units) to best fulfill demand. Provides the ability to discriminate quantity and quality of resource assets for best-fit utilization. | *Demand Sensitivity:* JIT responsiveness of the right resources at the right time. *Centralized Planning:* Asset trending and analysis of work and capacity usage. *Fit-for-Purpose:* Balancing asset usage with performance criteria. *Sustainment:* The availability and allocation of resources for work in business continuity situations. *Consolidation:* The real-time temporary allocation from an aggregated pool of compute storage and network assets. |

## Goals and objectives

The central objective for the NGDC effort is to minimize wasteful redundant efforts by various development and support teams to build what is essentially common functions that do not provide unique strategic value on their own. One must initiate the foundations for a cultural shift away from every application team needing to control all resources, which is the root of datacenter sprawl and waste. This cultural shift is required across all roles so that the changes that come as a result of this initiative achieve the proper acceleration throughout the organization.

The creation and packaging of technology as consumable NGDC services is a critical component in building and deploying an NGDC infrastructure. These services are the starting point to deliver Fit-for-Purpose operating platforms that are optimized to application workload types while respecting the IT physics that require close proximity for highly collaborative operating components. The effort to design these services will set in motion a larger cultural change where common services are designed, developed, and maintained to meet changing business demand.

## Execution

A series of iterative workshops must be conducted with participation from executive management. Infrastructure services will be defined based on business drivers, recurring problems in the operating environment, and development trends of the application teams. These workshops will produce service definitions, candidate consumers, service interdependencies, and enough details on what each service should do so detailed design can proceed. For many participants this will be a cultural shift away from making all infrastructure capabilities on a per-project basis. The senior staff will need to address this head on.

## Limiting sprawl

Application teams that build their own middleware that cannot be shared by other projects are a significant contributor to datacenter sprawl. Often this specialized middleware was designed to meet stringent performance requirements but was built quickly and specifically for that project. In most cases the primary design drivers assumed the need for special configurations. Once built, these services evolved into something so specialized that refactoring them to be shared with other projects becomes impossible. Each application would find the need to build such services from scratch, increasing sprawl, time to market, and reducing the funds available to other initiatives.

## Define success

Success is founded on active senior-level sponsorship that promotes NGDC as a critical component to business success. The CIO and CIO direct reports are essential participants for these workshops, as are the product line architects for each business line. Key systems managers for the critical targeted business applications should also be present.

## Service design inputs

The essential principle behind top-down infrastructure service design is creating services that will meet the requirements of the business. The only way to ensure that can happen is to utilize inputs that have been influenced by business requirements:

- The inputs used for the business support services (i.e., business value chain mapping, existing framework, and service documentation) are required in this workshop.
- Since the business support services workshops are initiated first, all outcome artifacts from those sessions should be used to frame the scope of the infrastructure services.
- A prioritized list of critical datacenter pain points is required to help shape the debate on which services must be created first.
- A prioritized list of key development pain points is also required to guide the priorities of service creation.

## Artifacts

Once the first service workshop has been completed and the required artifacts are produced and validated, subsequent workshops must be held monthly with a different consumer (i.e., line of business focus) so the holistic strategic path can be properly defined. This initial up-front investment is critical for success. Once all the lines of business have been explored in this manner it will be possible to establish a quarterly two-day workshop where the entire plan can be reviewed.

## Service description table artifact

This matrix lists all candidate services, definitions, service owners, and likely consumers along with other information that will be collected as the process matures such as level of effort, priority, and dependent services (Figure 5.6).

---

**How to Create: Service Description Table Artifact**

*x*-axis:   Service Table Header
            Software Factory
            Component [C], Service [S], or Framework [F]
            Component Number
            DIO Group
            DIO Subgroup
            Component Creator
            Component Name
            Component Description
            Target Production Date
            Dependencies (other group components/services)
            Business Products Supported
            Software Capabilities
            Issues
            Lifecycle
            Lifecycle Ownership

**Row:** The table seeks to compile a master list of all components, services, and frameworks existent within an organization. Not all questions will have an answer, and some cells will be left blank, but the user completing the table should seek to fill out as much as possible.

---

## Service description picture artifact

Figure 5.7 shows the defined infrastructure services and their relationships with consumers (e.g., applications and business support services). Emphasis is on information flow to highlight the dependencies. Business support services and applications can be depicted as consumers of infrastructure services in this manner.

## Service dependency map artifact

Figure 5.8 shows functional dependencies between consumers and infra-structure services, using quarterly phases. The nature of the dependency is not shown—only that there is a dependency. As more services are introduced through the transformation, large-scale visual tools become critical for executives and designers to keep track of the investment progress. Automation of these drawings is highly encouraged.

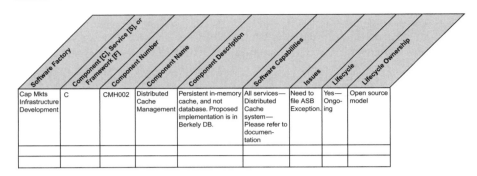

| Software Factory | Component [C] Service [S], or Framework [F] | Component Number | Component Name | Component Description | Software Capabilities | Issues | Lifecycle | Lifecycle Ownership |
|---|---|---|---|---|---|---|---|---|
| Cap Mkts Infrastructure Development | C | CMH002 | Distributed Cache Management | Persistent in-memory cache, and not database. Proposed implementation is in Berkely DB. | All services— Distributed Cache system— Please refer to documen-tation | Need to file ASB Exception. | Yes— Ongo-ing | Open source model |
| | | | | | | | | |
| | | | | | | | | |

**Figure 5.6** Service Description Table artifact sample.

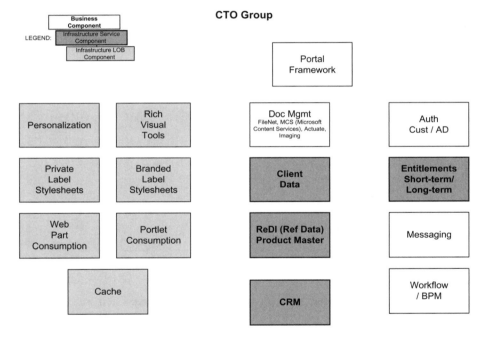

**Figure 5.7** Infrastructure services.

## Stakeholders

Service design is such a critical step toward successful transformation that some attention must be paid to the stakeholder list:

- The CIO, CIO direct reports, and the chief architects from each line of business are key stakeholders.
- Another group that must be in these sessions is the team that will spearhead the design and be responsible for the implementation and *long-term support* of these critical cross-business services. This team must not reside in any one business unit

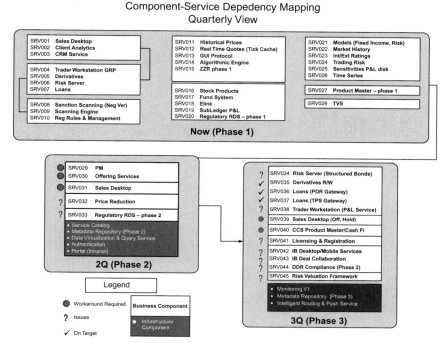

**Figure 5.8** Service dependency map.

but instead will be the seeds of an internal product development group that is associated with architecture and governance functions.
• It is strongly recommended that senior technical members of the datacenter operations team be involved at this stage to add their insight on the current operations of critical cross-business functions.

## Steps

Service design is iterative and relies heavily on workshops in its initial phases. The following are steps to consider:

• Prior to the workshop, gather and understand all of the inputs as they are critical in guiding the initial process.
• Ensure that the CIO and CIO direct reports are in the initial meetings to set direction about the culture shift, state their view on the strategic imperative, and provide focus for the first candidate services and the consuming applications.
• During workshop execution, ensure there are lots of visual aids and encourage active participation through whiteboard drawings or alternative means. Have dedicated note takers and facilitators, and ensure that session documentation is sent out within days of the session.
• Set up the iterative session process to foster progress.
• Have offline sessions with the smaller team of stakeholders to refine the thinking.

- Have a public checkpoint with all key stakeholders. Ensure that the range of services to cover is well known to the stakeholders. Iterate as necessary, while encouraging the start of follow-on activities from other elements such as service qualities and road maps.

## Usage

Use the artifacts as a guide to take some important next steps:

- Perform detailed design in smaller collaborative workshops with the service design architects and application team architects.
- Leverage the service design artifacts to refine the definitions with service design qualities elicited from line of business representatives.

## Do's

- Keep senior IT engaged and vocal.
- Encourage offline collaboration.
- Document decisions.
- Make a big picture of how it all fits together.

## Don'ts

- Don't let a small group dominate the debate, even if they are right (remember this is political).
- Don't let political agendas dominate, and when in doubt, ensure that the CIO and CIO direct reports address them.

## Political and organizational guidelines

Successful design and implementation of infrastructure services will increase the degree of sharing and reuse among different applications. It will also be a cause for concern for many IT teams where tight delivery timeframes are a driver. Generally it has been more difficult to convince teams to use shareable services for infrastructure due to a variety of factors, including loss of control, response to problems, and requests for new capabilities. There is a need for coordinated change control that respects the needs for all stakeholders; this includes the fact that some teams are aggressive early adaptors that drive change, and others are severe laggards. Coordinated change control means that teams should be accommodated but must also keep reasonably current so that the design team is not supporting five-year-old releases.

The application teams will be concerned about trusting a third party with whom they have no direct influence to deliver the required services on time and with the right level of quality. Loss of control for a project team is one of the scariest scenarios, especially if tight delivery timeframes are consistently involved. The workshops and follow-on sessions need to focus on ensuring that key stakeholder concerns are addressed.

Despite concerns from the application groups, a separate *product development group* must be created to design, build, and maintain these infrastructure services, and this represents a loss of control to application development groups. The product development group must not reside in any one business line. Unfortunately, this arrangement has been tried in many financial services organizations, usually as an office of architecture function. These architecture groups are often stereotyped as ivory tower thinkers,[4] so this must be avoided in perception and fact, as the formation of a competent product group is essential to success. There must be an identified budget for this group, which provides visible evidence that executive management is serious about this investment.

## Infrastructure service types

Other types of infrastructure services that should be considered as a result of the alignment exercise include the following:

*Message Processor:* Focus on non-business-related processing of incoming or outgoing messages in order to decouple the complexities of reliability, performance, validation, and transformation from business logic.

*Authorization and Authentication Services:* Have a range of security services that perform at high speeds (wire speed). These services provide policy enforcement through the introspection of messages to determine fine-grained authorization and third-party authentication in conjunction with corporate human resources information.

*Data Transformation Service:* Transform multiple, arbitrarily sized and formatted data sets from one representation to another. The transformation rules can be varied and complex and are subject to frequent change.

*Multilevel Distributed Transactional Cache:* Accelerate the throughput and/or response time for many types of applications by keeping frequently used objects in memory (to avoid expensive disk retrievals). These objects are subject to changes from multiple sources; therefore, these changes must be propagated to all users and all copies upon the change event. Subsets of this cache might need to persist in levels as the distance from the source becomes greater, and the subsequent items of interest become smaller in range.

*Directory Naming Service:* Provide server names in a way so the actual location is transparent to the searcher. This address broker is critical to successful operation of any global operation. Many large organizations grew through mergers and acquisitions, each with its own trusted name domains. Negotiating these various domains is not trivial.

*Service Broker:* Facilitate the resource allocation of a virtual operating platform in real time so dynamic responses to incoming business demand can be configured, deployed, tuned, and then monitored in real time. Such a service would require configurable sampling windows that can be stated in milliseconds, with rules that can be tied to tangible events such as messages-per-second thresholds. Policies should be designed for recurring intervals that range from daily to monthly and specific hours in a given day.

*ESB:* Specify the intent behind application message interaction goals (e.g., send to many recipients, guarantee the delivery) without having to code the specific protocol behaviors. An intermediary is required to align the service requirement with available mechanisms so applications can decouple messaging logic and configuration tasks from business logic.

*Data Federation:* Provide location and format transparency for multiple data sources in multiple formats in order to decouple applications from details that add complexity

[4]Mathews C. Enterprise architecture: 4 steps to building it right. CIO.com. 2006, November <http://www.cio.com/article/26231/Enterprise_Architecture_Steps_to_Building_It_Right>.

to any design. Views must be created quickly and disseminated in a timely fashion. The data sets may be very large and the backend systems disparate.

*Discovery Service:* Find services through a directory by name, service type, and contract so the service location can be transparent to the requestors.

*Transaction Broker:* Coordinate among system workflow engines using a large-scale workflow manager in order to provide enterprise integration capability for transactions across an enterprise. There will be a need for ACID transaction semantics and varying levels of response to avoid cross enterprise transaction timeouts.

*Protocol Gateway:* Process financial transactions with multiple business partners serviced by external applications. These external applications use a variety of protocols, with high throughput in a secure manner. Internal STP of transactions should also be supported through disparate internal systems with little intervention and an efficient protocol gateway could be leveraged for this work.

*Information as a Service:* Build an information service provider that aggregates data from many sources (often in different formats) in order to provide a uniform view of this disparate data. Such an effort, using other services such as data federation, will reduce the proliferation of database copies that significantly contribute to database server sprawl. Having a consolidated information source for queries reduces the urgency that causes uncontrolled database copying that many global financial services firms experience.

*Application Configuration Service:* Represents a facility that allows a practitioner to package an application once, and then deployment many times without changes. The facility includes a library of approved and standardized deployment packages. Such services will set up application personas that can be loaded onto bare metal, which will repurpose a machine for scheduled or real-time deployment.

### 5.3.3   Service design qualities

A quality as applied to systems is a defined, measurable, or demonstrable requirement that is attributed to a software or hardware asset. The asset can be as small as a component or as large as a service or an entire application. A quality can be directly influenced by the business (e.g., availability, number of transactions to process) or indirectly derived by the designers as a result of interpreting direct business requirements (e.g., the number of events that must be processed per second, as result of transaction traffic).

This element explores how the service requirements will be defined so they can be measured through the use of qualities. Being able to specifically define qualities improves the designer's ability to build what the business needs, measure them as the business demand changes, and make sustainable changes that will support that demand.

Qualities are used by service designers so they can understand the operational constraints that the service must conform to. Qualities must be elicited from the business representatives as a starting point and will be used to craft SLAs with specific targets.

It is essential to define specific qualities and how they will be measured for any service to be built. It is the only way to understand how to optimally design that service so that it is not overengineered in the attempt to satisfy consumer requirements. Chapter 2 makes a clear case that overengineering is the typical response that IT provides to a set of operational requirements that are not known or difficult to characterize. Overengineering is a major cause of datacenter sprawl because the result of sprawl is a rigidly implemented infrastructure that is hard to change or repurpose when idle. Only by understanding qualities can we balance the three essential aspects of Quality of Experience (QoE). Table 5.4 presents a list of service qualities.

## Goals and objectives

Services must be designed to meet a range of operational characteristics that can be measured through qualities. The following are the goals of eliciting service qualities:

- Identify the measurable qualities for the defined services based on the line of business that will consume them.
- The qualities must be defined in tangible business terms that promote dialog between business and IT, fostering better alignment.
- Service quality definitions help avoid the trap of overengineering, which has caused many current datacenter issues.

Achieving QoE means balancing the user experience (e.g., response time, time to market, availability) with cost and efficiency. QoE cannot be achieved by continually spending money on infrastructure as problems arise. Understanding what the business needs and being able to measure those attributes are critical to achieving QoE. Without measurement there is no opportunity to control the environment to meet demand in real time, which is the critical mandate of the digital supply chain. The digital supply chain is the analog of the business value chain, so it must respond to business demand in real time if the organization is to become a real-time enterprise. Measurement through quality definition leads to understanding, Fit-for-Purpose engineering, and real-time responsive control to meet demand.

## Execution

The elicitation of qualities for services that applications consume is critical to ensure that these services will operate on Fit-for-Purpose optimized platforms. As the scope of any service is defined, it is useful to engage the stakeholders in understanding what operational requirements the service must meet and how they will be measured. The NGDC team should use the line of business drivers as a starting point and ask specific questions about performance, security, and the day in the life of the consumers of that service.

## Define success

To properly define measurable service qualities a number of key steps must be taken in a variety of workshop forums. The key to these workshops is making people feel comfortable with the level of detail that must be collected. In organizations that endure pressure to produce, deploy, and maintain applications, these workshops may be viewed as a waste of time. However, without the baseline information that is gathered in these workshops and other activities, it will be impossible to track progress and clearly show success. These activities will also detail where problems are happening in the environment, especially subtle ones that are hard to find that are often caused by datacenter sprawl. Very visible executive sponsorship is critical here. Some of the activities would be greatly aided if benchmarks from the legacy datacenter modeling exercise could be obtained.

Those eliciting information should create a list of questions regarding key qualities that are likely to be relevant on performance, hours of operation, and availability requirements. It is important to ask pertinent questions and get specific numbers (see the "Additional Supporting Information" section for some details that should be explored).

When eliciting qualities, it is important to compare classes of applications that exhibit similar behavior to avoid the problem of everyone believing his or her application is unique. This work becomes the basis for the creation of patterns, which will be explained further in the section on service design patterns later in this chapter.

## Inputs

Service qualities need to be elicited based on an understanding of business demand. The following inputs will aid in getting reasonable measures for these qualities.

- The previously defined service design artifacts are required.
- Any supporting metrics from the current operational platforms should form the basis for discussion.
- Any existing SLAs should be included; SLA compliance reporting is important as well.
- The daily lifecycle of the consuming applications, including heavy activity periods.
- Business value of the consuming applications focused on what impact slow or interrupted service will have on the business.

## Artifacts

There are numerous views that need to be created in this element. The reason so many views are required is because this very critical topic must be conveyed to a variety of key stakeholders and decision makers in appropriate detail.

### Business value chain service delivery framework matrix artifact

IT alignment with the business means multiple stakeholders must understand the datacenter dilemma from a similar point of view. This picture brings together all of the key concepts regarding business value chain, service requirements, and typical infrastructure supply. This picture would be created after much iteration in workshops for a specific organization. It is an excellent guide for how supply will need to be built in response.

The senior executive summary view characterizes lines of business and the business value chain to provide a broad basis of operational characteristics.

Figure 5.9 provides a good executive level summary that can be grasped quickly. This broad view will also aid in pattern creation discussed in a subsequent element.

---

**How to Create: Business Value Chain Delivery Framework Matrix Artifact**

**x-axis:**  BVC Category {BVC Sub-Category}
Research {Research}
Sales and Trading {AES, Equities, Fixed Income, Foreign Exchange}
Risk {Market, Credit, Counter Party, Trader}
Back Office {Reporting, Settlement}

**y-axis:**  Category {BVC Capability}
Demand {Service Requirements, Processing Requirements}
Supply {Implementation Patterns, Resource Consumption, Infrastructure Components, Infrastructure QoE Measurements}

**x-y Cell Question(s):** What are the QoE characteristic expectations?

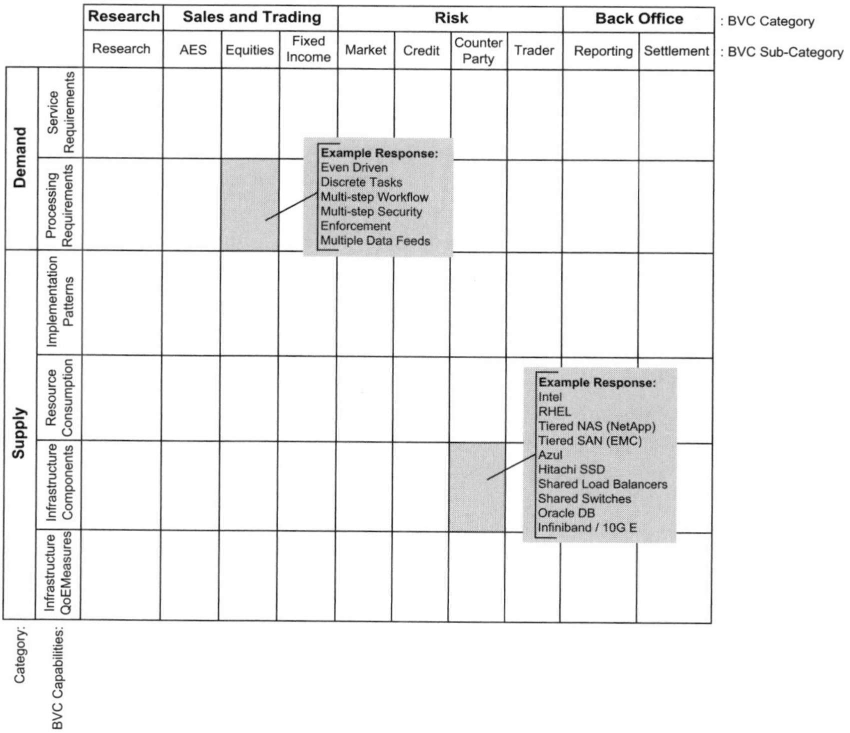

---

**Figure 5.9** Business Value Chain Service Delivery Framework Matrix artifact sample.

## Business value chain capabilities and key qualities matrix artifact

This view is also for the executive where quality requirements such as the need to drive throughput, minimize latency, and have elevated security are depicted per business value chain (Figure 5.10). This grouping reinforces the message that types of work have different consequences on the demand.

---

**How to Create: Business Value Chain Capabilities and Key Qualities Matrix Artifact**

*x*-axis: Business Operational Requirement
Minimize Latency
Drive Throughput
Maximize Concurrent Calculation
Process Large Data Volumes
Optimize Tight Operational Timeframes
Policy Based Security Enforcement
Minimize Disk Delays
Minimize Failure Recovery Time
Optimize Operational Platform Footprint

*y*-axis: Line of Business {Business Function}
Sales {Research, Client Screening, Client Relationship Management}
Trading {Trade Execution, Order Management, Market Data, ECN Connectivity, Scenario Analysis, Portfolio Management, Sell Side Trading}
Operations {Compliance, Asset Management, Accounting, Settlement, Clearing, Connectivity}
Risk {On Demand Risk, Client/Market/Firm Counterparty/Cash Management}
Report {Regulatory/Client/Management/Financial}

*x-y* **Cell Description(s):** Each cell in the matrix is focused on answering one primary question: Is the Business Operational Requirement applicable to the Business Function? The answer choices are either "Not Required," "Required," or "Variable." The objective of the exercise is to gain a course grained overview of the environment and not get into too many details.

---

The most important factor to consider here is to not delve into too much detail. The primary objective of this exercise is to get a coarse-grained overview and gather enough information so future discussions around setting direction can ensue.

| | Minimize Latency | Drive Throughput | Maximize Concurrent Calculation | Process Large Data Volumes | Optimize Tight Operational Timeframes | : Business Operational Requirement |
|---|---|---|---|---|---|---|
| **Sales** — Research | | | Not Required | | | |
| **Sales** — Client Screening | | | Not Required | | | |
| **Sales** — Client Relationship Management | | | Not Required | | | |
| **Trading** — Trade Execution | | | Required | | | |
| **Trading** — Order Management | | | Variable | | | |
| **Trading** — Market Data | | | Variable | | | |
| **Trading** — ECN Connectivity | | | Not Required | | | |

Line of Business: Business Function:

**Figure 5.10** Business Value Chain Capabilities and Key Qualities Matrix artifact sample.

## Service design qualities effects on supply matrix artifact

One of the key recurring themes throughout this book is that IT must align itself to the business. Qualities are a critical place to start, especially if the relationship between business demand and operational consequences are concretely shown. That requires a certain level of traceability through the detail so architects and other IT practitioners can speak about the relationship between demand and supply. Figure 5.11 drives down to tangible detail what will resonate with IT practitioners.

---

**How to Build: Service Design Qualities Effects on Supply Matrix Artifact**

*x*-axis:  Line of Business {Line of Business Function}
  Sales Functions {Research, Client Screening, Client Relationship Management} [Visual Experience, Accessibility to Content, Quality of Search, Availability/Convenience, Geographical Regulations.]
  Trading Functions {Trade Execution, Order Management, Market Data, ECN Connectivity, Scenario Analysis, Portfolio Management, Sell Side Trading}
  Operational Functions {Trade Execution, Order Management, Market Data, Scenario Analysis, Portfolio Management, Sell Side Trading}
  Risk Functions {On Demand Risk, Client/Market/Firm Counterparty Cash Management}
  Reporting {Regulatory Client/Management/Financial}

*y*-axis:  Demand Characteristic {Business Service Requirement}
  Performance {Latency, Availability, Throughput QoS, Throughput Load}

---

Data Usage {Data Aggregation, Interim Data Persistence, Data Distribution}

Storage {Swap Utilization, Disk Consumption}

Memory Consumption {Memory Consumption, Memory Volatility, Distributed Memory Coherence}

Compute Characteristics {Compute Data Set Size, Data Transformation, Rendering, Workload Size}

I/O Consumption {Event Intensive, Input Intensive, Output Intensive}

Security Requirements {Machine to Machine Internal, Machine to Machine External, Geographic Data Restrictions, Role Based Cross Machine Access, Role Based Access, Policy Management, Policy Enforcement}

Supply {Fit-for-Purpose™ Network Ensemble}

*x-y* **Cell Description(s):** Each cell in the matrix is focused on answering one primary question: What is the Business Service Requirement for each Line of Business Function? Depending on the demand characteristic category or subcategory, the type of answers will differ. In some cases, a Yes/No answer or High/Medium/Low answer is sufficient. In other cases such as Latency, the answer set consists of "Milliseconds, Microseconds, Standard, or N/A." Throughput QoS revolves around whether or not the system LOB Function needs all data (Full Rate), major differences (Conflated), or delayed feeds. In that case, the answer set consists of "Full Rate, Conflated, or Delayed." Other demand characteristics such as Fit-for-Purpose Network Ensemble are answered by matching the LOB Function to the appropriate ensemble.

The primary objective of this exercise is to obtain a coarse-grained overview of the demand characteristics for each line of business (LOB) function in order to match them to ensembles that will most readily meet their needs.

## Business value chain function requirements and characteristics artifact

It is important to understand the operating characteristics for business functions within a value chain. The functions in this artifact are grouped by value chain component and the operating characteristics are called out (Figure 5.12). This type of categorization will be used to associate function groups with ensembles for optimal workload type assignments. The value chain associations show likely collaborations between functions that require optimized communications. These associations will aid in assigning ensembles to Processing Execution Destinations (PEDs) to optimize interensemble communications. PEDs were introduced in Chapter 4, and the design process for PEDs will be discussed later in this chapter.

| | | Sales Functions | | | Trading Functions | | | | : Line of Business |
|---|---|---|---|---|---|---|---|---|---|
| | | Research | Client Screening | Client Relationship Management | Trade Execution | Order Management | Market Data | ECN Connectivity | : Line of Business Function |
| **Performance** | Latency | | | Standard | | | | | |
| | Availability | | | High | | | | | |
| | Throughput QoS | | | Conflated | | | | | |
| | Throughput Load | | | Low | | | | | |
| **Data Usage** | Data Aggregation | | | Low | | | | | |
| | Interim Data Presence | | | Low | | | | | |
| **Security Requirements** | Machine to Machine Internal | | | Yes | | | | | |
| | Machine to Machine External | | | No | | | | | |
| | Geographic Data Restrictions | | | Yes | | | | | |
| | Role Based Cross Machine Access | | | Yes | | | | | |
| **Supply** | Fit-for-Purpose Network Ensemble | | | Information Integration | | | | | |
| | | Demand Characteristic: | Demand Characteristic Subcategory: | | | | | | |

**Figure 5.11** Service Design Qualities Effects on Supply Matrix artifact sample.

## Stakeholders

Defining the service qualities is an important cornerstone of the NGDC transformation process. Since this must be done early in the transformation process, it is vital to get the right set of stakeholders involved. Here is a recommended list:

- The CIO and CIO direct reports must be present in the early workshops to set the tone and direction.
- Product line architects from the businesses whose applications will consume the service must be present.
- The designated design and implementation team must be present.
- Business analysts and system owners from the consuming applications must be present to verify their understanding of the characteristics of business demand and the current consequences of meeting that demand.

## Steps

A series of workshops must be conducted to further refine the previously defined services to include specific measurable qualities across line of business functions. These qualities form the basis for usage patterns that will be utilized in the architecture, patterns, and ensemble elements discussed later in this chapter. During the workshops a discovery and definition process will occur:

- Define how different classes of applications, by line of business, consume the infrastructure. In financial services, it is not unusual for a small percentage of the

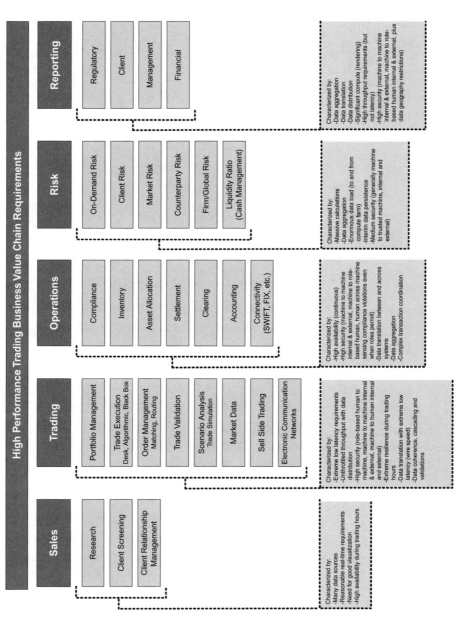

**Figure 5.12** High-Level Business Value Chain Function requirements and characteristics.

applications to consume a majority of the infrastructure. Examples of such financial services applications include the following.
- Internet-facing applications for client self-service.
- Trading platforms including market data, order processing, and proprietary trading.
- General ledger and statement generation applications.
- Define how users of those applications expect to be serviced, how the work they do varies over the day, and how that variance affects consumption.
- Classify applications by the type of work they perform, by business line, and business function.
- All the definitions and findings must be arranged in an intuitive fashion with many layers of detail. This will take time and iteration.

## Usage

Multiple stakeholders need to view layered details of qualities, business value chain requirements, and the impacts on supply. These details will emerge from the service design quality workshops. The artifacts listed in this section provide multiple views that can be used to engage the business, senior IT executives, and architects in the investment discussions. Utilizing these artifacts will foster a better understanding of the business demand and its consequences on supply which is critical to building optimized Fit-for-Purpose operating platforms to run applications.

## Do's

- Be specific about quality values—see the additional notes section.
- Challenge conventional wisdom about values.

## Don'ts

- Don't allow application owners to pigeonhole their applications into specialized classes. There is a tendency among owners of very high-performing applications to consider all aspects of their application unique. Make sure the work is decomposed enough to challenge those assumptions.
- Don't accept broad statements about 24/7 availability without some business qualification.

## Quality categories

There are many categories of qualities that can be considered, and not all categories will be appropriate for all lines of business. Within these categories there are many quality attributes, and not all of them are applicable for every service or application. The categories of qualities that should be considered for most applications in a financial services organization include the following:

*Performance:* Attributes that measure the speed, size, and efficiency of the work that is processed. Performance is one of the most significant drivers in all aspects of financial services, so the performance category of qualities will be expanded as an

example of the depth that will be required to be explored for all categories. Some
examples of performance attributes are described in the following sections.

- *Latency:* The maximum acceptable time it takes to process a unit of work (e.g.,
  transaction). Since this category is usually relevant for low latency applications,
  the expectations are that answers would be in milliseconds, and this is expected
  to be measured to ensure that the latency expectations are maintained. This
  measure usually applies to the area of control that the application can exert. It is
  not sufficient by itself to guarantee a certain response time.
- *Throughput peak characteristics:* Throughput needs to be carefully analyzed,
  as it is too often quoted in a single number (e.g., 10,000 messages per second,
  1 million records per day). Neither of those examples is sufficient to perform
  proper demand analysis. Proper demand mapping requires that the peak be put
  into context by stating (1) extent (e.g., 10,000 messages/second for 30 minutes),
  and (2) frequency (10,000 messages/second for 30 minutes, three times a day).
  Without extent and frequency, it is impossible to properly engineer a platform to
  meet the demands of an application, without overengineering.
- *Throughput and service design:* It is important to remember that in most services
  and applications the number of input messages does not correspond one-to-one
  with the number of output messages generated, so some consideration must be
  given to the ratio of input to output when reviewing the impact of this quality.
- *Response time:* This implies that there is an entity (human or other application)
  that is expecting a response. Expected response times are measured from the
  time a user or application initiates a request till it gets a response (this could be
  through multiple systems). It is a critical visible factor in the QoE.

*Availability and Failure Recovery Expectations:* Failure recovery needs to be carefully
understood. Hard facts are important to elicit to avoid design flaws or underes-
timating the need. Percent availability can be deceptive (e.g., 99.99 percent), as
uptime for a 24/7 application still could mean three-plus hours of downtime in a
year. It is just as important to understand maximum acceptable time to recover during the critical peak time (e.g., recovery in under one minute for a trading application during trading hours). This is very different from 24/7, but it is very stringent.

*Security:* The number of security related functions that this service must perform as
part of its contract. The broadest set of security attributes to investigate includes
authentication, authorization, identify management, and encryption. Other details,
such as national restrictions on data movement and users having multiple roles,
also may be considered in broad services that span a global financial enterprise.

*Integration:* The amount of varying protocols, information sources, and formats that
this service will be expected to process. The degree of integration that must be performed will greatly influence the design of the service, especially if the number and
type of protocols, sources, and formats are expected to change frequently. This
could be the case if the business expects a higher degree of mergers or an increase
in external partners.

*Speed of Deployment and Change:* As discussed in Chapter 2, the financial services
business needs to respond to new opportunities quickly. Deploying new functionality, new products, or rearranging processes are attributes that can be measured in
terms of time and efficiency.

*User Experience:* In this case the user could be in the form of a client-facing application
where the service is providing content or the user is affected indirectly because the
service is providing information to a client application that performs the bulk of the

presentation transformation. In either case, there are attributes that should be investigated. One attribute to consider in a global financial organization is the degree of *geographical dispersion* of users. This attribute will raise issues of time zones, performance, security, and human language translation of real-time messages and events, all of which will have overhead in processing, I/O, and potentially storage.

*Workflow:* In many areas of the financial industry there is a push to convert traditional end-of-day batch processing to real-time straight-through-processing (STP). This driver is especially true for well established business products in capital markets and fixed income, where the speed of the settlement and confirmation process becomes a competitive advantage. Introducing new business products that have slightly different processing rules or sequencing is becoming necessary. In addition, these tactics provide a basis for design discussions. One attribute to investigate is the degree of *exception processing* required. The desire to have business rules managed external from the service programs, as well as the testability of business rules, have considerable implications for the flexibility of design and testing.

*Service Levels:* Service levels are defined agreements that must be met in areas such as performance (e.g., response time, throughput) or availability. Understanding the consequences of not meeting these levels (e.g., penalties, loss of business, government regulations, harm to brand) affect the decision-making process in making a Fit-for-Purpose platform to meet the needs of the candidate application.

## 5.3.4   Service architecture patterns

NGDC service architecture patterns are platform independent models representing the collaboration of identified components designed to solve a problem set. An architecture pattern employs reusable frameworks and services to minimize the amount of custom software required to solve business problems. NGDC service architecture patterns are never implementations or reusable services. They are represented in visual (block components) or tabular (functional decomposition) form. This is usually augmented with lists of attributes, capabilities, and constraints of the pattern and act as guides for implementation. Patterns should be viewed as platform-independent models that have value as the codification of deliberate decisions. Patterns are realized by program code running in ensembles that optimize the workload characteristics of that pattern. PEDs are platforms that optimize communications between ensembles.

NGDC service architecture patterns are part of a larger reference architecture that is used by an organization to define design principles. This reference architecture is used as follows:

- Provides a basis for communicating "good architecture" to the stakeholder community (developers, managers, executives). Good architecture meets requirements; there is no single "good" architecture; it is solution and constraint based.
- Establishes a common language for stakeholders to design and discuss the benefits of the designs.
- Defines design principles to guide and evaluate the architecture as the business evolves.
- Enables applications to be integrated by assembling instances of relevant parts within the reference architecture.

- Facilitates a means to ensure applications are not built entirely from scratch, reducing risk, saving time, and cost.
- Ensures institutional knowledge and investment are reused.
- Acts as a guideline that can be used in parts so any given application will use only the parts of the architecture it requires.

The NGDC service architecture patterns must be discussed by all key stakeholders, including the CIO and CIO direct reports, business line architects, and development teams. The service patterns must be conveyed in several formats exhibiting incremental levels of detail to ensure that credible discussions can take place.

An understandable services architecture that includes business decisions from the start will have longer-lasting value than any program or product that is installed. A services architecture that captures the needs of the business is working from stable principles that are aligned to business direction. Such architecture represents the digital supply chain, which is the analog of the business value chain.

Properly designed services, represented as architecture patterns, provide the guiding blueprint to build services with the right flexibility and growth points. This architectural foundation is fundamental to NGDC success.

## Goals and objectives

The goals of service design architecture patterns are to provide guidance to all stakeholders so ensembles can be built from the patterns. Service patterns document the following important decisions:

- How services will be assembled, including the types of functional components to use.
- All of the constraints that the pattern must work under.
- Specific operational qualities derived from the business.
- All of the tradeoffs that can be foreseen when building the realized version of the pattern.
- Provides a basis for prioritizing a product road map.

The NGDC service architecture patterns provide the critical guidance to ensemble creation and subsequent PED integration. The patterns are platform independent models that reflect business requirements and therefore are less volatile than the changes in datacenter hardware. These patterns are blueprints that are grounded in alignment with the business.

## Execution

Once the services are defined and the service qualities are elicited, patterns should be defined based on how the consuming applications expect to utilize the services. Small iterative workshops with the service design team and representatives from the consuming applications are required. This process requires a combination of structured meetings and offline design work over a number of weeks. Senior IT management checkpoints should occur monthly. As designs mature attempts to validate them with focused "proof of concept" integration labs should be undertaken.

## Define success

A delicate balance must be struck between focusing on the depiction of a platform-independent model, even as preparations should be made for testing design assumptions in the lab. All critical decisions need to be documented, as these are as valuable as the design. The other balance is between too much analysis and a rush to implement. Taking one service at a time in the early stages is critical, even if the candidate applications require more than one defined service before they can cut over. Finally, it is important to remember that this is a cultural shift, and some people will inject their "loss of control" bias in the design discussions. Impersonal tradeoff analysis based on explicit requirements is the best way to get over these types of obstacles.

## Inputs

Architecture patterns are created from the work already done on service design and service qualities: service design and service quality definitions, including priorities, and existing framework or service designs that have similar functionality.

## Artifacts

### Extract translate load architecture pattern artifact

There is a need to aggregate many sources of data into preconfigured information hierarchies, categories, or record types (Figure 5.13). The data must be transformed to summarize the disparate sources, making it available for display in a cohesive structure. The ETL is designed to transform multiple, arbitrarily sized and formatted data sets from one representation to another. The transformation rules can be varied, complex and are subject to frequent change. There are many packages that perform this set of tasks. While implementations will vary per vendor, client size, and industry, there are recurring themes of behavior in such a large-scale pattern. These behavioral themes are represented by three functional patterns defined by the following. Each has different operational characteristics. The details of these patterns might be hidden by the particular vendor implementation, but they must be addressed. Figure 5.13 illustrates many of the operational design challenges that are faced when engineering this type of application and how these characteristics stress a typical deployment that uses a static resource allocation scheme.

**Data Aggregator (*Extract*):** Designed to aggregate many sources of data into preconfigured information hierarchies, categories, or record types. This pattern will typically summarize already existing information or collect data from many sources in order to transform or display it in a uniform manner.

**Transformation Engine:** Focus on the transformation of data between sets of representations. Input & Output streams could be multiple. Typically utilizes reference data to retrieve transformation rules. Could employ context-driven rules to execute transformations.

**File Transfer Integrator (*Load*):** Designed to produce the files at specified intervals. Uses a data repository to persist the incoming and destination files. Since files are being transferred and transformed according to a specification, there is little need for the

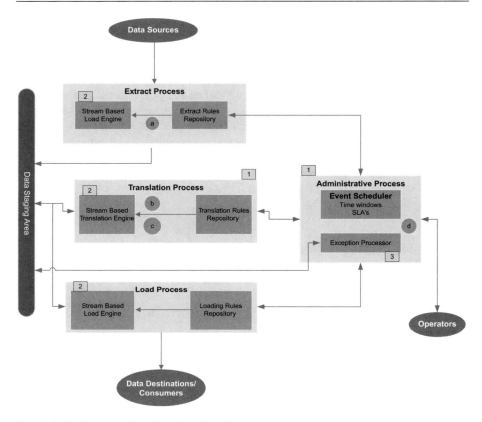

**Figure 5.13** Extract, Translate, Load architecture pattern.

applications that collaborate this way to know the internals of their collaborators. FTI does not need internal knowledge of collaborators either.

1. *Driving forces.* There are multiple input and output streams that require different workload profiles. There are unexpected peaks that cannot be determined until the load process is started. Each stream will have its own service delivery option. Extract, translate, and load could all have peak loads simultaneously.
2. *Resource contention at peak causes service-level violations.* Statically assigned resources prevent the flexible allocation of those resources to process unexpected increases in workload for a particular data stream. If an increase in one stream cannot be accommodated, the entire load process could be violating SLAs.
3. *Resource contention due to an unexpected increase in high-priority error processing.* With static allocation of processing resources, longer-running workloads such as exception processing (which is usually higher priority) could starve resources from normal-running workloads because static allocations for error processing are usually small.

## Tradeoffs and constraints in a static allocation model
1. Processing multiple data sources for multiple consumers, with different SLAs will increase the scheduling complexity, especially if data quality is not predictable.

2. Complex translations with high throughput volume requirements will contend for resources with less compute-intensive workloads. Solving this problem can increase operational complexity.
3. Within a workstream, the mix of workload units could be large. In a static allocation model, a workstream will not be able to use freed resources to divide the workloads by duration. Efficiency is not achieved.
4. Failover considerations get more complex for large data sets, where a cold restart is not an option.

This architecture pattern shows the essential functions of an extract, translate, and load (ETL) architecture pattern, highlighting the component interconnections and the typical driving forces that designers of such a pattern encounter. It shows this pattern running in an operating environment whose resource allocations are fixed so the consequences of demand, which are the various bottlenecks, can be demonstrated. This pattern offers no particular solution; it is platform independent and reflects experiences with such tools (commercial or in-house built) in a static environment. It forms the basis for discussions about designs that would leverage an RTI environment. A companion pattern would need to be drawn showing how each of the problems pointed out in the static pattern would be addressed utilizing components from RTI. This solution-oriented drawing should make assertions about fixing each problem that could be tested.

This would be part of the basis for pattern development and refinement. The scope of this book does not include a detailed discussion of patterns, but there are excellent books that refer to this subject for pattern development and refactoring existing applications into patterns.[5,6]

The concept of refactoring applications into patterns is a critical one, because many large-scale applications that a global enterprise uses are comprised of several patterns. ETL is often found as one of those patterns, as illustrated by the next artifact.

## Application pattern decomposition artifact

As discussed in Chapter 4, the long-term goal of the NGDC initiative is to have critical applications run on optimized platforms that are fit-for-purpose aligned with the application workload. Critical applications are often complex entities that perform many functions that have different workload types and therefore can be decomposed into patterns that reflect that workload type.

Even if the application (such as ERP shown in this artifact) is commercial off-the-shelf software, the exercise of decomposing the workload types is the first step in understanding how to optimally run that package. It is an idealized view that will challenge conventional thinking for various internal teams such as operations, the service design team, and the support team. In addition it presents the opportunity to have meaningful discussions with the commercial vendor about how to optimally run the product.

[5]Fowler M. *Patterns of Enterprise Application Architecture*. Addison-Wesley Professional; 2002, November 15 [Signature series].
[6]Kerievsky J. *Refactoring to Patterns*. Addison-Wesley Professional; 2004, August 15 [Signature series].

Figure 5.14 shows an ERP application composed of four fundamental patterns: portal server, numerical processor, enterprise application integrator, and ETL (from the previous example). Each pattern is again shown in the static allocation model with each pattern's attendant problems exhibited for analysis. The figure also includes definitions for each component.

### Service architecture pattern workload analysis matrix artifact

An essential part of the pattern mapping exercise is to establish gross operational requirements of the patterns used an organization (Figure 5.15). Patterns will be divided into usage scenarios, each of which represents certain workload types. Each workload type will then be used to map to specific ensembles based on their distinct operational characteristics.

---

**How to Create: Service Architecture Pattern Workload Analysis**

*x*-axis: Workload Characteristic {Workload Characteristic Subcategory}

- Performance {Low Latency Required?, High Peak Volume, Long Volume Duration, Frequent High Volume Peaks, Fast Response Time}
- Scaling Tactics {Multiple Concurrent Input, Partition Workload Possible}
- Workloads {Decomposable, Workload Data Size, Workload Duration}
- Quality of Experience {Tight SLAs Defined, Volatile Demand}
- Compliance {Concurrent Usage Restr. Req?}

*y*-axis: Usage Scenario {Usage Scenario Category}

- Grid Broker {Complex Calculators, Time Driven Value Calculators, ETL, Web Service Broker, Mainframe Offload}
- Service Broker {Web Server Content Servicing, J2EE Distributed Application, .Net Distributed Application, IOC Container & POJO Distributed Applications, Distributed Transactional Data Caching, Data Federation, Content Management, Business Intelligence, Web 2.0/RIA Content Interaction, Real Time Event Correlation, Enterprise Service Bus, Straight Through Processing Workflow}

*x-y* Cell Description(s): Each cell in the matrix is focused on answering one primary question: Does this workload characteristic apply to this usage scenario? The answer set is binary, consisting of a Yes or No.

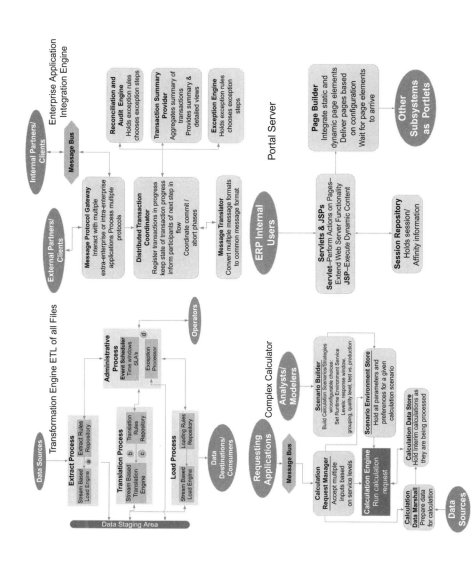

**Figure 5.14** ERP application depicted in patterns.

| Usage Secnario : | Usage Scenario Category : | Performance | | | | Scaling Tactics | | : Workload Wharacteristic |
|---|---|---|---|---|---|---|---|---|
| | | Low Latency Required? | High Peak Volume | Long Volume Duration | Frequent High Volume Peaks | Multiple Concurrent Input | Partition Workload Possible | : Workload Characteristic Subcategory |
| Grid Broker | Complex Calculators | | | | | | | |
| Grid Broker | Time Driven Value Calculators | | | | | | | |
| Grid Broker | ETL | | | Yes | | | | |
| Grid Broker | Web Service Broker | | | | | | | |
| Grid Broker | Mainframe Offload | No | | | | | | |
| Service Broker | Web Server Content Servicing | | | | | | | |
| Service Broker | J2EE Distributed Application | | | | | | | |

**Figure 5.15** Service architecture pattern workload analysis sample.

The key thing to take away is that the preceding creation description and sample table are a starting point for any organization to decompose its workload characteristics. Many organizations will require additional usage categories to consider. Additionally, it's important to get enough information to fuel further discussion without getting in too deep.

The usage scenarios above are divided into grid broker and service broker scenarios. Grid broker scenarios have workloads that are compute intensive, can be parallelized, and benefit from the concurrency management a grid broker provides. Service broker scenarios consist of container based applications that benefit from the type of container lifecycle management and dynamically assigned resources that a service broker provides based on business demand.

## Stakeholders

The stakeholders for architecture patterns are as follows:

- Service design team
- Senior business line architects (product line architects)
- Architects from consuming applications that will later form the basis for a product steering group as the long-term transformation takes hold
- Senior IT management that dictate the investment strategy

## Steps

Architecture patterns are created through a series of iterative steps:

- Small workshops to start with the design teams
- Offline work to include research, validation, and consolidation of ideas
- Validation of choices in the lab using quickly created proof of concepts to examine assumptions and potential bottlenecks and tradeoffs

## Usage

The link between applications and PEDs goes through patterns, then to ensembles, and finally to PEDs. Most large applications like ERP have components that can be configured to run in an NGDC optimized footprint. This optimized footprint is best realized as ensembles running specific patterns aligned by workload type, collaborating on a PED that optimizes interensemble communication, lowering latency, and improving performance, increasing efficiency while lowering costs and energy consumption.

**Patterns and Applications:** Since the first publication of *Design Patterns*[7] in 1994, there have been hundreds of pattern books written, and they have advanced the field of IT architecture tremendously. Many of these publications have defined a significant number of patterns at a variety of scales. There are good rules of thumb to be found in many. Pattern matching to applications is not an exact science nonetheless; experience has taught us that even unconscious efforts to develop applications have yielded some trends in pattern to application ratios that are a function of managing complexity. Applications of sufficient size that warrant consideration for NGDC services are composed between three and five architectural patterns.

## Do's

- Iterate through design workshops, validate in the lab as decisions mature.
- Use expressive visual aids; don't be afraid to use large, colorful sheets to convey information to executives.

---

[7]Gamma E, et al. *Design Patterns: Elements of Reusable Object-Oriented Software*. Addison-Wesley Professional; 1994, November 10 [Professional computing series].

- Treat conflicts with facts such as requirements, document decisions, and publish them, especially contentious ones.
- Remember that architecture is an investment that yields value.

### Don'ts

- There is no single good architecture; instead, realize that architecture is good when it can be shown to meet the requirements.
- Do not have only a product-specific architecture; the service architecture patterns will be most valuable if they are platform independent.

## 5.3.5  Architecture ensembles

According to the Software Engineering Institute, an ensemble is a defined collaboration of components that solves a specific business problem.[8] The ensemble defines the types of components involved and a pattern of interaction, along with driving forces, constraints, and tradeoff decisions. A component ensemble is a realized instance (at a point in time) of an architectural pattern, where the requirements for that pattern have been addressed by measurable capabilities.

Ensembles are integrated components that have been tested to work within certain measurable conditions. They are designed to perform optimally for a certain class of problems that exhibit patterns of behavior. An example is an ensemble designed to process all of the work (compute, interprocess communication, persistent, and interim storage) for low-latency applications that support the trading environment.

Any NGDC infrastructure service consumer will transparently use ensembles when they consume the services. Ensembles are used by service consumers to achieve a Fit-for-Purpose solution for specific types of application workload that is not over-engineered to meet their quality goals.

The ensemble is designed to balance the QoE factors of cost, efficiency, and user experience that the consumers require. It is the QoE that senior executives care most about, because they are trying to align costs with revenue growth. Ensembles are the most effective means to deliver services in a dynamic real-time enterprise because they are designed top down to operate on a focused problem set that exhibits well-defined operational characteristics. The integration of ensemble components is designed to work together to solve certain application pattern types that are characterized by a defined range of work characteristics. This design focus will optimize the QoE.

### Goals and objectives

The primary objective of creating an architecture ensemble is to provide a top-down, demand-driven operating environment that effectively processes all

[8]Clements P, et al. *Software Product Lines: Practices and Patterns*. 3rd ed. Addison-Wesley Professional; 2001, August 30 [SEI series in Software Engineering].

aspects of a defined set of architectural patterns that possess similar working characteristics. Ensembles solve distinct application pattern operational characteristics. Ensembles should be designed top-down to meet demand, but must be able to be tailored bottom-up to meet specific application and service needs through configuration and business policy rules. Ensembles should be integrated and instrumented sufficiently so that performance guarantees can be stated within certain parameters. An example of such a guarantee is detailed following.

**Latency Sensitive Ensemble:** More than 1,000 messages per second can be sustained for eight hours with a latency of less than 40 milliseconds provided that the processing of each incoming message will result in only updating one database record. In addition, the maximum size of input and output messages is less than 200 bytes.

Ensembles are focused building blocks that optimally operate specific application and service workload types. Ensembles realize application patterns by providing an operational platform tailored to that pattern's work characteristics. Ensembles enable the designer to validate component choices based on the top-down blueprint design. Ensembles are integrated into PEDs that facilitate interensemble communication, ensuring that highly collaborative applications with different work characteristics will be able to optimally operate.

## Execution

In previous elements, the operational characteristics of key application patterns were discovered, and the infrastructure services were defined. As a result of these efforts, the work exhibited by the key consuming applications has been characterized. The consuming applications and the defined services have also been characterized through patterns. It is now possible to design the solution building blocks that will enable RTI.

## Define success

Successful ensemble design results in blueprints that can be used to incrementally construct the ensembles as specific custom and commercial components are integrated. The designs should be clear, and the top-down design assumptions well documented so parameters of execution can be understood by consumers (e.g., if an ensemble will only be able to process 1,000 messages per second for 10 minutes, that needs to be known; if configuration changes can alter the throughput, then they must be specified along with the consequences). The ultimate success criterion for ensembles is widespread adoption.

Success during design is an incremental approach to integration once the top-down design has been formulated. Integration, measurement, and simulation will ensure that the top-down design will have the appropriate amount of tailoring to meet consumption needs.

There are few types of ensembles required to operate the working characteristics of most financial services applications. It is important to get agreement early on scope and start with the four ensembles mentioned in Chapter 4 as a basis.

Any new ensemble types should be subjected to a reasonably detailed analysis. In the additional supporting documentation section, the four ensemble types are summarized. In Chapter 4 these ensemble types are explained in detail.

## Inputs

Ensemble design builds upon the previous work on patterns and services and thus requires the following inputs:

- Architecture patterns defined through the workshops and iterative design.
- Service definitions and service qualities.
- Output from a legacy datacenter mapping, including infrastructure dependencies and metrics for applications that will consume the service.
- If these ensembles are going to operate currently running services, then those benchmarks are critical as well.

## Artifacts

### Business requirement workloads and ensemble choices artifact
It is important to remember key concepts from the alignment discussion in Chapter 3, specifically the importance of the business value chain components, the business functions that support the value chain, and the resulting service requirements that those functions need in order to operate properly (Figure 5.16). Business functions generate demand that must be fulfilled by the IT digital supply chain. The migration to a real time enterprise will enable better fulfillment of business function workload types by running on ensembles that interact within

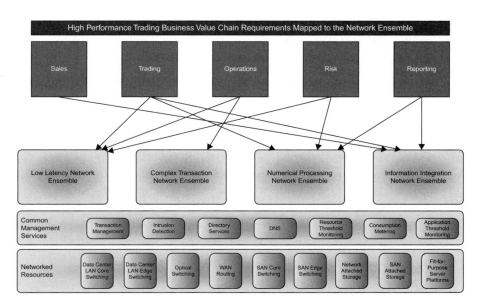

**Figure 5.16** Relationship between BVC and ensemble types.

PEDs. A visual review of the relationship of business value chains, business functions, and ensembles would reinforce these ideas.

Note how high-performance trading, normally only associated with strictly low latency operational requirements, has more than one workload type associated with it. If the assumption were made that all trading functions only ran on low latency ensembles, massive waste and inefficiency would ensue, and performance would suffer. Paying attention to business demand is essential.

## Service design solution ensembles artifact

Figure 5.17 shows the culmination of many workshops and design sessions that result in four general ensembles optimized to process all of the work types that a financial services organization is likely to need. The four ensembles are low latency, complex transaction, information integration, and numerical processing. These ensembles were introduced and detailed in Chapter 4. As can be seen in Figure 5.17, the ensembles are designed to process specific workload types and contain components that would optimize the operation of that workload, along with the appropriate compute, network, and storage facilities. The ensembles are shown as part of an architecture that includes common management services and networked resources that these management services make available as needed.

The ensembles are designed to be used collaboratively to support lines of business that have different work type characteristics for the different value chain functions. How those collaborations are optimized is discussed in the NGDC PED element section.

### *Stakeholders*

A product steering group needs to be formed that consists of key technical leaders from both the consuming population and the design and implementation teams. This steering group should meet regularly—at least once a

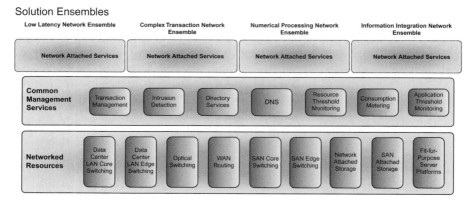

**Figure 5.17** Example services.

month—to discuss how ensembles are being designed. This discussion would also include reporting on services and patterns.

### Steps

Using the preceding inputs, incremental design working sessions must be established to utilize the characteristics of application workload and patterns, along with the defined services to take a first cut at the types of ensembles.

- Focus on the most critical application and service types first, going over the work analysis, operational characteristics, and driving forces. Be aware that applications will likely exhibit more than one workload type, so it is critical to laboratory-test the behavior of the application while running on the target ensemble.
- Be conscious of the possible product choices for these ensembles to understand potential gaps in integration and measurement.
- Product choices should include internal as well as external components. It is important to consider hardware as well as software. An ensemble will be delivered as a comprehensive unit. The consumer does not get to pick and choose pieces of the ensemble; this is an important consideration in design. A lab area needs to be created to do three things: Let potential customers try the ensemble by testing it, create new ensembles, and revise and test existing ensembles.
- Benchmarks using characteristic application patterns must be run so other consumers can review results similar to their applications. This prevents a constant stream of formal benchmarks from consuming the team's time.
- The creation of a quick start team is critical to ensure rapid adoption.

### Usage

Ensembles need to be treated as products by the development teams. The concept of IT product development and evolution within a financial services firm needs to be introduced, as it is unlikely that any such firm uses that discipline currently. The practice of IT product development has been covered by the Software Engineering Institute (SEI) in detail in the book *Software Product Lines* by Clements and Northrop.[9] The SEI also teaches courses on the subject.

Four distinct ensembles were introduced in Chapter 4. Each of them addresses a certain workload type: latency sensitive, complex transaction, information integration, and numerical processing. Each ensemble optimizes these workload types because the ensembles are realized from application patterns that describe the workload type and its associated driving forces.

Ensembles should be designed to evolve as new technologies are made available. That is why it is so critical to treat ensembles as products, whose operating characteristics can be tailored based on parameter settings. The tailoring is critical to attract a range of consumers with similar workload characteristics.

---

[9]Clements P, et al. *Software Product Lines: Practices and Patterns.* 3rd ed. Addison-Wesley Professional; 2001, August 30 [SEI series in Software Engineering].

It should be made clear to all consumers that ensembles are delivered as a whole product, not subject to piecemeal selection. The major reason for this is reduction of maintenance and improvement of service as ensembles evolve.

Application teams might be reluctant to take on the whole ensemble because they may feel they do not need all of the features. This is where an on-boarding team is needed. The on-boarding team should be created to assist all stakeholders in moving to all aspects of the new infrastructure. The initial on-boarding team will be the seed to create a discipline for the organization. This team will accelerate consumption of the services by coordinating application assessments, integration tests, providing guidance on documentation. This team also needs to work with the service design, platform engineering, and operations teams to ensure that it is clear how to operate and configure ensembles. As applications are placed onto ensembles, the on-boarding team should also make sure the instrumentation team is benchmarking the results.

## Do's

- Consider integration strategies and how to provide measurable repeatable results.
- Documentation, design, and integration testing are critical and must be understandable to ensemble creators and consumers.

## Don'ts

- Ensemble definitions are not static; they must be designed and documented so they can be altered.
- Ensembles are delivered whole, with a defined range of capabilities that should be tuned. Do not allow consumers to pick and choose ensemble pieces.
- Don't assume the old habits of documentation; testing and design will suffice for the creation and maintenance of successful NGDC ensembles. Attitudes and skills will need to be changed to think about documentation, including test results as a valued asset.

## Key concepts

Ensembles are realized platforms that are designed to run certain patterns optimally and the initial attempt to establish a product discipline to IT. This requires a larger amount of initial work that will have long-term payoffs. This product view of IT will force more formality in documentation, integration testing, and design.

The link between applications and PEDs goes through patterns then to ensembles and finally to PEDs. Most large applications like ERP have components that can be configured to run in an NGDC optimized footprint. This optimized footprint would be best realized as ensembles running specific patterns aligned by workload type, collaborating on a PED that optimizes interensemble communication, lowering latency, improving performance, and increasing efficiency, while lowering costs and energy consumption.

### 5.3.6   Infrastructure processing execution destinations (PEDs)

NGDC infrastructure PEDs are the optimized operating footprints that integrate highly collaborative groups of workload-specific ensembles to minimize communication delays. PEDs contain this operating footprint which optimally balances the three pillars of QoE (user experience, efficiency, and cost) by respecting the realities of IT physics.

IT physics concerns itself with the energy utilized to perform the totality of work. Energy concerns include the effects that distance has on collaborating components—the heat generated by all the hardware, the cooling required to dissipate the heat, the space that servicing the workload requires. A consequence of datacenter sprawl is that distances between physical tiers of an application grow larger, impacting performance by increasing the overall execution time required to perform the work. This performance impact tends to be addressed by adding more hardware, which in turn increases cooling and power requirements, while introducing operational complexity, and increasing the need for higher network bandwidth to ensure that highly collaborative components can communicate effectively. The ultimate result of all these compensating factors is that latency between highly collaborative components impacts performance, requiring further compensation, all of which increases the total cost to execute. It is a degrading spiral.

Close proximity between collaborating ensembles results in less network hops and less switch traversal. Reducing hops and switching is critical to meeting performance requirements and preventing excessive engineering quick fixes, which tend to create long-term maintenance problems in the datacenter. The value is that the proper construction of PEDs reduces datacenter sprawl. Properly designed PEDs have lower power and cooling requirements and as a result can pack more capacity into a smaller physical area. PEDs optimize communication efficiency and are the physical manifestation of ensemble groups brought together to fulfill specific business demand, which is logically viewed as a suite of applications. This logical view of an application gets preserved in the business operations context because the resources in the ensembles and PEDs are abstracted through virtualization. Having context for a logical view of the application supports the premise raised in Chapter 3 that *tangible* logical business models are a competitive advantage. By placing these highly collaborative ensembles together in a single footprint, PEDs optimize communication efficiency and therefore improve all aspects of QoE for that application suite.

PEDs have integrated communication switches, special cooling facilities that allow for greater density of blades servers, and accommodations for specialized appliances, which, when assembled, provide a pool of resources that can be shared to optimize workload while respecting IT physics. This sharing will occur in real time in reaction to incoming demand. The sharing will also extend to repurposing, where applications that only run during the day relinquish their resources to be used by applications that run only at night. All of these capabilities are part of the RTI strategy.

Applications and infrastructure services are deployed within PEDs which use the management services listed in Table 5.1 to create an adaptive operating RTI for ensembles. These are the management services that aid in flexible deployment of applications and services to the right level of resources:

*Dynamic Application Deployment and Activation:* Packaging an application or service once that can be deployed many times, based on events.

*Dynamic Infrastructure Service Provisioning:* Managing the lifecycle of service or application instances in order to invoke more instances or retire them.

*Dynamic Runtime Service Orchestration:* Allocate resources based on real-time demand and business policy. These allocations are made based on defined business demand thresholds such as messages per second.

*Utility Resource Management:* Assign work to the right kinds of resources, based on an association of type. An example might be to direct certain kinds of risk numerical processing workloads to processors with chips that can greatly accelerate that type of work (e.g., FPGA).

The processes involved in designing PEDs use all of the design work elements presented in this chapter and leverage the alignment work highlighted in Chapter 3. Business value chain service requirements drive PED design, as does the work on *service design* and *service qualities*. Architecture patterns, which define functional solutions, are then realized by ensembles that are tailored to fit types of workloads. PEDs make it easier for different workload types, running on different ensembles and on optimized platforms, while enabling fast, efficient communication and providing footprints that can be delivered as whole units to manage the transformation.

PEDs are the tactical lever required to enact RTI strategy; without the PEDs many of the RTI goals will not be achieved. They also represent a considerable investment for which the CIO must take responsibility. Therefore the CIO, CIO direct reports, and senior datacenter personnel (including the CTO) are all critical stakeholders and need to see the documentation and be concerned about PED development.

The service design team, product steering group, the on-boarding team, and product line architects all must become conversant in the use of PEDs. PEDs are the physical backbone of the NGDC operating model.

Ensemble design and creation are not enough to achieve an NGDC transformation that enables RTI. Without the use of PEDs, ensembles that must heavily collaborate may be placed in arbitrary parts of the datacenter, using some physical resources in the more traditional datacenter deployment method. PED design introduces the often overlooked aspect of IT physics that includes the efficient use of energy and the optimal communication between disparate workload types.

PEDs provide the chance to place the new NGDC platform into an existing datacenter as a focused pilot. PEDs are self-contained and can be placed in the datacenter with minimal disruption to existing operations. This is one of the great advantages of PEDs.

## Goals and objectives

The critical goals in PED design are as follows:

- Design a PED to optimize the workload types across an entire application, or suite of applications, across a business value chain.
- Introduce architecture tradeoff analysis to ensure that designs are grounded from business requirements, while making the tough tradeoff choices required to deliver optimized operating platforms.
- Use PEDs as a lever for change agency in existing datacenters.

PEDs solve a major tradeoff problem, because they allow designers to decompose an application into distinct workload patterns, optimize each pattern, and yet enable fast, efficient communication. In essence, the designer can optimize local and global behavior, which has been difficult to accomplish in distributed operating platforms.

## Execution

The process should include work from the ensemble designs where an application or a suite of applications within a business value chain are assigned ensembles. Since it is likely that the ensembles represent different workload types, the PED design would explore the key operating characteristics and metrics on business demand to assign the correct level of resources to a PED. This design is iterative and requires laboratory-based validation.

## Define success

Success is defined by the introduction of a PED into the production environment, where the executing applications and services can be instrumented and managed in real time. Success is the introduction of processes that enable applications to be on-boarded, processes that clearly delineate how change is managed and an integrated metrics dashboard for the PED. The PED should be a model for how the datacenter will evolve to an NGDC that enables the *real time enterprise* through the operation of an RTI.

## Inputs

PEDs require the input of all previous design activities discussed in this chapter. Here is a summary of the inputs needed:

- All design work from the ensemble workshops (including all operational qualities).
- Initial processes for on-boarding applications.
- Metrics for the candidate applications including all network related data requirements.
- Architecture patterns and dependency maps for the candidate applications.

## *Artifacts*

### PED design artifact

This artifact is the result of the iterative design workshops. Figure 5.18 shows two PEDs—one for capital markets front office functions and one for capital markets middle office functions. It is important to show the reasoning behind the PED and ensemble choices.

The front office PED has varied high-performance needs including low latency market data and algorithmic black box trading. The high-performance characteristics of algorithmic trading require many calculation iterations until an answer is achieved. In some cases the calculations will be time boxed. This workload type is best suited for a *numerical processing* ensemble. Market data is concerned with the low latency processing of incoming messages that cannot be throttled. A *low latency* ensemble is best suited for it. Algorithmic trading receives constant messages from market data. It is clear these two functions collaborate highly but require different localized processing. The front office PED optimizes the local workload but respects IT physics.

### Platform engineering analysis matrix artifact

Platform engineering plays a role because ensemble and PED configurations must be repeatable, traceable, teachable, and accessible in order for the enterprise to have a dynamically managed infrastructure. Configuration decisions must be recorded because they will evolve along with the ensembles and PEDs. PEDs are an advance in operating platforms, but they are not magic. All of the work discussed in Chapters 3 and 4 indicates that there is significant groundwork required in requirements analysis and design to realize PEDs. While ensembles and PEDs take a top-down design approach, individual application patterns will have a range of operational characteristics that must be accounted for by tailoring certain parameters for optimal performance. As an example, consider two risk-calculation engines that use a numerical processing ensemble:

- One calculator might perform long-running calculations whose duration might be expected to last 30 minutes and require 10 megabytes of data for just one calculation request. It might be expected to handle a dozen simultaneous requests.
- Another calculator might be expected to perform calculations that take less than 2 minutes but are expected to handle 100 simultaneous requests where each request requires 10 kilobytes of data.

There are nuances in operating system and caching configurations that would optimize each of these workload types. This kind of configuration analysis would typically be performed by a platform engineering group that is used to configuring an entire suite of *dedicated* hardware for one application. There is a mindset shift when working with ensembles and PEDs that requires this platform engineering group to think about application and service personas that are provisioned on bare metal to be deployed as needed.

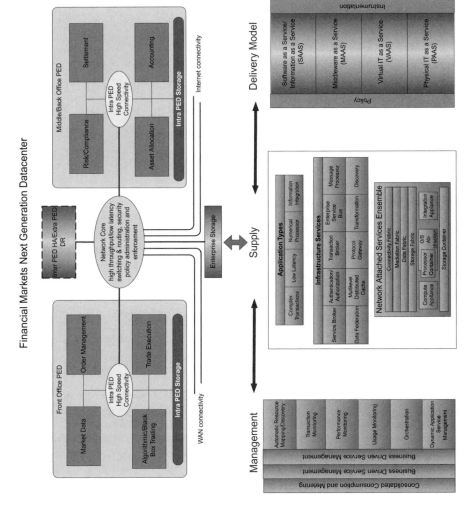

**Figure 5.18** Two PED examples.

The importance of platform engineering analysis can be summed up in the following question. Would any competent system administrator configure a database server and a market data server the same way? The answer is no. The same is true for information integration and low latency ensembles.

Ensembles and PEDs require that intelligent analysis of configurations must be performed to optimize all parts of an ensemble, while taking the varied operational characteristics of an ensemble suite into account for optimal PED configuration. Choices about network, disk usage, caching, and default server allocations must all be considered by the platform engineering team.

The platform engineering artifact is a living document that captures how different platforms are tailored to meet operational requirements. The types of configuration decisions are too numerous to mention or analyze in this section, but what follows are examples of decisions that need to be codified.

Operating system types for each ensemble, page file sizes, swap file sizes, and what kinds of operating system utilities are included are example configuration decisions. Since ensembles are aggregations of several hardware types, including application servers and caching servers, it is possible that there could be conflicts in guidance from the vendors regarding optimal operating system configurations. Some conflict resolution may be needed to find the optimal workload strategy. When the conflict is resolved, those decisions need to be documented for future use. This kind of activity has a distinct product management focus. The artifact must be in a table form, preferably captured in a database that is accessible to all qualified practitioners. These decisions become vital intellectual property and must be considered as such in the framework of a product development culture.

## Stakeholders

The stakeholders for PEDs transcend the IT organization, and they include the following:

- Service design teams
- Team members from the candidate applications, including the architect(s)
- Datacenter operations teams
- Platform engineering

## Steps

The PED design process starts with candidate applications that have been mapped to patterns and ensembles, have metrics based on their current operating environment, and have written SLAs that they must meet.

A series of small, focused workshops must be conducted to drive down the PED design. Participants should include members from the following groups.

- Architects from the application team
- Platform engineers that configure ensembles
- On-boarding specialists
- Operations specialists familiar with the various new hardware that runs in a PED

- The central architecture group
- The infrastructure services design team

This team will drive through the design issues presented by combining the different ensembles representing different workload types into one operating PED. This exercise would be an extension of the application profile work done as part of the legacy datacenter modeling. The typical issues that will arise in these design workshops include the following.

## Data transfer

- Data transfer rates expected within the PED between collaborating ensembles during a typical 24-hour period.
- The data transfer issues need to be characterized into synchronous, asynchronous, streaming data, and bulk data rate transfers.
- Expected data transfer into and out of the PED during a typical 24-hour cycle.
- It is important to understand the impact of overlapping peaks.

## Data retention

- How much data needs to be retained in the PED on a daily basis?
- How long is the totality of the retention cycles?

## Deployment and repurposing events

- What does the daily cycle of application starts and stops look like?
- Are there aberrations to that cycle that could require a time extension?
- Are spikes in daily workload easy to determine in advance of deployment?

## Application recovery, including disaster recovery

- Understanding the criticality of this application suite will aid in determining how to effect an optimal DR strategy, assuming the primary PED is not operational.
- Understanding the relationship of the application suite running in the PED to other applications that would migrate in the same class if a DR event happened.

## Peak fluctuation

- Each ensemble is optimized for a workload type, but if peak load has wild swings in business demand, the PED designers need to account for that to best utilize dynamic real-time allocation across ensembles and potentially PEDs based on business priority and need.

## *Usage*

The PED design is a living design that must be updated and referred to as the transformation proceeds. It must be integrated with ensemble designs and the services road map, as PEDs are the operating unit of the NGDC.

## Do's

- Ensure that SLAs are leveraged as part of the PED design process. The design should assume the SLAs can be enforced through definitions of business policy, which can be managed dynamically.
- Use the lab frequently to test PED design ideas.
- Remember that the initial PED model is a first step to the larger goal, so it must not be overanalyzed. While success is critical, introducing the proof of concept into production is the key to transformation.
- Remember that a PED will contain several technologies inside the physical container including network attached processors, solid state disks, network appliances, specialized CPUs, its own switching, and so on. The entire operations team must think about problem identification holistically. That will include changes to processes and metrics gathering.

## Don'ts

- Do not allow old operating models to sway PED design.
- Do not forget that DR needs to be considered in PED design.

## Quality conflicts and tradeoff analysis

Design tradeoffs were mentioned in this section as a key to building PEDs. These tradeoff discussions center on how best to fulfill requirements and qualities. Each quality could be very important for a particular service in a given line of business. It is likely that when exploring service qualities that conflicts will arise, making it difficult to determine how best to proceed.

- Any service that must process incoming market data traffic must be capable of transforming those messages with as *little CPU effort as possible* (the definition of low latency processing) while *handling massive uncontrolled throughput*. Another absolute requirement associated with market data is that *availability* must be extremely high. Achieving these three service qualities *simultaneously* is difficult, requiring special skills and constant adjustment, especially as demand continues to increase.
- There are tactics to achieving a balance between these quality requirements that have been detailed in *Software Architecture in Practice*[10] and *Evaluating Software Architectures*.[11] Employing these tactics requires an architecture tradeoff analysis.

The key to employing the tactics and any analysis is to elicit the qualities for the services to be designed. The reason for that is simple: There is no absolute good design. A design needs to be judged based on its ability to meet the balance of quality requirements, such as performance, availability, and security. Favoring one quality over another without business context will lead to

[10]Bass L, et al. *Software Architecture in Practice*. 2nd ed. Addison-Wesley Professional; 2003, April 19 [SEI series in Software Engineering].
[11]Clements P, et al. *Evaluating Software Architectures: Methods and Case Studies*. Addison-Wesley Professional; 2001, November 1 [SEI series in Software Engineering].

a perception of a poor design, no matter how sophisticated or elegant it really is. Imagine an SUV biased for maximum speed, say 100 miles per hour and minimal fuel consumption of say 50 mpg. It will have to either cost so much to produce that no one could afford it, or the car manufacturer would have to leave out most of its interior amenities such as TV, DVD, and stowaway seating and interior storage capacity. This is the true essence of tradeoff analysis. How much of one quality do you emphasize to the exclusion of others?

There are always nuances in tradeoff analysis, especially when determining the optimal choices for qualities such as availability, latency, and throughput. Patterns help these processes because they highlight the issues with platform-independent models of the problem. Ensembles and PEDs provide virtualized resources that are abstracted from the implementation just enough to allow for changes in technology to be introduced that can change these tradeoff balances.

- Optimized PED and ensemble design will include tactics and technologies that make it possible to achieve the necessary performance, availability, security, and flexibility while balancing cost and efficiency.

### 5.3.7  Service design framework

The NGDC *service design framework* is the definition of an ITIL influenced service management and service support model that integrates into an organization's existing and planned support model. This framework must include strategies for the appropriate instrumentation, tooling, and reporting necessary to operate a successful shared service platform. The framework lays out specific principles and processes across the range of IT to enable the transformation to NGDC. Here are some examples:

- Product development (for ensembles and PEDs), including management, readiness assessments, harvesting of internal assets, and release tactics.
- On-boarding for new consumers of services, including coordination and escalation.
- SLA and OLA construction, incident resolution and tracking.
- Roles and responsibilities that support all key activities.

It is used as a process guide, but it is a living guide that will be refined after initial definition. The framework sets roles, responsibilities, and processes grounded in the key business imperatives of a line of business. Properly defined, communicated, and enforced, it relates processes back to the fundamental notion of why an action is important to the business. When properly enacted, it can change the IT culture.

This framework touches most roles in IT from the CIO through developers, testers, and operators. It provides guides for product testing, application on-boarding to the real-time infrastructure, instrumentation, and development. It incorporates a product development mentality with a business-focused view of running IT.

Sustainability of the infrastructure is the overriding goal. An NGDC transformation will take years. As services are added and new concepts validated, they need to have a place in the framework so that partial solutions have grounding. Without the grounding of the framework, the initial release of an ensemble could be followed up by a piecemeal offering in the second release, where consumers can pick and choose parts of the ensemble. If this happens the cohesion of the ensemble is lost, making it less than a product. It will not have long-term survivability under those circumstances.

## Goals and objectives

The goals in a service delivery framework are very straightforward. It is designed as a bridge between IT and the business:

- Provide the foundation to make changes to the infrastructure sustainable by providing the proper supporting processes to introduce, maintain, instrument, and innovate services.
- Provide a measurement mechanism so senior IT executives can make informed investment decisions to foster the transformation.

It is too easy for an organization to fall back on old operating habits following the surge of activity associated with the launch of the NGDC. The key to sustainability is a cultural shift that can measure and enforce accountability. The service design framework requires comprehensive changes in people skills/behaviors, technology, and an overhaul of processes. The service design framework brings all of these disparate parts together and shows how they work together.

## Execution

The framework will be created through a series of iterative sessions that will enable the organization to implement a service delivery model that ensures the quality of the shared service platform and user experience, while balancing cost and efficiency according to business drivers. The initial structures of the framework will be defined in a workshop with appropriate senior level sponsorship. Follow-on workshops will occur as the service portfolio evolves and the RTI grows. The framework should be subject to regular review, typically monthly after the initial definitions. Comprehensive quarterly reviews by senior executives are required.

## Define success

The old ways of operating need to be challenged in light of the new tools and services that will be introduced. As the first services are introduced it is important for stakeholders to understand how operations will change. Roles, responsibilities, and instrumentation will change. The early services will provide a test for how easy it is to break from old operating habits, especially if silos are torn down. Explicit scenario definition will help, lab simulations will also help. The CIO must be a strong advocate for this change, especially since two operating models might have to run simultaneously until there is a sufficient critical mass of services and consumers operating in the new paradigm.

## Inputs

The Service Delivery Framework leverages previous work that had existed before the transformation projects started and any lessons learned gleaned from any of these projects.

- Current operating models
- New service design road map and service definitions
- Existing SLAs and OLAs
- Current testing and release processes
- NGDC maturity model as defined to date to understand the long-term goals and get a holistic view of challenges

## Artifacts

It is important to remember that the artifacts depicting the role and process descriptions described following will evolve as the organization places services into production and applications consume them. Early services must have a template to work from, so having a process framework is helpful to get started. The following artifacts are required to ensure that the framework can be articulated.

### End-to-end operations management model artifact

As mentioned in Chapter 2, each layer of technology in a datacenter manages its own pool of resources quite well. The difficulty occurs in understanding how to find an application problem when all layers report no trouble at all. Figure 5.19 puts the individual layers of application and datacenter responsibility

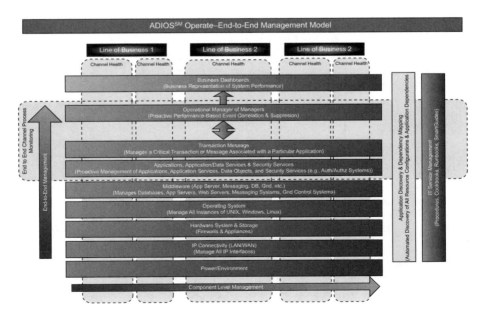

**Figure 5.19** End-to-end management model.

into the larger context of line of business health. This picture is a template with which to call out specific responsibilities, escalations, and roles. The final product should be crafted after several workshops.

## NGDC engagement processes artifact
Using the *maturity model* and *end-to-end operations management model* as inputs, all key processes that support the NGDC utility model must be fleshed out. Figure 5.20 is a high-level list of the key processes that must be defined for the NGDC transformation to be successful. The critical high-level processes shown are component planning, application diagnostics, architecture review, application on-boarding to the utility, and product architecture. Each of these processes has deliverables and stakeholders and must exist in some form as the NGDC migration moves forward. Each organization has some of these processes, but they must be coordinated as part of the NGDC transformation. The degree to which an organization defines and drives these processes will depend on its maturity model's current and target state, but if these processes are not taken seriously, the NGDC transformation will not be sustainable, as old habits will take hold with new technology. Each process will require several collaborative workshops to define and drive consensus.

## NGDC utility sourcing assessment artifact
A migration toward an NGDC requires a certain amount of rigor, which, when accomplished, presents some options to the business in terms of reigning in the costs of datacenter expenditure. As will be discussed in Chapter 8, one of the considerations is alternative delivery models through an enterprise cloud and other external clouds. While outsourcing datacenter operations has been a trend, getting rigorous SLAs in place and enforced is not an easy task. This artifact would be created during a series of iterative workshops and would use the maturity model and NGDC engagement processes as input. The purpose of this document is to explore utility operations at a finer level of detail than the maturity model in order to define the maturity production, assurance, service fulfillment and process readiness in general. The assessment is important to establish how realistic it would be to outsource some of these activities (Figure 5.21).

### Stakeholders

There are many roles that have a stake in service design frameworks. Those most closely associated with it will also be changing the artifacts as NGDC service maturity proceeds. CIO and CIO direct reports set the tone and direction for all three sets of artifacts. Some of these discussions will be considered very sensitive, such as the utility sourcing assessment, so the CIO will need to consider whom to have in those workshops.

*End-to-End Operations Management Model:* Senior operations staff and key line of business architects and system managers.
*NGDC Engagement Processes:* Operations, service design teams, and key line of business architects and system managers, product steering group, architecture office

| NGDC Lifecycle Phase | Macro Process | Purpose/ Objective | Why | Key Success Factors | Critical Deliverables | Process Owner |
|---|---|---|---|---|---|---|
| | | | ADiOSSM Sustain—Utility Engagement Model—Micro Processes | | | |
| | Component Planning | Create and maintain an integrated view of the future state of how all applications and components fit together | Identifies which components can be common across applications | Mapping business capabilities into application components | Component Master Inventory Future State Map | TBD |
| | Application Diagnostics | Identify root causes of applications problems | Reactively assist lines of business in resolving application problems | Application performance analysis | Application Forensics | TBD |
| Engagement | Architecture Review | Assist lines of business in assessing the architectural needs of existing applications | Proactively assists lines of business in bringing applications into architectural comliance to reduce risk | Understanding the business implications and risks introduced by identified architectural issues | Architecture Review Findings Business Impact Analysis | TBD |
| | On Boarding | Assist an application team in transitioning to use new Adaptivity products | Application teams cannot readily adopt new Adaptivity products (due to learning curve) without support | Line of business teams will need to acquire skills and knowledge of how to use and best leverage new components in parallel with On Boarding support | Service Request Application Deployment | TBD |
| | Product Architecuture | Determines the Reference Architecture | Need a blueprint to ensure that products meet business needs, and that they will fit and work together | Reference Architecture must separate pattern functionality in sufficent detail to guide product definition without being product specific | Conceptual Architecture Funcional Architecture Reference Architecture Pattern Specifications | TBD |

**Figure 5.20** Key processes of the NGDC utility model.

| ADIOSSM Sustain — Utility Sourcing Assessment | | | | |
|---|---|---|---|---|
| NGDC LC Phase | Macro Process | Micro Process Activities | Maturity Level | Suitability for Sourcing |
| Utility Operations | Readiness | Service Desk | Ad Hoc Process | Potential Suitability - Operations |
| | | Change Management | Defined, Repeatable Process | Potential Suitability - Operations |
| | | Security Management | Defined, Repeatable Process | Potential Suitability - Operations |
| | | Service Instrumentation | New Process | Potential Suitability - Operations |
| | | Service Performance Management | New Process | Potential Suitability - Operations |
| | | Special Projects | New Process | Potential Suitability - Operations |
| | | Network Capacity Management | Ad Hoc Process | Potential Suitability - Operations |
| | | Resource Capacity Management | New Process | Potential Suitability - Operations |
| | | Supplier Relationship Management | Ad Hoc Process | Not Suitable – Governance Control |
| | Fulfillment | User Change Management | Existing, Repeatable Process | Potential Suitability - Operations |
| | | Service Release Management | Defined, Repeatable Process | Potential Suitability - Operations |
| | | Service Configuration & Deployment | Defined, Repeatable Process | Potential Suitability - Operations |
| | | Service Activation | Defined, Repeatable Process | Potential Suitability - Operations |
| | | Network Capacity Allocation | New Process | Potential Suitability - Operations |
| | | Resource Provisioning & Deployment | Defined, Repeatable Process | Potential Suitability - Operations |
| | | Asset Inventory & Configuration Management | Defined, Repeatable Process | Potential Suitability - Operations |
| | | Supplier Sourcing & Order Management | Defined, Repeatable Process | Not Suitable – Governance Control |
| | | Supplier SOW Change Management | Existing, Repeatable Process | Not Suitable – Governance Control |
| | Production | SLA Performance Reporting | New Process | Potential Suitability - Operations |
| | | Chargeback | New Process | Potential Suitability - Operations |
| | | Workload Scheduling & Monitoring | New Process | Potential Suitability - Operations |
| | | Service Execution Management | Existing, Repeatable Process | Potential Suitability - Operations |
| | | Service Logging & Log Maintenance | New Process | Potential Suitability - Operations |
| | | Network Management | Defined, Repeatable Process | Potential Suitability - Operations |
| | | Resource Consumption Reporting | New Process | Potential Suitability - Operations |
| | | Resource Event Monitoring | New Process | Potential Suitability - Operations |
| | | Dynamic Resource Brokering | New Process | Potential Suitability - Operations |
| | | Resource Administration | Existing, Repeatable Process | Potential Suitability - Operations |
| | | Supplier Operations Oversight | Existing, Repeatable Process | Not Suitable–Governance Control |
| | Assurance | Help Desk | Existing, Repeatable Process | Potential Suitability - Operations |
| | | Support – Level 2 | Ad Hoc Process | Potential Suitability - Operations |
| | | Support – Level 3 | Ad Hoc Process | Potential Suitability - Operations |
| | | Support – Level 4 | Ad Hoc Process | Potential Suitability - Operations |
| | | Incident Management | Existing, Repeatable Process | Potential Suitability - Operations |
| | | Service Problem Management | New Process | Potential Suitability - Operations |
| | | Service Quality Management | New Process | Potential Suitability - Operations |
| | | Service Continuity Management | Managed and Predictable Process | Potential Suitability - Operations |
| | | Resource Problem Management | New Process | Potential Suitability - Operations |
| | | Resource & Network Discovery | New Process | Potential Suitability - Operations |
| | | Resource Performance Optimization | New Process | Potential Suitability - Operations |
| | | Supplier Performance Governance | New Process | Not Suitable – Governance Control |
| | | Supplier Process Auditing | Ad Hoc Process | Potential Suitability - Operations |
| | | Network Problem Management | Existing, Repeatable Process | Potential Suitability - Operations |
| | | Security / Emergency Incident Response | Defined, Repeatable Process | Not Suitable – Governance Control |

Figure 5.21 Utility Sourcing Assessment.

and governance teams. There will be numerous workshops required to flesh out each of these processes.

NGDC *Utility Sourcing Assessment:* This being quite sensitive, initial workshops would be restricted to senior level operations staff, CIO direct reports and line of business product architects. Any discussion of outsourcing will likely cause political posturing, so these sessions need to be managed discretely so that the focus is on the strategic end goal, which is to optimize IT investment.

## Steps

An initial workshop is required, likely two full-day sessions, where senior IT executives attend to set the ground rules and vision about the new service model, which will include breaking silos, new levels of documentation and testing, and new roles and responsibilities.

- Current pain points from all stakeholders should be put into play, including frustrations with release cycles, deployment delays, and the biggest issue—trust and support for the new services. Prior forensic analysis details should be leveraged to ensure the discussion remains fact-based and unemotional.
- Iteration of current processes is necessary, clearly indicating where new roles or responsibilities need to take effect.
- Respect for transitions to the new service delivery framework must be included, so that it is clear what new and old processes need to coexist.
- Drive consensus on what to measure first.
- Get the processes ready with issues to explore in further depth in follow-up sessions.
- Ensure there are clear actions from the initial session, with a follow-up scheduled within a month. During the first year it is critical that this group continue refinement once a month as new services and consumers are introduced.
- Actively publish the processes and drive discussions around their adoption.

## Usage

This is a living document that may take years to smooth out. If the CIO and CIO directs do not make this a top of mind agenda it will not propagate. This is part of the blue print for transformation. It should be used as a reference when a problem is being addressed in the old or new operating model.

### Do's

- Senior executives need to promote this framework and drive change from it.
- Service designers need to view it as their in progress operating model.
- Make the measurement process work for the change agents.
- Remember that "trust is the currency" that will make this process flow, building trust is fundamental to the process.

### Don'ts

- Don't assume this set of processes will just seamlessly fit into the environment. It will take active senior sponsorship to inject this into the DNA of the IT organization.

- Don't assume documentation and process is enough to affect this change, even after it has been running for a while. On-boarding is high-touch, and while it follows a process, it needs to be thought of as a boutique offering, hand-holding reluctant and captive consumers all the way.
- Don't race to automate processes until they are functioning well; otherwise, you run the risk of simply making bad things happen faster.

## 5.3.8   Service design road map

An NGDC Service Design Road Map is a picture that depicts a time phased introduction of the infrastructure services that were defined in the service design workshops. The road map is an important visual tool used by multiple stakeholders to track when services will be delivered, what the services contain, how the services relate to each other, and how the services fit into a longer term architecture picture. This road map must explain the following to all stakeholders:

*Timelines and Milestones:* Indicate when services will be delivered.
*Dependencies:* Clearly indicate the dependent relationships among services so that strategic direction can be monitored.
*Releases and Capabilities:* What defined capabilities will be delivered in each release for each service.
*Priorities:* A clear indication of priorities, so that dependencies and priorities can be properly assessed.

Once the services have been defined and the qualities of those services have been established, there is considerable detailed design, development, and integration testing that must be performed before the services are consumable. In most cases a number of services will be developed simultaneously, and it is crucial that expectations are conveyed as to when those services will be available. Application project teams have time frames they must adhere to and must know when to expect a release, and what it will contain. Senior executives are committing investment resources to build these services, so they need to see a big picture of when the services are being made available.

This road map is used by senior IT executives to track the range of services that are being invested in. Application architects and project managers will also use this road map for a view of the expected delivery date. Service developers will use it to coordinate service releases, and understand dependency impacts.

### Goals and objectives

Provide a clear understanding of when services will be delivered to a variety of stakeholders, at multiple levels of detail. The road map is a living document and must be updated regularly so that it is standard by how service introduction is progressing.

The road map provides a visual communication mechanism for senior executives to see how investments are realized. The road map is one visual source to convey how the NGDC strategy is progressing. The road map also shows how each service fits into the larger architecture that will be created for NGDC.

## Execution

Once the services are defined in the workshops, detailed design on the chosen services must proceed. There could be several design and implementation teams working in parallel, and their efforts need to be coordinated, since some of the services might have interdependencies. As the designs become hardened in preparation for development, it is critical that the road map is updated frequently to ensure that management of expectations is consistent. The road map should reflect a rolling one-year view.

## Define success

The keys to road map success are that it is used by all the key stakeholders, it is updated monthly, it is widely communicated, and changes to the road map are well advertised. A program manager needs to be accountable for the currency and viability of the road map. Senior executives must use this road map as a communication vehicle across the organization. It is important to keep prior revisions of the road map so progress can be shown over any 12-month period.

## Inputs

The road map combines the efforts of many elements described in the chapter. It is one of the visual overview and coordination components to the transformation process. The road map needs specific inputs to be created.

- The service design definitions and service qualities created in prior workshops.
- Results of detailed designs for individual services, including estimates for production readiness.

## Artifacts

### Service design road map artifact

The road map must integrate service delivery based on time lines with service descriptions and the place where each service fits into the architecture (Figure 5.22). The many stakeholders involved force the creation of a multilayered road map that has high level executive views and more detailed views that can be used by project staff. This first artifact is the road map with all services listed by architectural layer. It includes release numbers and timelines. It is broad in scope, but lacks information about each service, which would require subsequent sheets.

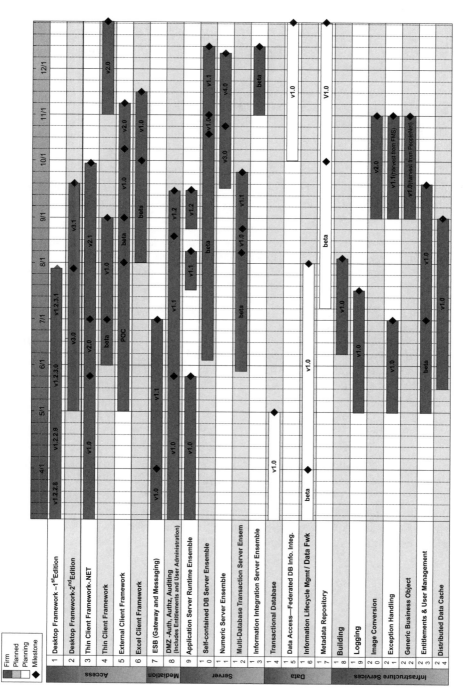

Figure 5.22 Sample service design road map.

## Stakeholders

The road map needs active stakeholders because it represents the coordinated delivery of IT investments. These stakeholders are critical to keeping the road map a relevant driver for change.

- IT executives who need to use the plan to track the strategic initiatives
- Project and program managers who will consume or create the services
- Architects who will consume or create the services

## Steps

Much of the road map development involves multistakeholder buy in and education. It is an iterative process. These steps lay out the necessary work.

- Once the first service definitions are created, the road map shell should be created with a layered architectural context so services can be easily classified not only by function but where they fit in the solution building blocks.
- The road map presentation is critical, so it must be reviewed and approved by key stakeholders.
- The road map owner should have initial meetings with IT executives and the service consumers and producers to lay the ground rules for success, including updates, conflict resolution, and dependency mapping.
- Road maps need to be iterated in the early creation stages so the level of detail can be properly structured. All stakeholders need to be involved as this represents a critical part of the investment strategy in RTI and NGDC.
- Once the road map process is part of the regular process, senior IT executives need to ensure that it is used for strategic investment discussions.

## Usage

The road map is the universal communication vehicle for conveying what services will be delivered when. All major stakeholders must have access to this and senior management should drive the strategy from it. The road map is the beginning of a product discipline, because each service has a place in the architecture, has consumers, and has release dates that must be tracked. The Service Design Oversight Program should use this road map as the master to track to.

### Do's

- There are multiple stakeholders, so it is critical that the road map have layered detail that will convey key meaning to the executives, while providing enough meaningful detail to architects. Multiple-layered views are critical.
- The road map owner must press service producers and consumers to indicate dependencies.
- Brief release feature summaries are critical to display on the road map.
- Any product or release must be shown to fit in the appropriate layer of the architecture.

- This road map is not just for in-house-built software, but it is also for any software or hardware products that will be purchased to support the NGDC strategy. Dependencies are vital to capture.

### Don'ts

- A road map is not a substitute for a project plan; each service initiative must have a project plan.
- A road map is not an issue list or design decision document.
- Do not underestimate the power of the visual map. It is powerful for executives and architects. Make sure the detail is provided in layers, top down just like the business design.

## 5.3.9 Architecture maturity model

The NGDC Maturity Model's primary objective is to provide guidance for transforming an organization's existing IT environment into a Real-Time Infrastructure Environment. The Maturity Model defines the maturity of five evaluation categories (quality of experience, architecture, strategy, operating model, and runtime execution) across five levels of maturity (chaotic, rationalized, stabilized, optimized, and enabling) via a set of criteria qualities in the greater context of a real-time infrastructure. This model is a reference that establishes standards and guidelines across the industry. The specific terms just mentioned are defined in the section "Additional Supporting Information."

The entire NGDC strategy is centered on alignment with the business, so the business needs to dictate what level of maturity it wishes to achieve for each business line. Since such a transformation represents significant investment and cultures, thought must be given to milestones and timelines based on business drivers, current pain points, and the current state of operational maturity.

This model is used by senior business and IT executives in conjunction with internal and external NGDC advocates and experts. Executives need to grasp the various stages of maturity and its telltale signs to understand the degree of change that will be required to achieve the NGDC vision. IT architecture, strategy, and governance teams should also participate to foster alignment and provide a reality check about the operating environment challenges.

The NGDC maturity model presents a vision and a benchmark from which to grasp the current state of IT operations holistically. Any comprehensive plan of action of this magnitude needs to start with an understanding of where the organization is and what it will take to achieve the vision. This model also serves as a qualitative gauge for change.

### Goals and objectives

The goals of the Architecture Maturity Model exercises can be summarized as follows:

- Understand the current state of the IT organization and its relationship with the business on a holistic level

- Engage senior level executives in a discussion about how the business must grow, its constraints and drivers and the appetite for change to fix IT so that it can become the strategic arm of the business
- Utilize the standard model as a framework for actions that must be taken to achieve the level of maturity in an optimal fashion

The NGDC maturity model is the definition of a multiphase, multidimensional architectural, organizational, and process model that evolves in terms of maturity and realization as an enterprise matures toward the NGDC goal. It is one of the guides used by senior executives to gauge the degree of investment they should undertake to affect change.

## Execution

Once created, the NGDC Maturity Model needs to be reviewed on an annual basis to reflect the year's new technology and process evolution and to reexamine evaluation criteria for each of the five evaluation categories. As solutions supporting the foundations of NGDC develop, or as the business or technology landscape changes, the NGDC Maturity Model will need to be revisited. It is best to do this once a year.

## Define success

In Chapter 2, the reasons for the current state of most datacenters were explained. This must be remembered when the initial maturity model sessions start. It will be easy to look at the maturity model categories such as chaotic, and be embarrassed. It is clear from Chapter 2 that there is plenty of blame to go around, so it is critical that the CIO and senior business executives set the correct tone that this assessment is about the future. It is also important not to sugar-coat the current state, since it does no one any good. Finally, do not take an initial broad brush when evaluating; there are multiple dimensions, and they should be used to better understand the challenges and bright spots.

## Inputs

This is broad category where many aspects of the current state need to be analyzed. Any data that can aid in this assessment should be considered, because the alternative is anecdotal evidence, and that can be colored by recent events.

- IT budgets broken down by line of business, to include capital versus expense.
- Operational trends including incident reports.
- Anecdotal evidence about the day in the life for operations, developers, key revenue generators.
- Business drivers that are affected by IT.

## Artifacts

### NGDC maturity model
The NGDC Maturity Model is a living document listing various sets of criteria qualities used to determine an enterprise's level of maturity for the five

different evaluation categories, as described in the section. "Additional Supporting Information." See Appendix B for the full NGDC maturity model.

## Stakeholders

The stakeholders for the maturity model are relatively few, but the impact of this model is significant, so the focused attention of senior-level business and IT executives and IT architecture, strategy, and governance teams is critical.

## Steps

The steps for the architectural maturity model include initial model creation and recurring review on at least a yearly basis.

- Preparation of all input materials is critical and should be in all workshop participants' hands at least a week before the session.
- The standard maturity model should be sent as is to the participants along with objectives and agendas.
- The initial workshop is a full 2-day session off-site. The first day is about awareness and validation. The second day is about consensus building including an action plan. Each category must be reviewed in detail, with some emphasis given to line of business differences. It might be useful to have parallel break out sessions to discuss key topics among experts with periodic checkpoints during the two days. Follow-up validations within one week of the session are critical via conference call.
- Publication of the model and the plan is essential to drive the change.
- Monitoring on a monthly basis by executives must begin after the workshops with dashboard reporting.
- The model must be reviewed at least once a year; in the early stages it might be best to do it quarterly.

## Usage

Use the model as a communication vehicle and a call for change. It is a metric that establishes what the organization considers its baseline state in key NGDC capabilities such as architecture, strategy, operations, runtime execution, and user experience. This model illustrates the gaps that prevent the business from achieving its growth goals.

### Do's

- Reference the model as a sobering assessment and a vision for change.
- Use the model to drive discussions about the degree and speed of change. The model provides a basis for broad investment discussions.

### Don'ts

- Do not treat this as a static report. This model is a guide to the organization's investment direction.
- Don't be afraid to change the assumptions of the initial model. It is likely that as the transformation moves forward, assumptions that seemed reasonable when the model was first defined will need to be revisited. The model is not a manifesto; it is a strategy tool.

## Additional supporting information

In order to understand whether changes to the maturity model are required, it is important to understand the outlining concepts and spirit of what each level of maturity represents.

- The **Chaotic** level of maturity is the lowest level of maturity and represents a lack of readily available documentation and knowledge around direction, strategy, and operating environment in which IT resides, as well as a lack of insight into IT expenditures by the business.
- The **Rationalized** level of maturity includes the necessary steps to take before one begins considering shared services and strategic initiatives. The key factors to consider are that the Rationalized level of maturity implies a big discovery process has taken place and IT has started aligning with the business and that people in the enterprise are aware of what they have and where the problems lie.
- The **Stabilized** level of maturity is really the first level of maturity that seriously takes RTI into perspective. The key factor to consider is that the Stabilization level of maturity implies that major issues in the environment have been remedied and the enterprise can start taking its first strides in planning the restructuring of processes, reorganizing its people, and learning/adopting new technologies.
- The **Optimized** level of maturity represents a focus on continual improvement in the respective evaluation categories. Optimization implies that environments run smoothly and that significant time, effort, and funding can be diverted from day-to-day maintenance and operations and used for the planning and development of strategic initiatives and shared services to reach the next level of maturity. The key factor to consider is that the Optimized level of maturity focuses on best practices in terms of people, process, and technology having been applied pervasively throughout an enterprise and that major changes can easily be incorporated.
- The **Enabling** level of maturity is the ideal state of being in terms of RTI and should reflect more than just the best practices in the five evaluation categories. Business Enablement implies that IT functions in a highly optimized state and more focus is invested in understanding business drivers and business demand. At this level of maturity IT capabilities are collectively and automatically managed by business rules and policies based on synergy of business demand and IT supply. The key factor to consider is that the Enabling level of maturity focuses on IT being a strategic partner to the business as opposed to merely an expenditure.

Each of the above described levels of maturity will need to be applied to each of the five evaluation criteria. It is equally important to understand the definitions of the evaluation criteria.

**Quality of Experience** (QoE) is the balance between user experience, cost, and efficiency in an operating environment. In terms of maturity levels, QoE must first be brought into balance and then maintained. Should QoE fall out of balance, the primary focus is to not negatively affect user experience at the expense of cost or efficiency. Thereafter, the focus should be to realign cost and efficiency again once user experience has stabilized.

**Architecture** takes into account the architectures and designs created for shared services with a focus on technology and the actual architecture teams within an enterprise (including process and people adjustments). Both change as an enterprise progresses through maturity levels.

**Strategy** primarily focuses on the alignment between business strategy and IT strategy, as well as having an actionable plan to move forward with changes in people, process, and technology, without disrupting the balance of QoE. The business strategy to IT strategy alignment has a heavy focus on creating visibility into IT funding and how funds are translated into providing value for the business.

**Operating Model** primarily focuses around how the enterprise is run. One area of focus is the operations groups and their modus operandi in terms of how they are alerted of problems and reaction to them. Ideally a shift will occur from a reactive to a proactive approach. In addition to process changes, technologies that enable sufficient monitoring of the environment are a large factor, as well as gradual transition from operating the environment to having a larger team focused on architecture, strategy and governance.

**Runtime Execution** focuses on people, process, and technology in terms of how the environments are run. The focus is not only the possibilities that technologies provide, but also cultural (people) shifts within an enterprise that have to be achieved in order to implement new processes.

## 5.3.10   NGDC program design and oversight

Global financial services firms are used to running global programs on the business and IT side. Some programs integrate business and IT really well, such as when two companies merge. In such a circumstance, processes and mission critical data must be integrated in certain tight timeframes. Brand unification must also take place across 100,000 machines in multiple continents. Most of the time the executive management focus is so tight from all corners of the organization that these complex programs succeed. This fact alone will thankfully limit the scope of this section to some critical aspects of an NGDC transformation program.

The natural question then is this: If this transformation is so critical to the success of an organization and the business and IT executives can agree on a plan, why is there any concern about running such a program? The answer is complex, but Table 5.5 offers some quick highlights that will illustrate the difficulties.

The contrast is clear: The NGDC program is ambitious, long-running, has incredible upside potential, and is very complex. In Chapter 6, minitransformation programs will be discussed where business-focused playbooks are introduced to reduce scope and complexity to 90-day transformations. The remainder of this section will not dwell on the program management discipline as a whole but instead point out considerations that are strictly for any aspect of an NGDC transformation.

### Goals and objectives

The goals and objectives have a lot in common with any other program, but there are some others worth mentioning.

Table 5.5 Merger versus NGDC transformation

| Transformation factor | Typical merger program management | NGDC transformation program |
|---|---|---|
| Organization | In a merger, even a hostile one, the winners and losers have been determined before the work of systems transformation begins. The winners have power, and the losers have either accepted their fate or moved on. | In an NGDC transformation, the nature of the organization is in flux. New teams will be created to inject change; organizations will be aligned as the full impact of the transformation takes hold. |
| Timeframe | Even if that merger effort takes a year or two, there is a sense that the end is in sight, and that end is deterministic. In actuality this is usually not true, but the illusion tends to persist. | The whole point of NGDC is to transform the entire IT operating model, and even if it only takes two years, the purpose of the transformation is to make change a natural part of the operating order. As a result, challenges will be responded to differently. |
| Roles and Responsibilities | In the merger program, there will be new temporary roles and in the end some will be rewarded and promoted, but for most people there will be the perception of the return to normalcy. | In an NGDC transformation program, new roles developed for pilot projects will be seeded for new disciplines. These new roles and disciplines will be a direct challenge to the existing operating, peeling-away responsibility, and control. Many people will be forced out of their niche knowledge base to take on more holistic responsibilities, often taking them out of their comfort zones. |
| Technology | Even though the merger will cause two technology philosophies to blend, the basic principles will be the same, especially with Unix, Linux, Microsoft, and mainframe operating platforms running in more or less traditional modes. | NGDC is enabled by new technology that works in ways that are different from traditional implementations because it supports RTI. |
| Culture | While culture clash among merged companies can be fierce, the winners will exert enough influence to stabilize the culture of the winners. | An NGDC transformation requires culture change from within, and those types of changes have so many subtleties that they are hard to predict. |

*(Continued)*

Table 5.5 Continued

| Transformation factor | Typical merger program management | NGDC transformation program |
|---|---|---|
| | Some changes might occur as a result of absorption, but that is usually minor due the culling process. | Since there are no overt winners and losers from the outset, the difficulties mount because aberrant behavior is harder to shut down. In fact the change agents could be considered the problem. |
| Executive focus | A merger on the scale of a global financial institution will receive incredible external scrutiny, so the senior executives will drive through objections. | NGDC is so ambitious that executives will want to either drive it or make it low key. Only early and continued progressive success against cultural resistance will win public executive sponsorship. |

## Typical goals
- Ensure that the program is running on schedule with respect to individual milestones.
- General risk tracking and reporting.
- Multiple project coordination, including milestone tracking, budget targets, inter-project dependency tracking.

## Additional NGDC transformation goals
- Marketing and advocacy for change based on all of the work produced across all elements. This vision's potential needs to be reinforced constantly, even to those who gave approval.
- Move the organization toward a sustainment model through the institutionalization of new processes, disciplines, and behaviors. Each change must be nurtured to maturity until it can stand on its own.
- Advocate the culling of outdated processes, roles, technologies, and applications by establishing governance, portfolio management, and architecture as enabling disciplines that facilitate change and minimize risk.
- Aggressive risk-mitigation strategies that focus on the risk of adapting new technologies and the risk of not changing some technologies.

## Execution

The execution of Program Management and Oversight is similar to other program management efforts with the exception that there are more far-reaching goals and the program office should not be dismantled because NGDC transformation will continue to drive innovation. The fundamentals of rollup reporting from projects are no different from any other program. A notable addition that we recommend for NGDC transformation is that program management reporting must be more engaging for senior management and contributing teams. Status updates must include venues to engage executive management, often with visually compelling artifacts and demonstrations from all of the aforementioned elements to show the nature of the progress. Teams involved in all aspects of the design elements should be given the opportunity to present to senior management upon achieving key milestones. The amount of meetings will be more numerous because there are more major aspects to cover. The budget tracking must not only cover expenditures but must also obtain information about the value received. The bottom line is that the NGDC program management team must concern itself with the state of the investment and keep it as top of the mind to senior management.

## Define success

Success is defined by the program being visibly recognized and supported by senior management. Senior management should view program reviews as something to look forward to because it will inform them of progress that affects revenue, cost, and client satisfaction. Success should be able to be measured, because one of the key goals of program management is to show value received for investment.

When IT becomes the recognized strategic partner of the business the NGDC program is a success. That is realized when the Digital Supply Chain is the strategic arm of the Business Value Chain. Nothing less will do. In sports parlance, it is not enough to get to the championship round; once there, the only goal is to win. This effort is a large investment and cannot be squandered.

## Inputs

The inputs that make a program of this size successful are varied, because NGDC will produce many compelling artifacts. These are the most basic inputs to run the NGDC program effectively:

- Weekly structured project status reports from every NGDC team, which should include milestones met and missed, issues to resolve, risks encountered, and new milestones to add.
- Comprehensive risk analysis across all teams, with a special focus on technology integration and adoption risk and the risk mitigations defined.
- Project plans for all projects watched by the program.

## Artifacts

Unlike all of the other elements in this chapter, the program management techniques and fundamentals are not radically different for NGDC, so there is little need to delve into details about any artifacts. The artifacts that are mentioned following are well documented in the program and project management literature. Instead, some key artifacts will be mentioned along with some pointers to consider.

- Project plan with levels of detail, including roll ups and milestones—any good project management tool will do, although rollup capability will vary. It is useless to use automated scheduling, although entering dependencies and providing such a view are valuable for many stakeholders.
- Risk matrix—highlighting such factors as risk type, risk name, risk description, risk impact, impact date, and risk mitigation strategy. These need to be reviewed weekly at a minimum and must be reported to senior management in accessible, action-oriented form.
- Issues—these are unresolved items that need to be fixed or turned into open items. Issues need owners, open dates, required resolution dates, issue types, and descriptions. Issue resolution needs to be trended by the program management team. This trending should include rate of open issues and rate of closure to assess progress and the degree of inertia. Open issues mean that people cannot agree and they have to be fixed.
- Budget and value—these need to be tracked per project, and the nature of that exercise will vary greatly. Most executives want to have investments arranged by hardware, software, full-time, and consultant expenses. Understanding what executives need to see is critical, especially if multiple business lines are involved. Investments will likely be subject to interpretation but does include cost savings and avoidance. What is advantageous to quantify is speed to market, performance improvements, and better reliability.

## Stakeholders

The entire range of stakeholders in all of the elements described in this chapter is involved, but of particular interest are the following:

- CIOs and CIO directs
- All service design and implementation teams
- The on-boarding team and senior operations executives
- Target application teams

## Steps

The steps basically follow standard program management oversight best practices, but some responsibilities that should be addressed in NGDC will be called out:

- Comprehensive dashboard creation for multiple stakeholders.
- Heavy consideration must be given to senior executive–oriented visual reporting.
- Track new vendor assimilation including the streamlining of the typical legal processes, loaner agreements, and NDAs. It is essential that this group streamline the procurement process.
- Workshop coordination, as workshop participation by key stakeholders are a critical success factor.
- Education and training coordination, as many new technologies will be brought in over the life of this program review.

- Resource request coordination across all groups, since new teams will be established. Help those teams get established and grounded. Provide the communication support to get new processes running in support of those teams.

## Usage

The key recurring theme of this section is that program management and oversight for NGDC are transformative processes that have the lofty goals of aligning the Digital Supply Chain with the Business Value Chain. Once that is established, program management must ensure that the advantage realized by such a state is sustained. The following are a few guidelines to consider:

### Do's

- Use all of the strategy and alignment tools that are created as a vision for the program management team to use.
- Ensure that the program management and oversight team is viewed as the investment barometer, giving executives a true lens into the state of the program.
- The program must change focus as progress is made; it will grow and shrink in size and scope as the transformation proceeds.
- Ensure that there is a program management team focused on sustainment as soon as possible.

### Don'ts

- Don't allow the program team to become stale; make sure there is a rotation of the program management team. Treat it as a promotion and perk to be selected for a time. Send team members back to project teams so they can spread the information.
- Don't allow any senior management to become complacent about the oversight reports. Get feedback from management in order to find out how to keep them engaged.

# 6 Extreme optimizations and eco-efficiencies

## Key Points

Playbooks provide a guide to assist the project team to organize and communicate.

A *building block* is the organizational structure, technology solution, and operating model that result from executing the playbook.

As *building blocks* are put into place, they begin to interact with one another, creating the foundation of the NGDC.

IT organizations are increasingly challenged these days just to keep the lights on. In addition, the business is looking to cut costs, maximize efficiencies, and reduce spending during these economically challenging times. The attention span that can be devoted to any particular project is very limited, so scope must be tightly controlled. To assist with these challenges, the use of standardized playbooks can be leveraged to provide a guide for consolidation, rightsizing, outsourcing, and vendor rationalization to meet the objectives of the business within very finite timeframes.

The first projects of the transformation into a Next Generation Datacenter are critical to develop the confidence and groundswell needed to affect change. The use of a playbook implementation guide will maximize the chance of success of these first building blocks of the new operating model. Chapter 5 outlined the need to define the scope of the first changes to the environment into a project and how to collect the relevant vinformation (artifacts) needed to properly design the technical solution. The playbook is the guide to using this information to effect the change, without the need for a big bang (Figure 6.1).

## 6.1 Guidelines for playbooks

A playbook is used to detail a *lean disciplined blueprint* that will amplify the impact of the initiatives while serving as a guide to create a sustaining operating model. It's a targeted 90-day plan to attack a specific technical constraint in the datacenter environment. It considers the directed activities that must take place to analyze the problem in detail, guides the design to solve the problem, and concerns itself with the introduction of the new solution with minimal disruption to existing datacenter operations. Figure 6.2 depicts the relationships that can be leveraged to create increasingly more complex IT services.

© 2009 Elsevier Inc. All rights reserved.
doi: 10.1016/B978-0-12-374956-7.00006-1

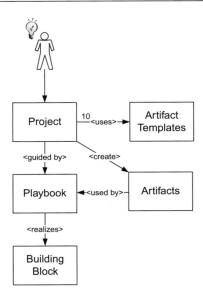

**Figure 6.1** Pulling together all the pieces to create a new operational building block.

## 6.2   A lean 90-day plan

IT leaders should execute the following 90-day plan to create a lean IT organization. The proven benefit of such a program can drive substantial gains over traditional approaches to cost and efficiency projects. Packaging as a 90-day program helps control the scope, sends the message to senior management that it can be enacted quickly, and has clear benefits to get senior level IT leaders' attention when budget requests are made. There are four fundamental elements to keep in mind while forming a playbook strategy.

*Know what you have.* Businesses must cope with a highly volatile and risky climate for commerce. To do so, successful organizations maintain "accurate to the minute" intelligence dashboards of what business they are doing, what resource capacity they have, and the associated dependencies of the workload. IT organizations must operate in the same manner. In the first 30 days, firms can leverage tools that self-discover and automatically document, inventory, and map thousands of applications and infrastructure devices with their associated dependencies. This data can be leveraged to show "exactly" where deployment designs or design inefficiencies can be quickly addressed to reduce infrastructure costs.

*Understand how it is used.* Businesses need to report to regulatory and shareholder bodies on how they invest capital, how it is leveraged, and how they derive returns and execute business. IT needs to incorporate such discipline. Most IT organizations do not track infrastructure usage in a "holistic" nature of correlating who is using what, for how long, where, and so on.

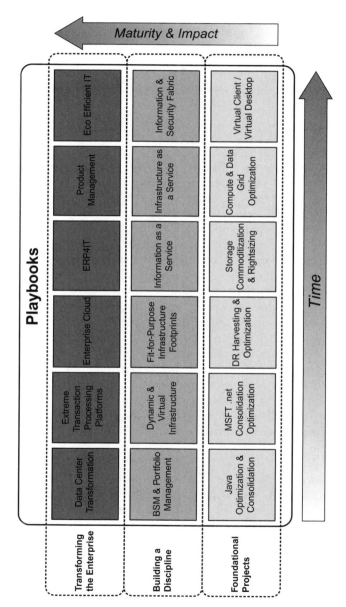

Figure 6.2 A sample collection of playbooks.

IT must implement a business-driven workload and consumption behavior analysis, and a tooling and tracking program (with factors of wall clock, calendar, special events, geography, and channels) that are then encapsulated in service contracts with qualities of experience associated to performance, priority, costs, and efficiencies needs of the business.

This then must be translated into a mapping and orchestration model of workload matched with qualities of infrastructure service units that are then transferred into optimized footprint configurations. In the first 30 days, firms can leverage tools that extrapolate log data from all tiers of the infrastructure and correlate these event logs to usage consumption by user, location, trends, and so on. This data can be used to "exactly" target high waste, inefficient usage, or, in appropriate workload balancing models, to reduce costs and drive greater consolidation, rightsizing, and efficiencies.

*Change how you manage it.* Firms must manage business in a real-time manner, adjusting their workloads based on customer demand. IT must incorporate this discipline into how they manage the workload of applications and services. Firms must implement dynamic runtime control and execution enforcement, ensuring that the right work gets done at the right time with the right resources. Virtual data, virtual access, and distributed availability are matched as infrastructure services with client and applications sessions based on policy and entitlement. (For example: In the first 60 days, implement and roll out such a management fabric and consolidate distributed applications onto a smaller footprint (1/5) while improving service level 30-fold.)

*Implement a "less is more" footprint.* Just because it ain't broke.... Well, you know the saying. Organizations can radically reduce costs, the consumption of power, cooling, and space, and deliver better performance if they institute the discipline and design efforts to create the "optimized footprint." Firms can incrementally and quickly implement an optimized footprint of a self-contained fabric of logical building blocks housed in a single footprint and interconnected with high-speed fabrics between each container. The building footprint container includes multicore processors, optimized memory configurations, multiple I/O fabrics (10 GigE, Ethernet, fiber-channel, Infiniband), optimal commodity disk (solid state and spinning), simplified storage with tiers of provisioning, processing appliances, integration appliances, connectivity appliances, integrated switches, networking accelerators—all housed in vertically cooled containers with DC feeds, simplified cabling, and a virtualized stack from the network to the transaction. In a 90-day plan, a firm can implement, test, and roll into production an optimized footprint of best of breed components that can reduce costs by 80 percent and improve performance by 50 times or greater.

This rapid transformation strategy can position organizations into a continuous improvement process of *lean it*. The pain and agony proved this kind of model works for any organization that operates distributed applications in support of a for-profit business.

# 6.3    The anatomy of a playbook

The playbook is a guide to the implementation of an IT service solution, which includes the people, process, and technology needed to create an operational model in the organization. Once realized, it acts as a building block on which additional IT services can be built. Note that in this context, the IT services discussed are at a very high level (in alignment with the top-down design approach). In several sections that follow, examples are cited from a sample playbook, *Optimizing Java Resources with Dynamic Infrastructure.*

## 6.3.1    Playbook description

Here is a brief description of what will be accomplished if the playbook is executed. It should be more expansive than just the technology such as describing the operating model enhancements that will be achieved. The reader should understand the main value proposition (e.g., how will it improve the business operation?).

Introduction of a dynamic infrastructure environment to run Java applications within; creates agility to respond to business events in real time and makes the environment more robust. The proposed dynamic environment decouples the application from the underlying OS to scale instances as needed and offloads the compute resources from the applications servers into an optimized appliance. The application resource structure can then move toward commodity blades augmented by solid-state disks for data sources and away from expensive SMP machines.

## 6.3.2    Business drivers/strategy

This is a brief description of why the business considers this important and how it will affect the business strategy. The purpose of including this information is to clearly draw a relationship between the actions promoted by the playbook and their relevance to the business.

*Client/User Differentiation:* The performance of Java applications is critical, as they face many clients and users.

*Environment Efficiency:* Improvement of the current infrastructure has broad positive impact on the inefficient resource utilization that negatively impacts enterprise datacenter productivity.

- On average up to 50 percent of enterprise applications and middleware services depend on Java environments.
- Java environments are a top three sources of datacenter sprawl and IT waste.

### 6.3.3   KPI improvements to track

A short list of *key performance indicators* that track the performance improvement from the resulting solution are listed here. Since we know we get what we measure, picking business relevant metrics to measure key performance indicators is critical.

*Time to Market:* 50 percent reduction
*Total Cost of Ownership:* 60 percent less in capital and operating expense
*Performance:* 50+ percent improvement
*Datacenter Productivity:* 70 percent reduction in packaging, deploying, and changing
   applications and infrastructure

### 6.3.4   Execution strategy

A short list of items that reflect how the environment will be modified once the playbook is executed should be included in the execution strategy. They should be aligned with the overall strategy of the datacenter transformation effort. This list can be used to rapidly understand the type of change the playbook will bring to the environment.

*Dynamic Management:* Manage current and new Java resource infrastructure dynamically.
*Reduce Resource Costs:* Cap legacy investment; employ lower-cost yet more efficient
   resources (e.g., multicore blades instead of SMP machines).
*Performance:* Optimized resources for execution of Java Runtime and removal of traditional processing barriers.
*Change What You Use:* Challenge traditional approaches; increased control of the work
   and where it executes facilitate its being serviced by optimized resources.

### 6.3.5   Key technologies

A simple list of the technologies that will be employed to realize the solution will act as a quick reference that can be used to derive the technology skills required to execute.

*DataSynapse's FabricServer™*
*Intel's® Multi Core CPUs*
*Azul's Vega3™ Java Compute Appliance*
*Solid State Disks*

### 6.3.6   Use cases and metrics

Use cases represent the typical usage scenarios found in the context of the playbook. They depict frequently identified approaches to solving business problems and the consequent consumption characteristics that these approaches must process. The playbook addresses the consumption characteristics with specific tactics that produce measurable results in a table. This information can be used to understand the benefits that can be expected under specific situations. Table 6.1 shows a few sample entries.

**Table 6.1** Sample use case and metrics

| Use cases and metrics | | |
| --- | --- | --- |
| **Service** | **Demand characteristics and consequences** | **Supply remediation** |
| J2EE Application Servers | Uncontrolled high volume of service requests during peaks that are hard to predict. Response times need to be fast and predictable during peak loads. Process complex business logic with high throughput. Typically transactions require multiple data sources from legacy environments (e.g., client, product). | Performance: 30–50 times improvement<br>• Throughput: increased 30–60 times<br>• Latency: reduced 10%–20%<br>• Response Time: is predictable, often reduced by 40%<br>TCO: 70% reduction<br>• Cost to Scale: linearly bounded to business growth rate<br>• Cost Reduction: 25% of original footprint for the same volume<br>• Cost Avoidance: reduced footprint, reduces power consumption, system administration resources, network connectivity, cap investment in legacy SMP machines<br>DC Efficiency: 25% of traditional footprint to process same volume using 25% of the power |
| Rules Engines | Longer-running calculations are mixed with short-term requests. It is critical to balance the processing so neither is starved. Rules engines need to keep a large information environment to process effectively, often running up against the 2 GB memory ceiling for Java applications. Complex rules with multiple logic paths must be processed quickly. Rule decision history will need to be accessed quickly to maintain quick response time at peak. | Performance: 40 times improvement<br>• Throughput: increased 50 times<br>• Latency: reduced 10%<br>• Response Time: is predictable, often reduced by 40%<br>TCO: 60% reduction<br>• Cost to Scale: linearly bounded to business growth rate<br>• Cost Reduction: 25% of original footprint for the same volume<br>• Cost Avoidance: reduced footprint, reduces power consumption, system administration resources, network connectivity, cap investment in legacy SMP machines<br>DC Efficiency: 25% of traditional footprint to process same volume using 25% of the power |

### 6.3.7 Technology or process optimization strategy

This section contains a high-level design for each Execution Strategy in section 6.3.4. It details the basics of how that strategy will be executed. Typically it consists of a high-level picture of how several technologies come together. It acts as the guidance to the team using the playbook, outlining how it can go about realizing the solution to reap the espoused benefits.

### 6.3.8 Idea in practice

Once the playbook is executed, the result is a strategic building block operating in the organization, including people, process, and technology. The implementation solves some number of strategic challenges the organization faces. The *idea in practice* section reviews the typical response the organization would have to these challenges, the problems with that response, and how the new approach improves upon the response. This helps with communicating with others as to why the new approach is superior to the traditional methods (Table 6.2).

**Table 6.2** Java/J2EE platform difficulties and tactics sample

| Problem | Typical datacenter design response | Consequences | Dynamic real time infrastructure response |
| --- | --- | --- | --- |
| Massive spikes in throughput are not predictable. | Overprovision key applications with enough servers to handle 2–3 times the historic peak load (scale-out architecture). | Dedicated systems are underutilized. Reports to senior management typically show server utilization at 20%. New hardware and space is hard to justify. | FabricServer™ from DataSynapse is a dynamic real-time service broker that assigns resources to applications based on business policy and real-time demand. This broker assigns and returns resources from the pool based on demand. Spikes are addressed, but other processes are not starved. |
| Seasonal or periodic upsurge of traffic causes temporary resource crunch. | Static resources temporarily assigned to process the periodic need, which includes B2C and B2B applications. | Increased staff load to deploy applications in a static environment add complexity and increase chance of errors into the deployment process, causing instability. | FabricServer™ facilitates deployment of extra instances through a repeatable build and deploy process. Once the instances are defined, they are only launched based on business policy, be that demand spikes or timed events. |

In response to the need to provide exceptional user experience for revenue generating or other critical Java/J2EE applications, more compute, network, and storage resources are added to the resource pool to manage the unbridled throughput of client-facing applications. This approach has unintended consequences and does not solve all of the problems it set out to address. The plan behind the Java Optimization playbook is a two-phased approach that handles the major problems faced by critical Java applications:

- *Change the way you manage your resources* better by introducing a Dynamic Real Time Service broker that allocates resources based on business policy and need.
- *Change the hardware you use* to maximize the legacy investment by solving the inherent Java memory constraints, virtually eliminating Garbage Collection (GC) pauses.

## 6.3.9 Project outline

The project outline presents a visual summary of the entire playbook transformation, including applicable phases, milestones, and signifcant deliverables. The outline shows the amount of coordination required to make the transformation successful and should convey a sense of urgency given that the time-frame is constrained to 90 days.

This project outline does not eliminate the need for a detailed program plan but instead acts as a template to construct a set of projects and their plans. This template is critical because the milestones are developed top down with a business focus. Any scope controversy can be resolved by referring back to the outline. The outline should be constructed with a prepackaged mentality so that once invoked into one line of business, it can be utilized in others. One can think of it as a franchise model for a specific problem. This kind of perspective will facilitate change in the larger organization because it is built with repeatability in mind.

### Audience

Senior IT executives need to understand the playbook's scope and impact and buy into the idea that quick adoption of a business-focused playbook will overcome inertia. They need to support it and influence the outcome. They need to *ensure* that money can be obtained quickly and that the usual vendor problems associated with nondisclosures, master service agreements, equipment loan agreements, vendor and consultant security clearance issues, and budget tie-ups do not get subjected to the usual large corporation inertia. Team members who will enact the change need to use the outline to build out detailed project plans that will meet each milestone and craft aggressive risk-mitigation strategies.

## Structure

The program consists of three phases to systematically deploy the new environment: the program kickoff, the production pilot, and the remaining applications to production. This is a crawl, walk, run approach to rollout that provides enough time for the support teams to become familiar with the environments prior to introducing the production applications. The project outline should delineate milestones for each phase and expected deliverables for that phase.

## Creation

Pick a defined problem that can be realistically fixed. One of the most useful to consider is a Java Optimization playbook. Java has strong penetration in many financial services organizations, and that has caused a proliferation of underutilized servers that ironically exhibit performance problems during peak times. The reasons for underutilization are many, including cultural ones regarding project control over hardware that was discussed in Chapter 5 and will be expanded upon in Chapter 7. The performance problems with Java are varied, but some typical ones are garbage collection pauses for applications that have high-throughput fluctuating demand. The Java playbook incorporates specific technologies to address performance and efficiency that will have a profound effect on cost.

### 6.3.10  Project mission statement, objectives, and benefits

On May 25, 1961, President John F. Kennedy created one of the most effective mission statements ever uttered: "I believe that this nation should commit itself to achieving the goal, before this decade is out, of landing a man on the moon and returning him safely to the earth." On July 20, 1969, only eight years after this incredibly bold statement, the U.S. astronauts set foot on the moon and returned safely to earth. The power of that statement cannot be underestimated. At the time of that pronouncement, the United States had still not sent a man into space. In eight years, the United States had to develop an infrastructure of innovation to make the mission happen.

### Project objectives

The project objectives define the direct actions that the playbook will undertake to make the transformation possible. Examples would include actions to fix the following areas:

- Reconfigure the existing blade server infrastructure as an optimized Java application hosting environment.
- Give hardware the ability to accelerate the execution of the JVM environments.
- Introduce solid-state disks to facilitate data-intensive operations, as needed.
- Address the slow responsiveness of the AAA, BBB, and CCC applications.
- Increase the performance of the environment by 40 percent.
- Decrease the power and cooling footprint by 30 percent.

- Decrease support personnel by 50 percent.
- Increase utilization of resources from 15 to 60 percent.
- Reduce 300 applications on 200 servers to run on 50 servers and 2 appliances.

## Project benefits

The benefits should show the results of the actions taken in the objectives section:

- *Performance:* Mention that the use of specific hardware and software products will be introduced to dramatically improve the responsiveness of the applications.
- *Efficiency:* Higher utilization of resources consolidates workload into a smaller footprint.
- *Time to Market:* Rapid deployment of new applications and changes to existing ones.
- *Flexibility:* Dynamic real-time response to business events is a competitive advantage.
- *Resiliency:* Replacement of failed resources faster than normal human response time to alert.
- *Control:* Centralized control of all deployed Java applications facilitates just the "right" amount of resources applied to any particular application and the rapid addition of other resources as needed.

## Mission statement, objective and benefits

The mission statement was simple, direct, visual, and measurable, but most of all it ignited excitement. The results were no less impressive, as the United States sent several missions to the moon in the next three years, landing a total of 12 men on the moon. The consequences of reaching such a lofty goal launched several new technology disciplines, including the need to consider microchip technology. The year 2009 will mark 40 years after the first moon landing. No other country in the world came close to repeating that first feat.

The objectives take the spirit of the mission statement and declare that certain accountable actions will be taken. The benefits must speak to the sponsors and act as a sanity check on project scope. The benefits will be the benchmark for project success, and such boldness will win endorsement.

### Audience

The mission statement is for senior business and IT executives who will provide the initial investment and continue the support of its rollout and the teams that will be directly and indirectly involved in the change. The objectives and benefits are first and foremost for senior executives.

### Structure

The structure is a simple demonstrative sentence that can be measured, that will entice a vision. It is clear that a mission statement for a playbook has to enact similar visions to the JFK mission statement. It should drive emotions and a call for action. For dramatic impact, consider using the KPIs mentioned in section 6.3.3. Use those tracking numbers as the basis for the mission statement, and add the urgency that the pilot program will only take 90 days to show results. Once the pilot is done, it can be rolled out across the organization. To a business executive, that is the same as a moon landing! The objectives and benefits are a simple list as shown in the beginning of this section (what does it convey?).

### Creation

Use business drivers and pain points as the key enticement. Use the guidelines about simplicity and measurement. Consider KPIs that the business needs to drive to become more successful.

The benefits and objectives need to be based on a realistic assessment of what technologies can be brought to bear and how they can be incorporated into a tight timeframe. Be too conservative, and the executives will treat it as another mundane request. Be too bold, and the project will fail. There is a delicate balance. Working with the vendors beforehand will help craft the best objectives.

### 6.3.11   Profile past successes

The aggressive timeframes of the playbook, combined with a set of objectives and benefits bold enough to garner executive attention, require grounding in reality. Failure in such a project could be a career-ending move. The playbook will be the marketing brochure for executives, so it needs more than product references. Real results that worked help bolster such a bold case for a playbook. The past success profile success story will need to show where some aspects of the playbook have been accomplished. Hard results must be shown.

Product promises are never good enough. Real-world installations are the proof. Any vendor that is chosen to enact the playbook must provide real references. The playbook should give strong consideration to combining technologies that have worked together before and can be referenced as such.

### Audience

Senior executives need to see that the components of a playbook have had some success before. If the technology is so new that it is not possible to demonstrate this, then numerous questions about risk need to be asked. The lack of past success is not necessarily a deal breaker; it just means that the risk is higher, and everyone needs to know that, including the advocates.

### Structure

A simple matrix of the challenges faced and how each aspect of the technology and process change helped that aspect is sufficient.

## Creation

Demand references from the vendors, and then call and/or visit the references. Validate the claims with vendor laboratory results, and then try to recreate them in your own lab.

### 6.3.12   Application patterns

As described in Chapter 5, application patterns are idealized models that exhibit certain workload characteristics. Applications are usually organized around patterns, even if it was not done consciously. Patterns represent these workload characteristics in a way that will allow for the analysis of problems in those workloads. As discussed in Chapter 5, those problems arise from trying to solve numerous operational qualities simultaneously.

The patterns that should be displayed in the playbook are those most likely to be encountered in the target applications that the playbook will address. For a Java Optimization playbook, this could be daunting, as a typical financial services organization will have thousands of Java applications. Those thousands of applications are the exact reason some patterns *must* be described.

It is useful to explore how patterns can help the playbook make its case. In the case of a Java Optimization playbook, it would be useful to point out that most Java applications in a financial services firm can be characterized as follows:

- Internet-facing transaction-oriented applications.
- Information query applications that need to obtain records from many disparate systems and place them into a coherent view.
- File manipulation systems that aggregate large amounts of data and then transform it into a format that can be accessed for reports.
- In the financial markets, high-throughput systems that provide multiple views to the trader.

There are many nuances and ranges for all these application types that can be categorized as operational qualities. Each of these applications has a few patterns that would be generally mapped to workload types. The Java Optimization playbook would be able to demonstrate applicability to a wide range of applications by showing how it could address the typical driving forces of recurring patterns.

## Audience

Architects and lead developers would be the most receptive to seeing patterns in a playbook. Patterns speak the language of an architect, and business line architects would be able to make the leap from single application relevance to a portfolio of applications where such a playbook could be relevant.

## Structure

There are just a few sections that would need to be created to make the pattern relevant to the audience. The first should be a brief description of the pattern. In the Java Optimization playbook, one of the more generic patterns to describe would be a typical J2EE application server pattern.

A *description* would be for use by applications that require commercially hardened features such as messaging, object/relational mapping, transaction support and connections, and/or connections to legacy environments.

## Demand characteristics and consequences
- Uncontrolled high volume of service requests during peaks that are hard to predict.
- Response times need to be fast and predictable during peak loads.
- Process complex business logic with high throughput.
- Typically require multiple data sources from legacy environments (e.g., client, product).

## How to tune or augment supply to resolve challenges
- **Control Throughput Processing**—A service broker provides dynamic (application deployment and activation, infrastructure service provisioning, runtime service orchestration, and utility resource management) deployment of workload to specific hardware to meet needs based on defined polices that specify event thresholds.
- **Reduce Response Time**—Java application heap memory can safely expand with no garbage collection pauses by using a network attached processor (NAP) providing 864 processing cores and 768 GB of shared memory, ensuring consistency and predictability of response even during peak times.
- **Accelerate Complex Business Logic Processing**—Use multicore processors that maximize efficiency of multithreaded applications and allow for bundling of single threaded applications that heavily collaborate with one another.
- **Accelerate Multiple Data Source Access Seamlessly**—Employ nonspinning solid-state disks, with capacity starting at 10 GB so interim and cached results can be stored and retrieved like regular files, significantly reducing access to large data sets; transfer rates are about 200 MB/second.
- **Visualization of Patterns**—Architects typically respond to pictures of patterns as opposed to just a text description. The pattern illustrated here is very generic, and the picture would add little extra clarity. Depending on the line of business and the nature of the pattern, it may be useful to add one.

## Creation

This would require research with vendor products, which will require significant behind the scenes preparatory work. This initial work will serve the playbook well as details about *how* the products work together need to be discovered so that the objectives and benefits can be grounded in reality.

### 6.3.13   *Key technology characteristics*

This section defines the types of technical challenges that the playbook will address in order to meet the project objectives and realize the playbook benefits.

It addresses the most important high-impact problems faced by the target applications. Here are some examples of prevalent problems:

- Latency
- Response time
- Concurrency
- Throughput
- Transaction processing

The purpose of this section is to describe what tactics will be used to fix these problems. The playbook defines KPIs, states a mission, and describes objectives and benefits. This section describes how the problems will be solved to meet the objectives and realize those benefits.

### Audience

This section is made by architects and lead developers and is used by them and all other teams described in Chapter 5, including platform engineers, operations, and the on-boarding teams.

### Structure

The key technology characteristics section should be a table that describes the details of the problem, such as latency, any software or hardware products that will be utilized to solve that problem, and the tactical implications of using that product. Each problem should be addressed separately, even if the product that fixes the problem shows up on more than one table. The tactics are too important to ignore, especially since these are used to guide the design of the playbook solutions.

### Creation

This section's content is the result of all the design sessions that eventually produced the first ensemble designs.

## 6.3.14  Maturity model

The techniques of using and assessing the maturity model are detailed in Chapter 5. The purpose of referencing the maturity model in the playbook is as follows:

- The model represents current state and can be used for a call to action that the playbook will address.
- The model should also reflect the target state that the senior executives wish to attain in some aspect (quality of experience, technology, strategy, operations, real-time execution). This playbook should use the model as a lever to reinforce that the model target state is being served by the mission of the playbook.

The maturity model is a direct statement from the senior leadership team acknowledging current state and future direction. Any playbook needs to use the explicit and implicit directions that the model states as a call for action.

### Audience

Senior executives need to see how their articulation of the model will be manifested in the specific targeted actions of the playbook. The change agents on the playbook team must internalize the maturity model's targets as they relate to the particular playbook in order to overcome resistance in the organization.

### Structure

An extract of the maturity model, discussed in detail in Chapter 5, should be used as part of the playbook. The audience should be senior executives and project leads. It is represented as a matrix that indicates the current state of the key operating aspects that the playbook will address and what the expected result will look like after the playbook has been successfully enacted.

### Creation

In the playbook, just extract the relevant portions. In the example of Java optimization, any references to current state execution and operation should be heavily emphasized. Current state should be leveraged as a baseline, with specific targets stated (see preceding mission statement) that will fix the current state and move it to the defined target state.

## 6.3.15   Reference models—development lifecycle

The reference model should convey to the organizations typical development and change processes that can be leveraged by the playbook transformation team. If none of the current processes can be leveraged at all, then a reference model of the project phases and steps needs to be created. The point is to get people thinking that although the mission is aggressive and ambitious, it is nonetheless feasible.

Anyone in the change process needs to know how to start, understand the roles and responsibilities for the playbook, and have a gauge for how they should be completed in each phase—in essence, a tailored version of the typical project lifecycle. The reference model is so important because the accelerated timeframes associated with the playbooks do not allow for much error and restart. New teams will be introduced, as described in Chapter 5, and very aggressive iterative approaches must be taken to meet the mission statement.

The change teams involved in the playbook program must have the grounding of a reference model to develop detailed project plans, which include the proper level of risk planning. The reference model should be related to the project lifecycle references used in the organization, with some important notable exceptions:

- The reference model that must be used for the playbook has to clearly indicate the iterative nature of the program.
- It has to use the milestones as anchors for the program.

Finally, the reference model needs links to the organization's development lifecycle, leveraging well-known terms so adoption is facilitated and people feel less disoriented. The rate of change acceptance in an organization must always be viewed from a conservative perspective.

Since the playbook represents a new paradigm in transformation, it is critical to start with the milestones and the aggressive timeframe and work backward. Iterate on making each milestone; create issues and risk lists that must be addressed by the sponsors. Understand the degree of design, programming, and testing that must be performed at each step, and relate it back to the organization's standard project lifecycle to help with references.

### 6.3.16 Reference models—reference architecture

The playbook defines an aggressive set of actions that manifest in a short timeframe, approximately 90–180 days. As such, it will be important to use an integrated set of products that has been designed top-down to reflect business demand characteristics. This integrated set of products needs to be configurable from the bottom-up to tailor the capabilities to meet the demands of individual applications.

The reference architecture is a blueprint that will be used constantly during all phases of the transformation to ensure that the roles of all proposed products are understood by the vendors and the transformation team.

For a Java Optimization playbook, all four previously defined ensembles (latency sensitive, numerical processing, complex transaction, and information integration) could have a role in transforming the performance, efficiency, and operational footprint of target applications.

A reference model is a vital visual tool for architects and other practitioners on the playbook transformation team. This model will be used during all integration discussions with vendors.

The design of those integrated set of products, called ensembles, is covered in Chapter 5. The reference architecture for the ensembles used in a playbook should be included as an architecture picture depicting the ensembles used, the details of their components, and their interrelationship to common management services and the networked resources that ensembles will consume in the service of the targeted applications.

This reference model is created through the iterative design sessions during the first pilot projects discussed in Chapter 5. The work sessions that defined service design and their qualities, the architecture patterns, ensembles, and PEDs will provide all of the necessary material to build the reference model.

In fact, the reference model should be built before undertaking the playbook. The use of the playbook should be triggered by the successful completion of key pilot projects that have tested the technology.

### 6.3.17   Reference models—quality of experience

The QoE is a key lens to view the entire playbook's premise. As mentioned in previous chapters (but worth repeating), QoE is the relative balance of user experience, cost, and efficiency. The balance will be different for each line of business, each component in a value chain and each application that addressed business functions. The playbook must report on which QoE measures it will address.

A Java Optimization playbook would be able to address all three aspects of QoE; a disaster recovery playbook would have a heavy focus on cost and efficiency. The whole point of the playbook is to get a business-focused transformation done in 90 days to excite the organization; it must be tied to balancing QoE.

The playbook needs focus, grounding, and executive support, and QoE is the means to achieve all three foundations. A playbook labeled the Java Optimization program will have greater executive appeal than an SOA strategy. Java Optimization is an easier leap for executives to make in terms of investment and return on that investment.

QoE is the key factor required to sell the playbook to senior executives. The playbook will likely be enacted for one business line initially; therefore, the playbook must use QoE to show why it can be the force for change throughout the organization. It should be a matrix showing the current assessment of the user experience, cost, and efficiency for the target business lines and the expected change.

The QoE model for the playbook must be fact based and tie back to the mission statement. It must show the assumptions that lead to the mission statements. In the case of Java optimization, fact-based measures from the current environment would be helpful in establishing the baseline pain points. Projections of the results, as mentioned in the KPI section and the mission statement, will tie QoE together.

### 6.3.18   Managing resulting building block to create a discipline

All of the lessons learned in the early pilot projects begin to coalesce in a playbook. Playbooks are targeted transformations that have a large impact in a short amount of time. They are essentially self-contained transformation processes that integrate technology, architecture, process, and new people skills into a powerful transformation engine that can be referenced to leverage repeatability. Playbooks also adopt a culture of flexibility and urgency that is essential to change agency.

Playbooks can be viewed as the building block of change because of all of the aforementioned attributes they contain. Each playbook project can be repeated in different parts of an organization as long as the team performing the transformation can enact it. This fact is both a benefit and a risk. The immediate risk is simple: How do you keep the team intact? The answer in the short term is incentives and promotions. The long-term risk is a very different matter. People get tired of fighting an organization's inertia year after year, and of course, people who have acquired new skills become very marketable. The real answer is to consider how to make a sustainable model that can continue to transform the organization.

Playbooks also provide the foundation to develop new disciplines. All of the activities in Chapter 5 clearly indicate that current ways of designing, instrumenting, testing, engineering, supporting, and operating need to be refined. Skills and processes will need to be adjusted, and so will behaviors. Playbooks give the organization the opportunity to experience a new set of interdisciplinary skills as they emerge around a common intensely focused goal. As the execution of the first playbook nears completion, thought should be given to codifying a new set of transformation roles based on the lessons learned. The pilot teams can act as a template for the entire suite of skills required to build or refine some key disciplines around the architecture and design of ensembles, platform engineering, on-boarding, forensics and instrumentation, and lab specialists.

These disciplines need the skills, role recognition, autonomy, accountability, training, respect, budget, and cultural guideposts to build a sustainment model for RTI. If the cost seems daunting, think about the playbook cost savings and the long-term impact that sustainable processes can have on the entire operating environment. A back of the napkin estimate would be about a 30-times return on investment.

The need for a move to key disciplines becomes more apparent as the true effort behind enterprise-wide transformation is explored in Chapter 7. Challenges of scale and sustainment are at the heart of that chapter. As all of the aspects of an RTI migration are explored, it will become obvious that leveraging disciplines makes sense.

# 7 Manage for scale and evolution

*"There is nothing more difficult to take in hand, more perilous to conduct, or more uncertain in its success, than to take the lead in the introduction of a new order of things. Because the innovator has for enemies all those who have done well under the old conditions and lukewarm defenders in those who may do well under the new. This coolness arises partly from fear of the opponents, who have the laws on their side, and partly from the incredulity of men, who do not readily believe in new things until they have had a long experience of them."*
—Niccolo Machiavelli (The Prince)

## Key Points

Through playbooks and strategic building blocks, it is possible to scale up the transformation programs to the scope of the whole organization.

The organizational change is not a finite process but is the seed to build a sustainable operating model for IT, where the IT digital supply chain becomes the analog of the business value chain.

This IT evolution positions IT to become the strategic enabler of business strategy. Once the first project wins and the key building blocks of the new operating model are in place, it's time to begin formulating plans for expanding the scope of the transformation effort into larger programs tailored to the needs of the organization (Figure 7.1).

This requires considerable senior management support, since the process alters how the organization operates. The primary outcome of this transformation should be the alignment of IT to the goals of the business, enabling the front and middle offices to react faster to business events. The secondary outcome ensures that the changes are incorporated in the enterprise culture so they become sustainable and promote the business needs.

## 7.1 Expanding the transformation program

Up to this point, the focus of the change has been on improving the performance of the pilot applications while placing the first building blocks of the new operating model in place. As experience shows, when exploring the concepts of the Next Generation Datacenter, it is tempting to think of it as *tabula rasa*, or a Greenfield design. While that opportunity may exist for a select few enterprises,

doi: 10.1016/B978-0-12-374956-7.00007-3

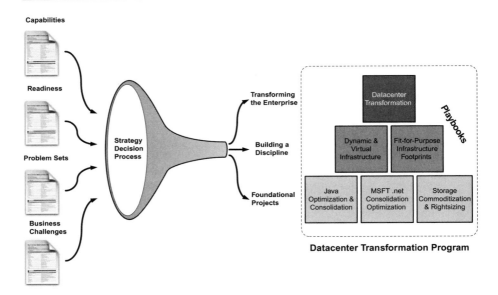

**Figure 7.1** Selecting playbooks to create a transformation program.

the reality is that the vast majority of firms must architect a program to gradually evolve their current environment toward an optimal state.

It is imperative that you have strong quantitative evidence of pilot project success. In fact, beginning the transformation program in such a manner and following with empirical evidence is an effective way of driving home the point. Once the organization begins to understand the capabilities of an infrastructure enabled to meet the needs of a Real Time Enterprise, a groundswell of demand will surface from those benefiting from the transformation and those jealous of peers who are getting an advantage. At the same time, expect resistance from the established hierarchy as it begins to understand the scope of the upcoming changes.

Make no mistake: The stakes are very high for everyone directly and indirectly involved. Individuals entrenched in the rigid legacy infrastructure will either bend or break; there is little room for a middle ground. While senior management interests are aligned with enabling a Real Time Enterprise, they don't necessarily have only one candidate team to execute the change. As a leader of this change effort, your personal risk is directly correlated to how well you manage the risks of the transformation process.

The best-case scenario is that you get a strong mandate from senior management to lead the transformation process. Although this is not a magic shield that saves the day, it helps establish credibility with peers where the real change needs to occur. Be on the lookout for teams and other leaders who benefit from proposed changes, and win them over to the transformation effort. They will provide leverage against those entrenched groups that resist the transformation efforts. It will take a coalition of many leaders to assist in the transformation process.

Senior leadership will be able to assist with the thornier political issues that are bound to appear, especially around reorganizing responsibilities and organizational structure. Managing up and being the first to report trouble will help formulate coordinated responses to raised objections from different parts of the organization. This can be particularly challenging in an environment where IT spans more than one line of business. Since IT is shared, there are some aspects of change that will affect the whole organization and thus require additional sensitivity.

As with any change management program, setting proper expectations and continually adjusting scope are critical. Not taking on change fast enough will stall the transformation effort, while taking on too much adds unwanted risk. Striking the balance is critical to success. As adjustments are made, it must be an imperative to continue the communication process. At any moment leadership must be ready to relay the vision and actual program status. Also, while keeping senior leaders in the loop is important, it's equally important that everyone affected by the transformation also be apprised. Communicating frequently reduces the chance for individuals to vector off on tangents, while reducing the fear quotient that the unknown sparks, not to mention baseless speculation in the absence of facts—the rumor will create them.

Clearly, any transformation process as large as this undertaking has hiccups along the way. How these challenges are managed as they occur is as important as avoiding them to begin with. The first inclination of any leader in this situation is to cover up shortcomings. This works against the transformation in two ways. First, it insolates the senior leadership from the underlying complexities of the change process, which makes it appear easier than it is. If at any point the program runs into significant difficulties, the program leader won't have the credibility of working though these difficult problems in the eyes of the senior leadership team. Second, enlisting judicious assistance from the senior leadership team embroils them with a personal stake in your success; the solutions to challenges will be theirs as well, and they'll want to see it succeed, too. This maximizes the transformation leader's chances for success, while keeping everything aligned with senior management's wishes and strategy.

The human factor of the transformation is absolutely perilous to ignore and is part of the underlying environment during the entire transformation. The most difficult time is in the beginning. As groups find their place within the new operating model, they act as additional building blocks that can be counted on as part of the transformed organization. As more make the transition and realize the benefits, resistance to the change begins to fade.

## 7.1.1 Setting the stage for an effective dialog

One of the biggest challenges facing IT executives and organizations trying to transform their legacy applications, infrastructure, and operations is the resistance to change. In many cases, this resistance to change will be defended with numerous explanations: shortage of time, skills, resources, or perceived disruption to the business. More often than not, though, the true cause of resistance is fear of the unknown, a lack of understanding of new technology and the state of poorly documented applications, systems, dependencies, and actual user experience.

The other big unknown is actually due to IT's inability to step away from solving today's problem and create a proactive planning dialog with the business that transforms the current relationship of support provider. A structured, open, frank mutual exchange about the current state of affairs and the development of a scorecard system to communicate how each participant is doing (as users or abusers and as suppliers or strategic partners) is needed. The work to document the current state of how the value chain of the business is executed against the technology platforms of applications, information, and infrastructure components with their associated workloads should help facilitate the development of the scorecard.

To address this dual challenge in implementing change and transforming legacy IT, firms need to employ both top-down and bottom-up approaches at the same time. Top-down begins with an executive dialog and exchange between IT and the business. It is important to understand fact-based, documented, and natural language defined service requirements. In return, IT should provide a similar, structured feedback as to gaps, misses, or disruptive decision making that the business employs that creates documented examples of behavior and their associated cause/effect. This limits IT's ability to deliver service that meets business needs. This is easier said than done, but it *has* been done. Moreover, this barrier must be broken at some point to ensure that the value chain of business and IT is integrated properly and operating optimally.

Bottom-up approaches that employ instrumentation, data gathering, and analytics with objective, factual data (that is captured, trended, and documented in illustrative visuals) will enable very powerful results. With real-time user experience, instrumentation firms can benchmark and identify true end–to-end quality of execution in terms of the IT components of the organization's value chain. Using application mapping, discovery, and dependency mapping tools firms can capture critical knowledge of what actually exists, how it is connected across the digital supply chain, and where there are limitations, barriers, or bottlenecks in terms of design. Tools that capture and correlate resource consumption of users and applications, infrastructure, and so on across factors of time, quantity, and location in a service-unit-like paradigm help create a clear understanding of waste. In addition, new tools should be considered that extend the current systems management tool suite, correlate real-time root cause, proactively identify upcoming problems, and make sense out of the chaos that exists in legacy IT platforms.

This dual-prong approach enables IT to remove or mitigate the obstacles of change—a lack of understanding the transparency and alignment between the business and IT *and* a lack of fact and data driven insight of the IT value chain and the cause/effect of how it delivers service.

## 7.2  Architecture migration

There is a shift in perception about how to approach current datacenter problems. The shift in focus is from the traditional analysis of individual troubled applications and services to the entirety of enterprise datacenter operations. The concepts introduced in Chapters 3 though 6 detail a foundation of individual elements that come together to enable a Next Generation Datacenter design (Figure 7.2).

The NGDC objectives discussed in this chapter are arranged in a spiral model in Figure 7.2. This spiral model shows four broad categories—Align, Execute, Operate, and Sustain—into which 12 objectives are arranged. The model shows progression from pilots and proof of concepts through the major building blocks that enable large-scale transformations. Each of the objectives shown is discussed from the perspective of how to achieve scale and sustainability. The following 12 objectives are a practical guide in creating a comprehensive transformation program that enables a real-time infrastructure.

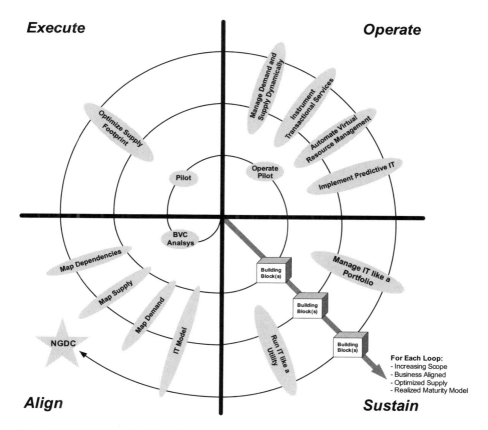

**Figure 7.2**  Realizing the Next Generation Datacenter.

## 7.3 Objective 1: establish an IT economic model

The economic model for IT can be thought of as the business and IT linkage of demand and supply. In particular, it is the interactive dynamic consumption of IT resources by the business and the fulfillment behavior of processing by IT. As stated in Chapter 3, the business sells products and services through the business value chain. IT is the digital supply chain that acts as the analog of the business. The IT economic model is important because the business must view IT as an investment that can be correlated to business drivers. The IT economic model is that vehicle and is a driver for alignment.

All of the other objectives in the Align, Execute, Operate, and Sustain categories take their lead from the IT economic model. The most critical goal of the entire transformation process is providing each business line the opportunity to balance Quality of Experience (QoE), according to its individual demands and drivers. QoE has three pillars: user experience in terms of performance and reliability, cost, and efficiency. Each line of business perceives QoE differently and therefore should be able to treat IT as an investment to achieve its goals. The economic model is the start to putting each business on the path.

### 7.3.1 The scope of the IT economic model

CIO's and their organizations need to think of their entire collection of service delivery components (people, process, and technology) as a digital supply chain. Like any other supply chain, this one needs to be managed against the economic realities of cost, growth, and agility. The entire IT operational model needs to account for the following five areas that correlate to at least one of the objectives in Figure 7.2.

*Demand Management:* The continuous identification, documentation, tracking, and measuring of business; what it expects; where problems exist; and understanding sensitivities to cost, bottlenecks, and timing constraints. In particular, this means service contracts defined in natural language that identify users, entitlement, expectations, geography, critical time windows, special business calendar events, and performance defined in terms of user experience.

*Supply Management:* The continuous identification, documentation, and tracking through instrumentation to capture "objective" factual data of which users; which applications they are using; consuming which applications, servers, network bandwidth, network QoS, and storage resources; and for how long. This information should be trended to accurately identify peaks, valleys, and nominal growth.

*Fit-for-Purpose Policies:* It is essential that organizations trying to build real-time infrastructure (or a more responsive IT platform and operation) and incorporate an operating level of policy management of how the IT platform matches supply and demand at runtime. This should include factors of wall clock, business growth trends, and service contract requirements matched optimally against runtime supply management trends. It is this operating level discipline that can radically reduce waste and unnecessary costs while lowering capital investment and improving service levels. It is here that most organizations fail to implement, execute, or adopt such a discipline at the right level of granularity. Instead, firms standardize infrastructure from the bottom up, using rule-of-thumb sizing and defining service levels in terms of recovery time objectives or availability.

*Role of ITIL/ITSMF:* ITIL 3.0 and the *IT Service Management Framework* are excellent guides for creating consistent end-to-end processes related to delivery IT as a service. Since they are guides, they are not the sole answer to resolving IT service problems or quality of delivery. Firms must still resolve issues of alignment and strategy, define sound architectures, and implement dynamic infrastructures before ITIL affects end-to-end process delivery.

*Sustaining Transparency:* Many IT organizations miss the mark when it comes to meeting and exceeding business expectations due to lack of transparency. The key components just outlined can contribute significantly to creating transparency. It is critical that IT organizations institute a discipline around tooling, data capture, and reporting procedures that consistently and accurately communicates to the business. Communication should provide a completely transparent view of what, how, and who related to the consumption of IT by the business and the delivery of service by IT.

In conclusion, each of the objectives has a goal that advances aspects of the IT operational model.

## 7.3.2   The IT economic model on an enterprise scale

**Maturity Model:** Given the broad categories of the operational model just described, the most important question that the business needs to ask is how much transformation are they willing to push though and how fast it should happen. This infrastructure transformation is time consuming and expensive in terms of real expenditures and opportunity costs, so the business needs to treat it as a long-term investment. The investment decisions must start with an assessment of the business and IT current state in order to get a sense for how far along the spectrum of change the organization must move. The organization needs to determine how fast the assessment and investment decisions must be completed.

Global financial enterprises are comprised of several business lines that may also be segmented by different national cost centers (e.g., commercial banking in two different countries). Each business line and national group has different drivers; therefore, the urgency to change will vary. Understanding, respecting, and leveraging these differences are critical to change advocacy.

The IT maturity model is both an assessment and guide for business and IT. The model measures the maturity of key aspects of the overall health of the IT and business relationship. These aspects include quality of experience, architecture, strategy, operating model, and runtime execution for each line of business and national group. This model guides the plan for the change each business line will undertake based on the current status and the perceived maturity that must be achieved. It will identify the greatest pain points and opportunities for change to take hold. Each of these aspects will be altered as NGDC objectives permeate the enterprise.

**Scale:** The maturity model mechanics are explained in Chapter 5, but to scale this, a mandate must come from the CIO and each of the business heads to drive through the initial chart. After the initial definition, it only needs to be reviewed once a year.

## 7.4 Aligning with the business

A constant theme in Chapters 2, 3, 5, and 6 is alignment with the business to achieve the vision of the Real Time Enterprise (RTE) that is operated on a Real Time Infrastructure (RTI). In Chapter 5 the subject of *legacy datacenter modeling* was introduced to gather baseline information on the first candidate applications that would be part of the pilot. This type of modeling must now be scaled across the enterprise. The first insight to that scaling is to realize that this modeling is so big that it needs processes and certain skill sets to be performed in a repeatable and consistent way. The second insight is that the modeling of legacy datacenters across the enterprise is expansive. It should be developed with specific areas of focus: mapping demand, mapping supply, and mapping infrastructure dependencies.

### 7.4.1  Objective 2: map demand

The mapping of business demand allows IT to understand the different work-load patterns that exist and how to best align and supply IT services to meet business consumption needs. Understanding current delivery, gaps, and potential issues from both business and IT perspectives is needed to make the shift toward demand-based IT alignment.

### Goals and objectives

*Mapping Business Demand Directly:* Produce a set of visual tools and metaphors that can be presented in layers of detail that become part of the language used by business analysts, architects, developers, and operations when discussing business service requirements.

*Application Profiling:* Produce a trend map of application and deployment process capabilities across a line of business so the applications can be viewed by workload type and the operating environment can be gauged.

### Challenges in scaling from pilot to enterprise

*Business Value Chain Mapping:* After the initial mandated workshop where the CIO runs it from beginning to end, it will become clear that this is a difficult exercise. The CIO must drive the agenda in the face of resistance due to travel requirements and the amount of time it takes.

*Profiling and Benchmarking:* In the initial pilots, applications were profiled with a small specialized and trained team, most likely with outside consultant help. It is likely that the project teams from the first profiled applications were willing participants because they needed the help or were being targeted by senior management. As the program begins to scale, there will be fewer early adopters, and fewer people will understand the effort involved.

## Approach

### Early iterations
- *Profiling and Benchmarking:* Have the same profiling and benchmarking team interact with all new clients. Supplement this team with a documenter, and ensure that senior management personally mandates the work.
- *Business Value Chain:* The large-scale demand mapping that includes business value chain requirements and capabilities should be completed with direct CIO involvement, engaging all senior IT system owners in the process. Initially one or two business areas receive the focus. Once done, it must be reviewed only yearly, unless there is an acquisition, and then this exercise should be done for the newly absorbed company.

### Late iterations
- Profiling and Benchmarking
  - As the scale grows, more practitioners need to be trained in application profiling and benchmarking. This needs to become a discipline. There needs to be a train-the-trainer program and, if necessary, help from the vendors.
  - Use the internal website to publish results and best practices. Highlight and praise application owners that cooperate. Post the stories on the web!
  - Invest in the right tools, and hold line of business product architects responsible for ensuring metrics are baked into the lifecycle.
- Business Value Chain Mapping: Once complete it should be reviewed yearly.

## Tool capabilities

- Application profiling can be accomplished through documents, but this data is too important to remain in that form. Some sort of database should capture this information.
- Benchmarking tools should be explored that can provide insight into end-to-end transaction latency and total application consumption across all server tiers. Report engines that benchmark and correlate disparate sources should be purchased.

## Best practices

### Do's

- Use the output of the business value chain demand mapping to make the case for change.
- Publish benchmarking data and correlate it to show how performance aligns with demand. Make sure this is accessible to senior IT and business management.
- Drive a vision to show how this data can be used to gauge the effect of business requirements on supply.

## Don'ts

- Don't use the application benchmark data as a stick; instead, punish the lack of cooperation.
- Don't assume that the profiling exercise will yield meaningful results at first. Any profiling data should be augmented with existing benchmark data.

### 7.4.2   Objective 3: map supply

Perform a thorough inventory of infrastructure resources supply. This work effort details the existing operational environment, including component locations (down to the row/rack/shelf level), who is using it today (what workload demand), and peak and average utilization characteristics.

### Goals and objectives

This information serves as a baseline of the enterprise infrastructure supply and is invaluable to the decision-making process for design, optimization, and run-time execution. An accurate supply map enables IT to be smarter about when it procures resources and how it provisions them to the business. Without supply and demand maps in hand, optimization and service quality achievement is just an accident.

### Challenges in scaling from pilot to enterprise

Initially a small team does this for a specific set of collaborating applications. To scale, this activity needs a consolidated effort across all datacenters to capture the information in a consistent manner using a common nomenclature and taxonomy (a description of wholes and parts). The data must be kept centrally, and the process must respect the fact that each datacenter is changing even as inventory is taken over a period of months. Expect that written configuration knowledge is sparse.

### Approach

The approach is to instrument and capture objective and factual data about the IT environment over a period of time so the team can trend the data to accurately identify peaks, valleys, and normal growth.

### Early iterations

- Take inventory of what is on the datacenter floor (applications, servers, storage, network), component location (down to row/rack/shelf level), who is using it, and how much is being used. Document the process and challenges.
- Ensure that a taxonomy and nomenclature are defined early, even if the information is in spreadsheets.

## Late iterations

- This information should be populated into an easily accessible database (i.e., configuration management database or CMDB) and will serve as the baseline for infrastructure supply.
- Application and engineering teams need to be engaged for applications with minimal staff and poor documentation. Incremental validations with the business will help spur cooperation, especially if configuration data looks excessive.

### Tool capabilities

Use tools that can produce configurations that can be imported. Tools should be able to either produce visual maps of configurations or provide the data so some other tool could draw them, perhaps using an interface like that of Microsoft Visio. The tool must be able to detect changes in the supply configurations and provide updates. The tools should be able to discover configurations by running on the network and investigating the configuration data on each node. In some cases such a capability will cause concern for some security departments. This needs to be addressed directly with senior management intervention. This kind of work cannot be done manually, as it is not sustainable, while allowing an administrator access to all of the machines to gather the same data poses other kinds of security risks. The tool should be given the opportunity to run a few days to develop the initial view. Then it should be allowed to run daily to detect the changes that it will report.

### Best practices

#### Do's

- Make every attempt to engage application teams.
- Ensure that the information goes into a living library.
- Make sure virtual server information is included so a true picture of the supply is obtained.

#### Don'ts

- Don't expect that any one group has a full picture of how an application runs on its supply; it could require multiple groups to get all the answers.
- Don't forget a disaster recovery supply.

## 7.4.3   Objective 4: map infrastructure dependencies

One of the most vexing issues for today's IT operations is understanding what resources are logically connected to deliver workload demand. Most topology diagrams are not sufficient given that more and more logical devices (via virtualization) and variance exist due to years of changes and infrastructure growth.

Combining this objective with previous mapping exercises enables an organization to benchmark and identify true end-to-end quality of execution. This information provides a clear understanding of the degree of overprovisioning (waste), flawed designs, and poor management. Without this knowledge, identifying opportunities for standardization and optimization is very difficult and risky.

## Goals and objectives

- Understand what IT resources are logically connected to deliver workload demand.
- Understanding an accurate picture of actual infrastructure dependencies that will enable IT to identify optimization and standardization opportunities.
- Automation of this process (and capture of the information to a CMDB) becomes a foundational capability for managing demand and supply in the datacenter of the future.

## Challenges in scaling from pilot to enterprise

- In the pilot phase, a small team is chartered to work with early adaptor application teams to identify the mapping. As this effort scales, the complexity of the interconnections grows. Despite getting good output from automated tools, this mapping team must validate findings with the application teams or else the data is not qualified.
- Some of the dependency mapping tools may be rejected by corporate security because root access could be required by the mapping program. That fight may be encountered in each country and each line of business, especially those with national data jurisdiction issues.

## Approach

The approach here is to use application mapping, discovery, and dependency mapping tools to capture critical knowledge about how IT components are connected across a digital value chain and where there are limitations, barriers, or bottlenecks in terms of design.

## Early iterations

- A competent team needs to be built that can create processes and exhibit patience with application teams.
- Success stories and case studies about unexpected connections and hops that impeded performance must be published internally.

## Late iterations

- The ownership of the interdependency mapping needs to become a role with processes.
- Mapping must be run every night, with changes made available to the key stakeholders.

## Tool capabilities

It is anticipated that the tools used to map supply will also be used to map infrastructure interdependencies, so similar capability guidelines apply. Tools should be able to produce visual maps of interrelationships that will be updated as a result of new data. The tools should be able to discover relationship data by running on the network and investigating the configuration data on each node. In some cases such a capability will cause concern for some security departments. This needs to be addressed directly with senior management intervention. This kind of work cannot be done manually, and allowing an administrator access to all of the machines to gather the same data poses other kinds of security risks. The tool should be given the opportunity to run a few days to develop the initial map. Then it should be allowed to run daily to detect the changes it will report.

### Best practices

There are some enlightening results of this activity that will help the migration toward change. One is that many application teams will discover undocumented connections to other applications and services that may be vestigial or are used very infrequently. This discovery is not surprising, since large IT organizations experience staff turnover and documentation is rarely kept current. Another result is the realization that some performance issues that could never be resolved occur because the original layout of collaborating applications has changed. The changes often cause excessive hops between collaborating applications, and in cases where there is more than one datacenter in a city, applications may be traversing these distances multiple times for one transaction.

### Do's

- Engage the application teams early in the process.
- Get feedback on how to streamline the validation process.

### Don'ts

- Do not let security prevent this tool from being deployed. Get business to intervene; this tool is critical in understanding bottlenecks in the datacenter.
- Don't underestimate how hard it is to maintain this data manually; an automated tool is required.
- Don't assume the tool can just run; each application's results need to be reviewed by both the mapping team and the application team to understand the full set of interrelationships.

## 7.5  Operate

Operation of the new platforms requires changes in thinking about the onboarding process for new applications, new approaches for day-to-day operations, the use of the integration lab, and the types of roles, responsibilities, and shared resource billing needed. Some of the big challenges will arise from the trend to share resources.

## 7.5.1   Objective 5: manage demand and supply dynamically

Introduce the sharing of infrastructure resources across multiple workload demands. To enable this, firms must create standard application packaging and development services (for both in-house and ISV applications), dynamic application management services (that support resource brokering, service activation, monitoring, and service-level management), as well as shared infrastructure services through technologies such as virtualization and grid computing. In addition, analytic services that support business and IT reporting, metering, and chargeback, and capacity planning and optimization functions must be matured and baked in to sustain and harden the environment.

### Goals and objectives

- Ensure that the right work gets done at the right time by the right resources.
- Reduce the deployment time from days to minutes.

By implementing a shared resource pool and dynamic management capabilities, the infrastructure becomes more responsive to changes in business strategy and operations, thus increasing business-IT alignment while improving overall performance within the IT supply chain.

### Challenges in scaling from pilot to enterprise

- Many objections will come from application owners with high-performance criteria combined with fluctuating demand.
- Loss of control will be a big issue, and that issue is so strong that many large financial services firms have multiple project grids. The use of metrics, business demand mapping, and characterization must be used to combat this entrenched thinking.
- Many of the applications that need the most help from shared infrastructure services are critical to the operation of the enterprise, and altering them will be considered risky.
- Many teams building high-performance applications are not encouraged by their business to share. They will undoubtedly get significant business support to be left alone unless senior IT management can get to the business first and explain the benefits for sharing infrastructure resources.

### Approach

Once there is an understanding of the business demand, the available supply of IT resources, and how everything is logically connected, the enterprise should begin sharing its infrastructure by implementing dynamic provisioning and execution management capabilities.

The cornerstone to this approach is a *service broker product* that should be bought, not internally developed. A service broker's biggest benefit to enacting change is the dynamic lifecycle management of application instances. Any application that is running in an application server can be managed by a service broker *without altering application logic or architecture*. The service broker makes it easier for critical applications to migrate to a dynamic infrastructure, show results quickly, and secure easy wins. Learning how to use a service broker properly will pave the path for running existing container-based applications faster and more efficiently.

A service broker is a critical element to a better-managed infrastructure, but it is not the only one. To achieve dynamic infrastructure management, the enterprise must deploy a common suite of services: application configuration services, application management services, shared infrastructure services, and analytics services. The need for these services will vary per business unit and value chain component, but there are some guiding principles to use in early and late iterations. Scaling is about putting services in place that make immediate tangible benefit. While some of these services might make sense to build, most should be purchased or licensed through an open source. They are enabling products that let the IT organization focus on business functionality.

## Early iterations

It is important to get results fast to show the power of the new approaches. The emphasis should be on helping applications in need by changing how the resources they run on are managed. These two services will increase efficiency, responsiveness, and overall performance without application changes, which is a key to early success. The following services will change how an application is managed without changing the application.

*Application Management Services:* The service broker. These services perform resource allocation that is managed in real time based on monitored workloads compared against service contracts. These services adjust allocation of applications, infrastructure services, and resources as demand changes throughout the operational day.

*Application Configuration Services:* Represents a package-once, deploy-many application facility, including a library of approved and standardized deployment packages. Such services will set up application personas that can be loaded onto bare metal, which will repurpose a machine for scheduled or real-time deployment.

## Late iterations

Leverage early success to get greater efficiency by *changing what is used*.

As the concepts of dynamic real-time management become part of the day-to-day operating model of the enterprise, additional services should be added that form the basis of a utility operating model.

*Shared Infrastructure Services:* Pools of infrastructure resources (processing, storage, caching, and communication) that are allocated in real time to the business as needed. This set of services reduces the proliferation of application infrastructure services that are difficult to design, build, test, and maintain. Many high-performance applications use them but often build them from scratch.

*Grid Brokers:* In some financial business lines, numerical processing applications that calculated risk became integral for the proper operation of the trading function. As a result, large-scale project grids were used to manage thousands of simultaneous calculations. In some institutions, grid broker products were used and modified.

In these instances, grid brokers were employed before service brokers, because grid brokers came to market first and the business opportunity called for its use. As an organization looks at dynamic infrastructure across its suite of applications, it will become clear that grid brokers can be used for a variety of application patterns, including image processing and large-scale statement generation. Grid brokers are suggested for a later iteration in general because it is usually necessary to alter the application to make best use of a grid broker. More will be discussed on this in Chapter 8.

*Analytics Services:* Supporting management services that provide the capabilities needed to assess the effectiveness and efficiency of the overall infrastructure based on business needs/consumption (demand) and IT performance (supply). These services can be used to provide reporting, metering and chargeback, capacity planning, and service optimization.

## Tool capabilities

Since the most critical tool for managing infrastructure dynamically is the service broker, its features will be summarized here. In Chapter 8 more time will be spent on describing the landscape of key technologies.

A service broker is designed to enable an application's specific Quality of Experience (QoE) to be met because the runtime environment can be configured to dynamically meet changes in demand.

- Service brokers have features to manage and execute services based on policies aligned to business priorities and workload demand.
- Service brokers allow organizations to build SLAs that can be adhered to.
- Volatile, unexpected demand can be processed, ensuring QoE is consistent and sustainable.
- A service broker manages a distributed environment enabled across available compute resources that facilitate an organization's ability to package an application once and then deploy many times.
- A service broker can ensure guaranteed, automatic recovery of service execution in the event of hardware failure.
- Attributes such as resource requirements, threshold activation, resource preferences, failover responses, and dynamic responses to behavior changes can be configured, deployed, tuned, and then monitored in real time.
- Service brokers require granular real-time monitoring to perform optimally. Therefore, one can expect that top-of-the-line service brokers will have very flexible monitoring that integrates tightly with the management of container instances. The sampling windows used by the monitors can typically be stated in multiples of milliseconds, and rules will be tied to tangible events such as messages-per-second thresholds. Business-defined policies could be set for recurring intervals that range from daily to monthly and specific hours in a given day. (These capabilities tie back to the strong need to elicit the lifecycle of events for a business value chain as mentioned in the "Service Design Qualities" section of Chapter 5.)
- Service brokers are evolving to include the mechanics of grid brokers. The tendency for the leading products will be to have a seamless operation across both broker types. What is unlikely to change is the need to alter applications that require grid brokers in order to realize maximum benefit.

## Best practices

The practices and artifacts are extensively discussed in Chapter 5, especially service design, but some rules of thumb are mentioned here.

### Do's

- Set up and use an integration lab extensively to validate designs and operational models.
- Encourage structured use of the lab by prospective clients.
- Iterate through designs, and engage stakeholders from operations and engineering.
- Consider open-source tools for some services.
- Integrate metrics into all aspects of the integration process.
- Document design decisions and integration processes.

### Don'ts

- Don't buy large-scale do-it-all products. They are too complex and are rarely flexible enough to let an organization progress incrementally. Vendors who sell such products also tend to sell the hardware, and this is a relationship to be wary of when the goal is a streamlined datacenter.
- Don't be fooled into thinking that virtualization is dynamic management. Virtualization alone will buy an enterprise very little in long-term efficiency gains. Virtualization has its place, but the task at this stage is quick wins with lasting impact.
- Don't think that the services defined in this section are easy to write; they are not. The central services group is needed (as per Chapter 5) to design the use of these services and then integrate a suite of them. Writing the services defined in this section is not a strategic win in a financial services institution.
- Don't think that integrating and supporting these services is a part-time job; these services take investments in skilled people who are motivated.

## 7.5.2  Objective 6: instrument transaction services

As the enterprise migrates toward a platform that can dynamically share infrastructure workloads, it becomes both a benefit and a challenge for IT operations personnel.

- If the new dynamic infrastructure-sharing capabilities are deployed properly, they will sense and respond to failures or impending SLA breaches with little or no manual intervention.
- However, that same capability may significantly hinder the operation team's ability to diagnose and repair transient faults or even to simply understand in real time how the environment is performing.

Therefore, it is critical to instrument the environment at the demand level to understand granular end-to-end transaction performance. Instrumentation must also be implemented at the resource level in order to quickly diagnose and repair faults when they occur. As the amount of shared infrastructure resources (supply) increases, fine-grained visibility into resource utilization is vital to minimizing operational risk.

## Goals and objectives

- Start the basis for comprehensive instrumentation that will clearly show the effects of business demand on infrastructure.
- Change the attitude toward instrumentation from a problem determination process to a discipline that is part of application and service design.
- Set the stage for the creation of dashboards that can show high-level correlated information that can be associated with drill-down detail. These dashboards should be a communication medium between executives and practitioners so meaningful dialog can occur regarding business demand and its consequences.

## Challenges in scaling from pilot to enterprise

- Most applications do not engineer instrumentation from the start and have no idea how to coordinate metrics across tiers. It is not part of the project plan or skill base.
- Most statistics are run by operations that only show various gross-level server utilization statistics.
- From this meager base of data and processes associated with instrumentation, a new discipline must be established. This lack of skills, processes, and data must be overcome by an education process that can produce results while training others.
- Numerous tools are needed, and multiple departments will be touched. This will involve politics, turf wars, and lots of bruised egos, especially as results emerge. This is a considerable investment, and the skeptics will be out in force. Expect some people to repudiate the results. Exposure to senior-level management will not necessarily be successful. Some senior managers will not like the implications of the truth.

## Approach

In the pilot phases, the emphasis was to use whatever tools the enterprise had on hand to establish the baseline. This should have worked because the pilot teams were either willing partners or were coerced with the implications of dire consequences. Beyond the initial pilot stages, a real assessment of the tools required must be performed.

### Early iterations

- Enterprise-worthy tools must be selected, which implies not only solid functionality but a vendor culture that will work with the enterprise to make the instrumentation project a success. Two initial tools need to be considered.
- One tool must be able to discover service traffic for transaction types so the latency of a transaction can be determined at each tier.
- Another tool must be able to measure resource utilization at each tier so total consumption effects based on wall clock events can be determined.

These tools will need internal experts that can be groomed by the vendor, which is why the vendor culture is so important. This initial expert team should be the basis for the instrumentation discipline.

Regular dissemination of measures and statistics must be published and polished for senior stakeholders. These measures must be relevant to the current problems at hand, emphasizing any improvements due to the introduction of shared services. This dissemination activity is a major goal of this activity. In early iterations this will be time consuming, but it is part of the investment strategy, and there is no alternative. Demonstrable, business-relevant facts drive change.

## Late iterations

- As discussed in the "Dynamic Infrastructure" section of this chapter, the aim of all these efforts is to create an operating model that runs like a utility. Utilities are run based on a pay-as-you-use model, which should foster usage responsibility among all the business lines.
- Significant correlation of large data sets must be performed in order to provide the basics for a utility model. A rules- and policy-based correlator must be obtained and used in conjunction with an OLAP type of report generator.

## Tool capabilities

- Service discovery in real time based on traffic.
- Multitier latency measures.
- Multitier consumption statistics.
- Correlation of large data sets into dashboard material that can be linked to levels of detail as needed.

## Best practices

Best practices can be summed up into some key components: training, education, tool vendor partnership, executive buy and reinforcement, and the hard, cold display of the facts. The facts are impersonal, although it is clear to acknowledge that the consequences rarely are.

### Do's

- Make sure that instrumentation efforts are in lockstep with service introduction.
- Get the vendors to sponsor regular chalk talks with material that people can access afterward.
- Build an instrumentation discipline, and invest in it: education, tools; servers; bright, committed people.
- Spend time on communication vehicles for executives and key technical people.
- Find success stories, and reward those brave enough to endure the scrutiny.

### Don'ts

- Don't be complacent, thinking that tool measurements stand on their own. Powerful, entrenched people who are resistant to change are threatened by the facts; make sure you have backup.
- Don't overestimate your organization's ability to operationalize new tools (it will take time).
- Don't think the tool installation is the end game. There must be an evolving data schema and metadata definition effort.

- Don't think individual tool vendors who cooperate with a large organization will cooperate with one another. The instrumentation team will likely need to build a federated database.
- Don't underestimate the size of the data involved (at a granular level, 1 Gigabyte/ day may be conservative).

### 7.5.3   Objective 7: automate virtual resource management

The word *virtualization* has been overused since 2005, and it is often associated with the solution to the current datacenter crisis. Nothing could be further from the truth. Virtualization is the abstraction of the logical running application from the physical resource it requires. The popular use of virtualization entails putting many instances of an operating platform on a pooled set of resources, packing multiple platforms into less physical servers. There are several scenarios where this makes a lot of sense, such as optimizing hardware for basic developer editing and debugging instances. For high-performance applications with fluctuating demand, this is not really helpful unless real-time assessments of incoming demand can be utilized to make optimal judgments about resource usage.

The adoption problem that is facing virtualization strategies stems from a bottom-up IT-driven approach versus a top-down business-aligned approach. Furthermore, the technology is limiting in value unless it is implemented as a "virtual service-oriented platform architecture" with a dynamic operational model.

### Goals and objectives

- The large-scale theme is *changing what you use*, to increase performance, agility, and efficiency, while capping the spread of legacy infrastructure. This change must be done with minimal negative impact to teams, so virtualization is critical.
- The aim of virtualization for the NGDC is to make each layer abstracted and therefore virtual so its usage is managed dynamically, which will provide the flexibility needed to meet the requirements of the Real Time Enterprise.
- Establish the designs and processes required to abstract all of the infrastructure supply at each level for all aspects of compute, network, and storage. This goal is critical for the NGDC to evolve as new technologies and tactics become available, such as network-attached processors and specialized network appliances.
- Prepare the processes and mindset necessary toward managing IT like a utility.

### Challenges in scaling from pilot to enterprise

- *Education about virtualization:* There are many entrenched misconceptions that can lead to very strong assertions that "we already do virtualization."
- *Loss of control:* The loss of dedicated machinery for critical revenue-generating applications will cause resistance for years.
- *Shift in roles and responsibilities:* Virtualization will cause confusion in well-established roles because clear delineations of responsibilities for applications or certain hardware groupings will need to be redefined. Accountability will be an evolving topic.

## *Approach*

### Early iterations

- Find target applications that run in different work cycles (day and night) that consume considerable hardware but have similar workload types. A good example would be a set of risk applications, some of which run during the day and others that run during the night. Build a focused repurposing project that will show tangible savings that can be measured and repeated.
- Introduction of specific intermediation technology that will alleviate specific bottlenecks, such as network-attached processors that remove Java caching problems by providing hundreds of CPU cores and hundreds of gigabytes of sharable memory. The virtualization tactic that introduces these technologies will expand as the optimized operating footprints are introduced later in this chapter. Placing new technology into optimized footprints will be discussed in more detail in Chapter 8.

### Late iterations

- Introducing Infrastructure as a Service (IaaS) incrementally will ease groups into the idea of the benefits that sharing can provide for application efficiency.
- Tools will be required to facilitate the creation of IaaS. The results will be that provisioning times for new releases will be reduced from weeks to hours with enough refinement. Other benefits will include policy-based reprovisioning of hardware to meet unanticipated spikes in demand.
- Introduce more specialized appliances that relieve stress on existing infrastructure, and allow the organization to cap investment in legacy SMP machines.

## *Tool capabilities*

- The tool selection is wide-ranging from bare metal provisioning to specialized appliances that provide caching, protocol gateways, and faster access to persistence (such as solid-state disks). The key is to use tools that minimize the need to change the applications but provide positive high-impact changes in performance and efficiency while reducing complexity.
- Understand that the tool vendors chosen might not have experience integrating with one another. The service design and on-boarding teams will need to drive these integrations.

## *Best practices*

### *Do's*

- Use best of breed products, and challenge them on the use of standards where possible.
- Strive to balance positive impact with minimal application changes; aim for changes in less than 90 days to ensure scope is contained.
- Vendors need to have a culture that will support the transition.
- Dedicated tool teams are critical to success, as is education.
- Make sure that the instrumentation team is in lockstep with any tool introduction.

### *Don'ts*

- Don't underestimate resistance; some of the tools will threaten secure positions.

- Don't get blindsided. Some of the tools will incite corporate standards groups to block on grounds of security and many other reasons. Fight with facts and usage scenarios.
- Don't forget that integration is critical to success. As tools come on board, they need to be integrated, eventually into ensembles and PEDs. This is complex with huge potential payoffs but only if the tools are abstracted from application programmers.
- Don't forget troubleshooting. Abstraction means that the responsibility for trouble-shooting falls on the integration team in terms of instrumentation, testing, and the ugliest responsibility in IT—"well-written documentation."

### 7.5.4  Objective 8: run IT like a utility

Running IT like a utility has strong implications for the need to change the typical enterprise IT operational model. As mentioned in Chapter 2, the data-center has traditionally been treated as both an infinite resource and a black box cost sink that has little correlation to business revenue or growth. The operational model of a utility is different by definition. Utilities have defined capacity that must be managed, and users must pay for levels of service. Utilities must accommodate demand, and while there are times when this cannot be accomplished (e.g., brownouts), priorities apply based on policies.

Policy-driven dynamic management of supply to meet demand in real time is the vision for the IT utility. This cannot be done with changes to technology, processes, and people's roles and skills. This cannot happen overnight, but the technologies and practices mentioned in previous sections pave the way. Focused executive sponsorship, alignment of business and IT, delineated roles, and organizational changes that include new ways to view compensation are all required to realize the utility vision.

### Goals and objectives

The migration toward managing IT as a utility should be guided by the following goals:

- Responsiveness
  - Become more flexible and responsive to the dynamic needs of the business.
  - Reduce the time it takes to build and deploy new business services.
- Reduce complexity
  - Eliminate dedicated silos of data, systems, and infrastructure as they exist today, making it possible to meet changing business demands dynamically.
- Better economics
  - Get more value out of project and operational IT expenditures in both systems and personnel.
  - Reduce costs while delivering improved service that can be measured.
  - Implement and sustain predictable qualities of service that the business can rely on.

## Challenges in scaling from pilot to enterprise

The challenges described in all of the previous sections apply here. They must be dealt with collectively as the movement toward the utility gains momentum. The challenges detailed in previous sections will be summarized here for clarity.

- *Loss of control:* As the utility grows, more application owners will be exposed to the utility and will need to be handheld to create SLAs they will trust.
- *Organizational changes:* Roles and responsibilities will be changing as the utility grows. Meanwhile, the day-to-day operations must continue.
- *New hardware and processes* will be introduced—in some cases increasing the perceived complexity of the operating environment.

## Approach

The enterprise-scaling problems must be overcome through the realization of incremental success, regular publishing of fact-based findings showing improvements, education, and behavioral changes through incentives and a culture shift.

### Early iterations
- New and old operating models must coexist as the utility takes hold. That includes reporting and problem triage.
- Introduction of new technologies and processes must have sufficient isolation and fallback to prevent initial growing pain errors from "spreading" to the older, established operating model.
- Metrics and early versions of dashboards must be made available to establish baselines, especially as it relates to SLAs.
- CIO directs for each line of business must be made accountable for their contributions to the utility, be it shared services that were harvested, applications migrated, or team members that contributed to the early adaptor teams (e.g., instrumentation, service design).
- The head architect for each line of business must play an integral role in the migration process, ensuring that the line of business is targeting applications that coincide with utility growth.
- The migration of utility services must be aligned with clients that need them. Giving each service an initial need to exist based on a specific application need reinforces the alignment strategy.
- All of the new teams mentioned in the previous sections—service design, on-boarding, instrumentation—must treat every step toward a utility as part of their professional mission. Compensation must be structured accordingly.

### Late iterations
- Integrated dashboards reporting on the progress toward QoE (performance, availability, efficiency, cost reductions, or avoidances) are key activities that must dominate as the utility model matures.
- The early enablement teams need to be converted to disciplines that are invested in with tools, official roles, and compensation structure.

- Compensation models that support utility evolution must be instituted top down—no exceptions. At the IT executive level, specific ties to the QoE pillars must be codified: cost avoidance, cost reduction, performance, reliability, time to market, and efficiency.
- Application migration and utility evolution should be tied to a portfolio management strategy. The architecture maturity should be reassessed as the utility becomes tangible and mainstream in the organization.
- As the initiative grows from pilots to large-scale migration, it is important to leverage external knowledge and skills to accelerate the rate of change and keep momentum going. The use of consultants in the beginning of the stages can help risk mitigation. Consultants should be used as advisors, not managers.
- Consultants are not the permanent answer to this kind of change. They should be used to only push the change. It is critical for full-time employees to take ownership in this initiative with appropriate incentives, accountability, and responsibility.

## Tool capabilities

The key to tool capabilities in a utility model is the guiding principle that managing IT as a utility means managing IT as a business. New technologies are an investment that must be constantly considered against the maturity model and the current understanding of the business (i.e., growth, revenue, demand, threats). The degree to which abstraction is achieved through utility construction will determine the ease of new-technology introduction.

## Best practices

### Do's

- Structure compensation to meet the challenges, skewing bonuses as a major part of compensation is necessary. This has tended to be more of an investment bank philosophy, but it needs to be broadened. Progressive cost reduction and cost avoidance can fuel very compelling compensation models.
- Integration is critical; it is the price one pays for flexibility and should be considered a strategic play that affects competitiveness.
- Deep and wide instrumentation is required, as is correlation of diverse data sets. All of this must be done to ensure that results are actively published.
- This journey is hard and fraught with setbacks, so educate, encourage, and paint the vision.
- Silos must be broken down.

### Don'ts

- Don't forget that this effort is as much a political fight as a design and engineering challenge.
- Don't assume vendor relationships will be the same, as some of the vendors in the RTI space are smaller and will have different drivers than large do-it-all vendors.

## 7.6   Execute

The activities in execution entail a combination of design, implementation, and integration. These activities are very iterative in nature and therefore have been combined to focus on the main intent, which is to deliver a set of operating environments that facilitate the migration toward the NGDC operating model that will be detailed in Chapter 8.

## 7.6.1   Objective 9: optimize supply footprint

In Chapters 4 and 5, the concepts of ensembles, PEDs, and specialized processing container-based racks were introduced. They represent an evolution in design because ensembles provide Fit-for-Purpose operating platforms that align with workload type, while PEDs integrate ensembles so heavily collaborating applications and services with diverse workload types can communicate optimally. Scaling ensembles and PEDs across the enterprise is yet another difficult challenge that must be undertaken.

Ensembles will require new organizational behavior if they are to be successfully utilized. Ensembles are integrated to provide a set of functional capabilities with guaranteed operational results. The guarantees are structured to work within certain constraints. Ensembles are delivered as products, which mean that the degree of testing and documentation is much higher than financial services IT organizations are used to producing. The advantage of the product approach combined with abstraction and virtualization is that as advances in technologies occur (e.g., new appliances, improved FPGA chips, and greater multicore chip capacity), ensembles can be updated with less potential negative impact to the consuming applications.

### Goals and objectives

The goals in creating *optimized supply footprints* are in complete alignment with the goals of the *utility operating model* and the NGDC. They are worth listing briefly here:

- Prevent overengineered solutions that waste energy, floor space, money, and personnel, and rarely provide the consistent performance needed.
- Drive a Fit-for-Purpose approach to building, acquiring, and integrating solutions that optimize workload-type operations.
- Lead with business requirements that are the best way to ensure that IT becomes a strategic arm of the business.
- Drive an SLA mentality throughout the enterprise that defines value for differentiated levels of service.
- Build an infrastructure that promotes agility, enabling the business to respond as market and other driving forces change.
- Harvest institutional knowledge as manifested in business problem domain designs and business components to extend functionality, leveraging investment.
- Increase speed to market by reducing design, integration, build, and deployment times.
- Reduce technology risk by leveraging well-integrated and tested repeatable solutions to recurring application patterns.
- Provide a platform that is better able to quickly leverage technology innovations with minimal disruption to consuming business services.

## Challenges in scaling across the enterprise

- In addition to challenges in all of the other sections in this chapter, the most significant challenge is instituting a product culture that will drive the development and sustainment of PEDs and ensembles. The product culture must fit into a bank's operating environment and requires a disciplined investment strategy where ensembles are planned, integrated, and tested rigorously.
- As already mentioned, there are many organizational challenges that must be overcome to scale.
- The degree of investment is larger than one would expect of a typical project because the reach of ensembles is far greater than even the most complex project.

## Approach

The general approach is to build on early pilot projects that used a variety of the newer tools. Establish the first ensembles from these projects by extending their capabilities to appeal to multiple consumers.

### Early iterations

- Build the first ensembles to accommodate dynamic service management, using a service broker, a caching engine, and a basic application server. This will establish a core asset, the low latency ensemble that can be used to build other ensembles.
- Add specialized appliances to appeal to a certain workload type with special operating characteristics.
- Engage the services design team and product steering group to flesh out the product road map so the proposed ensemble types can get the necessary feedback.

### Late iterations

- Expand the ensemble workload types to handle numerical processing, information integration, and complex transactions as the steering group sees fit.
- Establish the first PEDs as soon as multiple ensembles are operational and can be used to operate an application with diverse behavior or multiple diverse services.

## Tool capabilities

The entire suite of tools has a wide range of capabilities that are all designed to promote dynamic resource allocation based on demand. These technologies will be explored further in Chapter 8.

## Best practices

### Do's

- Get advice and instruction on creating a product development culture. A good source is the Software Engineering Institute, which has authored a book on the subject and offers on-site instruction.[1]

---

[1]Clements P, et al. *Software Product Lines: Practices and Patterns*. Addison-Wesley Professional; 2001, August 30 [SEI Series in Software Engineering].

- Ensure that the vendors you choose will cooperate by giving on-site education and will participate in joint design sessions with other vendors. Expedite the NDA and trial process so progress is not bogged down by "normal" legal timeframes. Executives need to push this.
- Making the labs accessible to consumers is critical, but safeguards must be in place.
- The special discipline teams must be very active in this entire process.

### Don'ts

- Don't be timid; move applications that matter so when change occurs, executives actually care.
- Don't underestimate vendor issues.
- Don't let instrumentation take a back seat.
- Don't let consumers try to piecemeal the ensemble implementations; they are delivered as a unit.

# 7.7    Sustain

Sustaining the RTI platform and the operating model is the key to long-term success. This mandates that the measurements of the environment are actively used in future planning, that investments in IT are viewed from a portfolio management perspective where ROI is gauged, and that investments are subject to governance. This requires a shift in thinking about IT. IT transcends its cost center status and becomes a strategic enabler of the business.

## 7.7.1    Objective 10: manage IT like a portfolio

Portfolio management is the discipline required to ensure that investments are guided by specific business goals. The guiding principle for IT portfolio management is that every dollar spent on IT is an investment. IT competes for investment dollars in an organization with every other department (sales, marketing, and client services). When a business makes an investment in IT, the business expects some or all of the following.

### Goals and objectives

- Increase ability to achieve revenue generation, improved efficiency, or risk reduction.
- Greater agility so the business can respond to market and regulatory pressures faster.
- Insight into the alignment of IT and the achievement of business goals so the correlation among IT investments and revenue, business growth, and profit can be understood.
- Transparency of reporting so the impact can be measured and value can be traced across all stakeholder groups.

## Challenges in scaling from pilot to enterprise

The major challenge is the integration of information from dozens of established sources of data that are embedded in production readiness processes, CMDBs, and specialized inventory databases that are used by a single department. None of these data sources were designed to work together, and they do not have the staff or investment to go beyond their current scope.

If these sources are not tapped, then a duplicate entry effort will occur and that will doom the project to fail. The new approach will be perceived as a burden with no advantages to the execution teams.

## Approach

A vision on what portfolio management can do for the business is essential, and executive buy-in is critical. This vision should include the fact that all current repositories will be integrated to maximize return and minimize disruption to current operating procedures. The vision must include a commitment to minimize dual entry of information.

### Early iterations

- Establish an architecture governance team that will establish architecture review guidelines, participate in service design, and assist the portfolio management team.
- Establish a portfolio management team that will develop a discipline and drive the ensuing activities.
- Get the top burning questions key executives would like to know about their asset base. These top questions will turn into use cases that drive the taxonomy, vendor choices, and integration. They will also serve as the test case for executives when initial pilots are shown.
- Get the nomenclature and taxonomy correct. It must be clear to all how services, applications, patterns, ensemble PEDs, applications, and components relate to one another. Questions such as "What is idealized?" "What is realized?" "What elements contain others?" must be codified. How all of the IT elements relate to business terms is also important to define. This includes business value chain components, lines of business, and other key business terms that are utilized in applications and services.
- Find a tool and start working with the taxonomy so design nomenclature can be influenced.

### Late iterations

- Enact the strategy that includes integration with CMDBs, code repositories, and measurement databases. This is a multiyear project.
- Ensure that road maps, application portfolio migrations, architectural prescriptions, and patterns are all included.
- Make the repository the link across stakeholders for information about services and platforms; include service reviews and synopses of service performance in measurable terms that compare against SLAs.
- Make this repository the facilitator of the internal IT marketplace where the currency to provide and consume services is *trust* because the data is transparent.
- Ensure that IT governance and portfolio management are established disciplines that influence product development, design, and discussions about IT investment.

## Tool capabilities

- The portfolio management tool must have an extensible database and taxonomy that can be used to accept and disseminate information from dozens of databases.
- It must expose an import and export API. Export and import capabilities must include spreadsheet compatibility.
- It must have a rich reporting engine, with the ability to craft special reports.
- It must be able to hold links to other repositories.
- Ideally the tool will have visualization capabilities to provide dynamic views of service relationships (all the users of ensemble X; all the BVC services enabled by PED Y).

## Best practices

The key to portfolio management success is multilayered communication to different stakeholders that occurs monthly. The entering of information cannot be onerous or require extended duplicate entry. Some of the best practices discussed here are derived from the discussion of portfolio management and IT governance in Chapter 4.

### Do's

- Quarterly strategy reviews should be held by the CIO to determine progress to plan on all investment tracks. Architecture and portfolio management groups should arrange supporting material for these reviews. These reviews should feed the strategy process for the CIO and the CIO direct reports.
- Monthly application user demographic reports should be produced for all applications in all LOBs to understand changes in demand and its potential effects on the strategy.
- A developer university internal site should be created as a repository for best practices, changes to technology, how to's on RTI, asset contribution, architecture reviews, and so on.
- The portfolio management repository should be used to show reports indicating contributions by LOB to the architecture, including the tracking of service consumption and contribution. Incentives should be structured from CIO directs on down to align with use of the asset base and contributions to RTI.
- Architecture reviews should be injected into the normal development process to accelerate best practices on RTI adoption. The Software Engineering Institute has excellent references on how to create performance reviews.[2]

### Don'ts

- Don't assume the organization will naturally adopt portfolio management. Despite its incredible usefulness, it is a very hard sell because the start-up investment seems high to those who can't envision its potential.
- Don't assume you can run an NGDC without portfolio management and governance; the technology is not enough. Just invoking process with technology is not enough. The processes need grounding, and the investment in technology needs transparent accountability.

[2]Bass L, et al. *Software Architecture in Practice*. Addison-Wesley Professional; 2003, April 19 *[SEI Series in Software Engineering]*.

### 7.7.2 Objective 11: implement predictive IT

Predictive IT is a maturity level that eventually needs to be reached within an NGDC to efficiently manage a virtualized operating environment dynamically and reliably. Predictive IT requires that self-learning components develop an understanding of normal behavior, automatically determine behavioral relationships, present proactive information, and then build a library of self-learned, adaptive problem models. Self-healing components leverage the self-learned, adaptive problem models to detect improper operations and initiate policy-based corrective action without disrupting the IT environment. Corrective action could involve a product altering its own state or effecting changes in other components in the environment. The infrastructure service as a whole becomes more resilient, since the day-to-day operations are less likely to fail.

#### Goals and objectives

- Manage complexity to deliver a balanced QoE.
- Enhance the ability for IT to manage SLAs effectively.
- Prevent problems from occurring by predicting their occurrence.

#### Challenges in scaling from pilot to enterprise

- Purchase a tool that has learning and predictive capabilities. It must be installed and trained over a period of time.
- The biggest challenge beyond picking the tool is getting the instrumentation team to train it and then getting operations to use it and trust it.
- Once the tool has proven its worth, operations needs to incorporate processes to react to alerts with well-defined actions. This is a nontrivial change and a departure from the current operational model. Comprehensive education will need to be provided. In addition, it is recommended to review roles and responsibilities, as the traditional definitions will not account for predictive tools.

#### Approach

The emerging tools that enable predictive IT will break down silos effectively early on, so once the tool is installed, there is typically just two to three months of data collection, dashboard building, and alert tailoring based on roles. Enterprise rollout is simplified in such cases. It is a matter of showing early success and then indicating how teams can be part of the initiative by allowing the tool to collect data.

#### Tool capabilities

This problem domain is emerging, and thus the functionality will increase over time. But there is some guideline functionality to consider.

- Correlation of disparate sources.
- A set of learning tactics such as neural networks, genetic algorithms, and fuzzy logic will likely be applied and will also likely be reluctantly disclosed by the vendor.

- An expectation that the learning is continuous, so new patterns can be discerned over time.
- Tailored alerts and dashboards.
- Integration to dynamic execution tools to facilitate automated actions should be strongly considered.

### Best practices

#### Do's

- Utilize the vendor heavily to get the setup correct.
- Pick areas that are problematic so the tool can be exercised quickly to prove value.

#### Don'ts

- Don't think this is magic; it requires the instrumentation team to be involved with the vendor and operations to ensure that events and problems are being interpreted properly.
- Don't underestimate the work required on the visual arrangement of the dashboards on a per-role basis. User interface is critical here, and that is an area not normally addressed for operations.

## 7.8 Objective 12: realize the next generation datacenter

It is clear that reaching the full benefits of NGDC will take years in a typical global financial services enterprise. It is no surprise that once a reasonable amount of this work is accomplished, the business realities will have changed. The good news is that all of the capabilities and techniques required to build the NGDC will help the business adapt to changes. The NGDC is not an isolated end goal but a vision that encompasses IT alignment with the business to become an active strategic ally to the business, not just a forgettable cost center.

As can be seen from the objectives in this chapter, it is a lofty goal. But it is also clear from Chapter 5 that there are techniques that can be leveraged that will make this possible. Technologies are moving in a direction to make the NGDC vision possible, and they will most likely be associated with the new buzzwords of 2009, which are *cloud computing* and *RTI*. Even as the technologies change and business reacts to new driving forces, the objectives described in this chapter provide a cultural, perceptual, and behavioral framework that can be used as a strategic tool to move the NGDC vision along as an organization sees fit.

Since NGDC is a long-term vision that is achievable, it would be useful to have a relevance test constantly applied so whenever the NGDC investment seems too daunting, its power can be put into perspective.

An example of such a relevance test was set forth by one of the founding fathers of the modern computer and the clear visionary of Artificial Intelligence, Alan Turing. In 1950 he wrote a paper titled "Computing Machinery and Intelligence," in which he proposed a test to determine if a machine has reached a level of sophistication that could be called "intelligent." The essence of the test is as follows. Place the tester in a room with two terminals, and have the tester converse via the two terminals, one at a time. One of the conversation partners is a human, and the other is a computer. If the tester cannot tell the difference between the two conversations, then the machine has passed.

# 8 Key strategies and technologies

## Key Points

The IT service delivery model needs to accommodate the rapid changes that the financial services industry continues to experience and balance user experience, cost, and efficiency.

The IT service delivery model must manage the degree of implementation volatility in the datacenter that is caused by the need to respond to changes. Traditional attempts to do so have contributed to datacenter sprawl.

IT needs to progress through a set of infrastructure maturity phases in order to create an aligned service delivery model that enables the RTE.

The first three chapters framed an argument that financial services has undergone significant change in the last ten years and the financial crisis that came to a head in 2008 will now force more changes to financial services companies, including some fundamental shifts in business models. In the face of the new economic and regulatory environment, IT must be able to align with business in order to become the strategic enabler.

## 8.1 The IT service delivery model and managing implementation volatility

The case has been made that IT tried to manage constant change, and the sum of all those attempts has led to the current difficulties in most financial services datacenters: sprawl, runaway costs, inefficiencies, operational complexity, and a constant scramble to maintain user experience expectations. So while IT delivers service to the business now, the cost of that service is not reasonably correlated to the business growth in revenue or profit. IT must change its *service delivery model* (SDM) to be more aligned, more responsive, and traceable in terms of investment. The IT SDM is the sum of all methods IT uses to design, implement, and operate the IT digital supply chain for the business. IT must change its service delivery model so it can manage the inevitable implementation volatility in the datacenter better.

Some changes to the IT SDM have been tried, including the outsourcing of development teams and some operational services. These changes were driven by cost, and the results have varied greatly, but they have not generally been viewed as positive due to the inability of IT to deliver consistency. The fundamental issue with this response to business change is that it doesn't directly

doi: 10.1016/B978-0-12-374956-7.00008-5

address agility and alignment. Under ideal circumstances these IT SDM changes have the potential to advance the IT operational maturity model toward a more stabilized state, but given the degree of business change and the fact that outsourcing of operational functions typically requires fairly rigid contracts, agility was rarely addressed. In the past decade, financial services business changes have caused applications to grow rapidly or have forced new applications to be implemented quickly. The growth in all hardware resources to accommodate such business change often outpaces datacenter planning. Holistic planning to accommodate the consequential volatility in datacenter configurations rarely occurred, as that would require focused design discussions with the business, CIO, and CTO organizations. Volatility in the datacenter is caused when the need to add new equipment outpaces the ability of IT to holistically plan how to accommodate that need. The result of such volatility is that development teams and datacenter teams each try to find a way to manage the impact of change separately. As discussed in Chapter 2 and summarized later in this chapter, the techniques used by each team can work disjointedly with the other, guaranteeing datacenter sprawl, driving up costs, and making it harder to achieve performance requirements.

The management of volatility is nothing new to IT; developers and architects have been struggling with this for decades, at the scale of applications or smaller scales. Datacenter staff has also managed volatility by organizing the datacenter based on device and server types. Neither effort included the concerns of the other group. In the last few years the development efforts to manage volatility have led to Service Oriented Architecture (SOA). SOA is part of the evolutionary path to managing volatility that IT professionals have discovered while creating solutions. Table 8.1 shows the degrees of volatility.

Table 8.1 shows the progression of thinking about how to manage volatility from a software architecture point of view.[1] Notice that as the progression toward a more stable workload unit increases, the scope of concern migrates to issues of distributed processing (components and beyond). Once issues of distribution become a concern, they are no longer just a simple software problem, as network issues enter the problem domain. As software architects struggled to manage volatility, datacenter personnel found ways to manage the constant change of adding new disks to specific application platforms by introducing abstractions for disk storage through the use of SAN and NAS. This abstraction, while useful, affected network design and eventually the floor design of the datacenter itself.

The techniques to manage volatility in either the software or datacenter domain involved the tactics of abstraction, containment, and isolation; in some cases more than one tactic was used. Those tactics are still viable. The only difference for the migration to RTI is that all aspects of delivering service (software, servers, SAN, network) must be considered holistically. This holistic view is the only way to achieve RTI, which will balance user experience,

---

[1]Coad P. et al. *Object Oriented Analysis,* 2nd ed. Prentice Hall PTR: Yourdon Press Computing Series; October 1, 1990.

Table 8.1 Managing Volatility

| Stability | Software Workload Unit | Volatility Example | Tactic | Remedies |
|---|---|---|---|---|
| Least Stable | Interfaces | The data exchanged between the interfaces needs to change because of new products and processes. | Abstraction | Abstract the interface to minimize attribute definitions; use self-describing lists. |
| | Business Processes | The order of operation needs to change often. | Isolation | Divorce sequence from functionality, encapsulate in objects. |
| | Business Data | Personal contact information has grown from two phone numbers to multiple e-mails and instant messaging addresses. | Containment Abstraction | Encapsulate in objects, provide coarse data sets. |
| | Business Objects | Object interaction can explode as abstraction and intermediation are used. | Containment Abstraction | Contain interobject collaborations through component orchestrator. |
| | Business Components | Business components tend to move to different machines. | Containment Abstraction | Expose coarse services; containers provide system services. |
| | Business Services | Business services encompass more than one application, with internal and external security look-ups and issues of failure notification. | Abstraction Containment | Ensure coarse-grain definition, robust look-up service, versions, and use SAML. For failover need special lookups. |
| Most Stable | Business Services Platform | Ensure that workload is optimized on fit-for-purpose operating platforms, while ensuring that communications are not compromised. | Abstraction Containment | Abstract the hardware and infrastructure to include issues of proximity of location and emphasizing the *transparency* of distributed processing. Use PEDs to optimize communication. |

cost, and efficiency. Given that premise, it is worth reviewing the progression toward RTI that has been detailed thus far.

## 8.2    Review of the RTI migration

This chapter focuses on the key strategies that will allow an organization to move toward a Real Time Enterprise, enabled through a suite of key technologies that transform the IT service delivery model. It is worth recapping what the book has conveyed so far in preparing for the strategy and core technologies discussion.

In Chapter 1, the changes to the financial services landscape were discussed and led to the conclusion that financial services firms must rethink at least some of their business models. In Chapter 2, the constant changes in financial services these past ten years was reviewed, because those changes had significant effects on the current state of the datacenter. In Chapter 3, the case was made for financial services firms to migrate toward operating as an RTE in order to make the necessary changes in the business models. Migrating toward an RTE requires a Real Time Infrastructure that enables the IT digital supply chain to be the analog of the business value chain. Moving toward RTI necessitates some fundamental rethinking about designing, implementing, and operating IT services. To that end, Chapters 3 through 7 demonstrated how to do the following:

- Align the *digital supply chain* to the *business value chain* to achieve common goals
- Design services that will make an RTE achievable
- Implement Fit-for-Purpose RTI solutions based on standardized playbooks and building blocks
- Managing the programs for scale and change on an enterprise level

With all of the building blocks in hand, it is now time to turn to the challenge raised in Chapters 1 through 3: *How does a financial services firm change its IT service delivery model?* The holistic answer is the Next Generation Datacenter. It is necessary to explore the implications, choices, and foundations of the NGDC.

## 8.3    An NGDC direction

The Next Generation Datacenter cannot be limited by the concrete walls of a particular facility or even the firewalls of the enterprise. Today's business trends drive toward the integration of content from different sources inside and outside the enterprise; this trend will be mirrored by IT, as the raw materials for the digital supply chain will be derived from a multitude of sources. The composition of these services will vary based on business policies, the magnitude and urgency of demand, response time, availability, and security, each of which comprise factors that must be considered in real time as infrastructure sourcing decisions and tradeoffs are made.

The reason IT needs to expand the digital supply chain outside of its immediate control is related to the economics of providing the necessary services at a cost that can be correlated to business growth in revenue and profit. In a changing market there are always going to be service peaks. The question business and IT must resolve together is the most feasible way to service those peaks. If the workload characteristics are analyzed by business lines and their associated value chain components and functions, it is likely that some peaks will be discovered that are periodic and predictable.

A good example is the need to have extra resources available at the end of each month to produce client statements. There is no doubt that this workload is critical for a two- or three-day period, with backup processors assigned to the task in the case of a large-scale interruption. The question for IT and the business in this new market landscape is whether all of the investments required to ensure timely delivery of these statements should be held in the organizations datacenter. These investments include all the costs associated with creating the statements including hardware, software, personnel, power, cooling, floor space, disaster recovery allowances, and many other factors.

The statements example just explained has many implications if their production were to be moved to another facility. Some of the implications include security and confidentiality of the data and the resources required to move the raw data to another facility and get the printable versions back. Other concerns would include the guarantees for timeliness and the long-term cost model. None of these are trivial issues, but given the continued rise in costs for a datacenter, the discussions and analysis should be strongly considered (Figure 8.1).

Any kind of the preceding analyses requires that business and IT focus on the business value chain workload characteristics that would take daily, monthly, quarterly, and other special processing lifecycles into account. These workload types need to run on platforms optimized for those workload characteristics, which have been defined as ensembles. Multiple ensembles may be required to match the total set of workload characteristics in an application. The ensembles within an application will likely have a high degree of collaboration, so their communication needs to be optimized. PEDs were introduced as the mechanisms that would enable optimized communication. The allocation of resources within ensembles and PEDs would be managed dynamically in real time based on business demand and defined business policy. This combination of workload optimization, communication optimization, and resource allocation optimization combine to respect the reality of IT physics that encompasses all of the energy involved in servicing the work necessary to provide a service. Business and IT need to work together to understand how best to service the business demand in through RTI so IT becomes the enabler of business strategy.

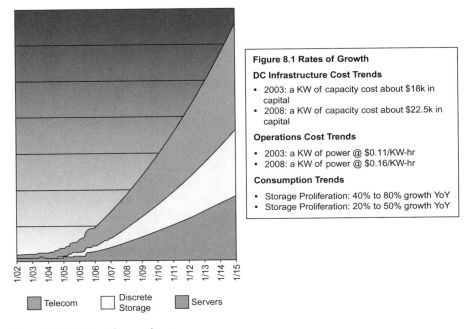

Figure 8.1 Rates of Growth

DC Infrastructure Cost Trends

- 2003: a KW of capacity cost about $18k in capital
- 2008: a KW of capacity cost about $22.5k in capital

Operations Cost Trends

- 2003: a KW of power @ $0.11/KW-hr
- 2008: a KW of power @ $0.16/KW-hr

Consumption Trends

- Storage Proliferation: 40% to 80% growth YoY
- Storage Proliferation: 20% to 50% growth YoY

Telecom    Discrete Storage    Servers

**Figure 8.1** Projected growth rates.

Within the enterprise walls there are many possibilities for delivery of infrastructure as long as business demands are met. Therefore, previously discussed concepts of PEDs that contain all the resources necessary for a particular type of workload can be delivered inside a single datacenter, in a shipping container at a warehouse, or at an alternate datacenter location that may or may not be owned by the enterprise. Realizing the capabilities of PEDs that can transcend the walls of an enterprise requires that an organization reach an elevated level of infrastructure maturity that will be outlined in this chapter.

## 8.4   Evolving into an NGDC

The bottom line is that an organization needs to evolve through several phases of infrastructure maturity, creating enough sustainable processes, skills, and infrastructure building blocks to manage an RTI first. Once that has been accomplished, the base has been set to manage IT as a *utility*. Once IT is managed as a utility, it is possible to consider managing IT as a *cloud*. Once a cloud is established, IT and the business can plan transformative business strategies that include using clouds outside of the firewall.

In the economic climate following the financial crisis of 2008, there will not be large investments available to take a "green field" approach, moving to a cloud from scratch. Instead, the use of the techniques mentioned in Chapters 4–7 will provide IT to migrate to various cloud strategies utilizing current datacenters.

The progression emphasized in the playbooks of Chapter 6 and large enterprise scale change approaches of Chapter 7 are part of a sequence of containment and isolation tactics that have been practiced by architects for over a decade at the scale of applications, services, and subsystems. The major difference in this evolution is that there is a drive to transform the datacenter top down. That top-down transformation used the abstraction tactic in addition to isolation and containment; the combination of those three tactics was described in Chapters 4 and 5. The key premise of the change is that you must respect the fact that critical systems are running every day to generate revenue and growth, even as the imperatives of transformation must proceed. This kind of migration must take into account current state operating models and application constructs, which means that when applications are profiled, tactics must be employed to consider large monolithic applications or those that are divided into subsystems. It will be important to pay attention to how applications in the current environment are constructed.

In order to evolve through those phases, IT must be able to create a series of building blocks that will form the basis for a migration to RTI and beyond. As mentioned throughout the book, these building blocks are a combination of process, technology, and people. The people and processes support the migration of applications and services through these various maturity models. These applications will be operated on an evolving set of technology that will mature to the vision of a cloud over a period of a few years.

## 8.4.1  NGDC technical building block taxonomy

A number of new terms have been introduced in this book. The terms have been defined, and pictures have been used to supplement the definitions. One term is new here: the *subsystem*. The subsystem is included because migration and evolution must respect the current state and work with existing applications. Some applications are monolithic, while others are broken into subsystems that do not have objects and components. This taxonomy section will briefly define the terms and show how these terms relate to one another.

### Definitions

*Application:* A collection of software systems that work together to facilitate one or more BVC steps of one or more BVCs. The collective systems are considered as a "unit" or "package" and are branded and managed as such.

*Subsystem:* Part of a complete application that can be separately compiled and deployed. It is not a service, as it is not generally discoverable. It often is composed of separately created components that it has control over. Traditionally, subsystems were created to run on separate hardware (e.g., they would be deployed in multitier environments, with each subsystem being a recognizable tier or functional block).

*Component:* A component is the smallest deployable piece of software. A component is a concrete implementation of an area of a system. It is important to note that components are expected to be deployable as a whole but cannot run independently. Components depend on an operating environment. Components are designed to produce predictable outcomes or defined errors. Component capabilities can be measured (e.g., various performance criteria).

*Service:* A service is a clearly defined autonomous operation whose definition is stated by a service contract that can be discovered and deciphered in a networked distributed environment through programmatic means. A service will have defined service levels that it will guarantee. This implies that a service must be instrumented and has facilities to allow operational parameters to change in order to meet its agreements. Services are defined to be coarse-grained; hiding the interactions among its constituent parts (e.g., components, applications, subsystems, or other services) is required to fulfill the request.

*Framework:* An instantiation of an architecture allowing components to be designed to interoperate. Two or more frameworks often need to be composed in order to fulfill the needs of an application.

*Pattern:* A pattern is an idealized design describing a set of communicating objects or classes that can be customized to solve a general design problem in a particular context. This problem tends to be recurring in a domain, thus the desire to abstract its essence in order to allow reuse.

*Ensemble:* An ensemble is a defined collaboration of components that solves a specific business problem. The ensemble defines the types of components involved and a pattern of interaction, along with driving forces, constraints, and tradeoff decisions. A component ensemble is a realized instance (at a point in time) of an architectural pattern, where the requirements for that pattern have been addressed by measurable capabilities.

*Process Execution Destinations:* PEDs are self-contained operating containers that can be placed in the datacenter with minimal disruption to existing operations. PEDs optimize the processing footprint by providing an adequate resource pool for ensembles to operate while meeting fluctuating demand.

## Taxonomy relationships

The following is a summary of many of the concepts covered in Chapters 4 through 7.

- Applications can be decomposed into several workload types characterized by patterns.
- Applications may be naturally decomposed into subsystems only, but if they are, those subsystems can be decomposed into patterns.
- Patterns are ideal designs that aggregate ideal components with specific rules of interaction.
- Patterns are ideal blueprints that guide the design of ensembles that optimally process specific workload types.
- Services abstract the details of interaction between applications, components, or other services.
- In some cases services can be used to isolate parts of an application and expose it for use to other applications.

- Applications will likely be described by more than one pattern and thus will be optimized if it is run on more than one ensemble.
- Ensembles are housed in PEDs that optimize interensemble communication and provide a pool of resources that these multiple ensembles can share to meet unexpected peak volume.
- PEDs can optimize the total workload of applications, interapplication communication. The details of the communication and all hardware configurations are abstracted from other applications. Optimizations to improve workload and interensemble communication are contained and isolated from other applications. Increased network utilization within a PED will not affect applications, services, or components outside of that PED.

### 8.4.2   Implications of the taxonomy on service delivery

The taxonomy relationships show a clear progression of abstraction, containment, and isolation. Ensembles and PEDs are an evolution toward a service delivery model that can meet the needs of the business, providing more flexibility, because the critical design principle of the service design contract is utilized. A service contract enforces behavior on the consumer and provider, essentially respecting a marketplace view of service; the consumer asks for a certain level of service, and the provider must deliver it. This notion of a service contract is at the heart of creating an aligned Service Delivery Framework (SDF). The SDF must consistently overcome all of the inherent problems that datacenters have encountered when trying to delivery service. But the movement toward a new model of SDF that will migrate toward an NGDC must be done incrementally.

PEDs provide the chance to place the new NGDC platform into an *existing* datacenter as a focused pilot; there is no need for a new datacenter to start this process. PEDs are the tactical lever required to enact the RTI strategy; without the PEDs, many of the RTI goals will not be achieved. PED design introduces the often overlooked aspect of IT physics that include the efficient use of energy and the optimal communication between disparate workload types. Without the use of PEDs, ensembles that must heavily collaborate might be placed in arbitrary parts of the datacenter, using some physical resources in the more traditional datacenter deployment method. When PED resources are managed dynamically to handle real-time fluctuations in demand and have tools that can accurately measure usage and predict failure, they become the basis for an RTI that can be managed as a utility.

## 8.5   Key strategies

### 8.5.1   IT service delivery evolution

As stated, the IT service delivery model must change. It is important to show the levels of maturity that should be considered in this change. Figure 8.2 shows

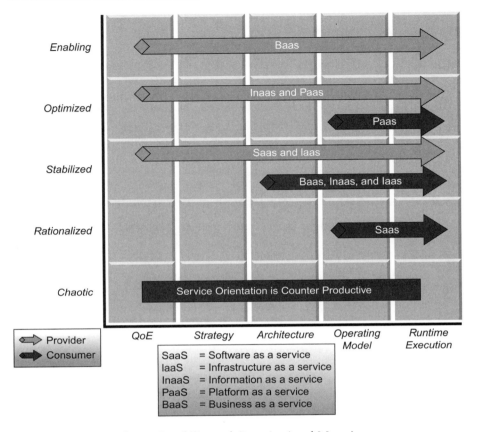

**Figure 8.2** Service Delivery Capability and Organizational Maturity

maturity along a variety of aspects such as operating model and runtime execution that were explored in the maturity model discussion in section 5.3.9 of Chapter 5.

The key concepts portrayed in this picture are that business value increases only if IT can competently deliver more abstracted services to the business.

- Each organization is different in their maturity level across these aspects and the level of capability affects what service delivery models can be adopted.
- Of particular note in this diagram is the fact that the capabilities for a consumer of delivery services have less stringent requirements than for a provider, which could encourage an entry strategy based on consuming SaaS.
- Nonetheless the diagram indicates that being a consumer of these delivery models does not come for free. It is unfeasible to be a consumer of (SaaS) Software as a Service, (e.g., consuming an expense report generator service) if the consumer infrastructure is so chaotic, that the user cannot be guaranteed of reliable results.
- It is clear that certain levels of maturity must be reached to realize the success of consuming or providing any service, even if providing this service is strictly internal.

Many scenarios are worth considering.

- Providing IaaS infrastructure as a service is useful to smooth the fluctuations in demand so user experience for client-facing applications can be consistent, while keeping costs contained.
- Consuming SaaS for nonstrategic, non-revenue-generating applications creates the possibility that these services can be removed from an organization's datacenter, reducing power costs and floor utilization, reassigning personnel to strategic initiatives, and stalling the need to build a new datacenter.
- Given the new business model for many financial services firms, it may make more sense to offer the considerable investment in risk analysis platforms to emerging hedge funds as a business service platform (BaaS).[2] In fact, this business model may be necessary to enact in order to capture new revenue streams, given the new regulatory environment.

As important as providing IaaS is, the cost savings in consuming SaaS for a large global organization can be enormous, especially since the target applications do not generate revenue. The third scenario, BaaS, represents the chance for IT to become an enabler of business strategy.

The adoption axis shows the tactical levels of maturity that must be achieved. The ability to sell business as a service will depend on that maturity, although in the scenario shown in Figure 8.2, an intense focus by a business line could provide such a service, so that business line need not wait for the organization to catch up, provided that certain aspects of the global infrastructure (e.g., network, security) will not impede reliable operation.

## 8.5.2  Service delivery models

There is a level of infrastructure maturity required to reach the delivery models shown in Figure 8.2. These infrastructure maturity levels can only be achieved through improvements in all five aspects of the maturity level. As those aspects are addressed, three broad levels of infrastructure maturity can be achieved. The following is a description of those maturity levels.

### Real Time Infrastructure (RTI)

An organization must achieve some level of RTI in at least one business line in order to start the migration toward an RTE. Grids have been implemented since 1998 in commercial enterprises, financial services being one of the heavier users. Though this technology has been around for some time, there is considerable confusion over the term, so to provide some clarity, it can be described as a pool of networked resources that distributes processing across a distributed infrastructure. The problem domains to do so are varied.

---

[2]Bishop T. Enterprise IT as a marketplace—infrastructure as a service, *Network World*. <http://www.networkworld.com/community/node/34497>;. Accessed 27.10.2008.

- *Improve Performance:* Solve complex computational problems in a fraction of the time to meet tight operational timeframe requirements.
- *Improve Overall Server Efficiency:* (i.e., server utilization) Share common resources across multiple workloads.
- *Improve IT Resiliency:* Reduce the impact of server failures.

What had started out as a definition of grid has now moved to the need to consider an RTI, which is a logical model for how the grid infrastructure operates. The essentials of grid technology are a foundation of the NGDC. As initial grid implementations evolved into isolated grids, it became clear that grids as initially implemented are not an end unto themselves, and much more is required to satisfy enterprise-level business demand.

The potential for grid computing is only realized when all of the principles of the NGDC design approach are applied to the underlying infrastructure. The NGDC design approach produces an abstracted *logical model* of the grid called RTI. RTI aligns the enterprise's business demands with IT resource allocation and scales services based on business metrics and priorities. The NGDC logical RTI design framework provides dynamic and automated provisioning, configuration management, and real-time metering and runtime control of application platforms and services across the physical and virtual infrastructure. The NGDC RTI transcends the historical association of grids with batch workloads because the NGDC RTI design approach is dynamic, extensible, and *application agnostic*. The NGDC logical RTI design unlocks the potential for grid computing, stopping the tendency for organizational inertia to continue the creation project grid silos.

## Managing IT like a utility

When you think of RTI, you are designing an environment that will convert to a utility when properly managed. This is not just about computational needs but about storage and network bandwidth utilization. The idea of a utility has been around for centuries, whether speaking in ancient times of Roman sewers or more recently of electrical power or telephone. There are universal attributes of any utility that are worth reviewing; they are available to anyone who is entitled to use it, and the utility is never designed such that all potential consumers may use it simultaneously. Instead, the utility relies on statistical averages for concurrent demand and throttling mechanisms for those rare occurrences where historic peaks are exceeded. When viewed from this perspective, *IT utility* becomes more than a collection of technologies; it becomes a business model.

The concept of an IT utility as just described is quite simple; but its creation and operation are not. It requires more than the simple resource sharing capability of grids, as it must now take into account a much larger universe of business workload demands, various processing paradigms, and all aspects of IT service delivery. Using a simple analogy to an electric utility, grids correspond to power generation plants, but it is the network of cables, transformers, and control systems that makes electricity a true utility that anyone with a standard power plug can access. The utility business model not only forces the organization to look at application efficiencies but the state of how the physical datacenter is operated and its power usage. For instance, recent studies have shown that when datacenters are carefully inspected, there are many optimizations that can be pursued in floor cooling by just looking at the nature of where cooling vents are located. Sometimes server proliferation occurs so quickly that air flow is blocked.[3]

To continue the analogy, the network, specialized infrastructure resources, and, most important, the dynamic application service management software tools that match workload demand with the available supply of infrastructure resources based on business policies must be closely examined. And just as the cost of a kilowatt/hour governs the rational use of electricity, operators of an IT utility must also understand and eventually charge for infrastructure service units to ensure the best use of available resources.

In IT, the utility has one other complication: The entitlement to use it does not mean one is able to use it. Unlike an electric utility, a simple appliance plug is not sufficient to get a consumer started. There are processes that need to be in place that were discussed in Chapter 7 to prepare the consuming application to run on a utility. A more complete analogy to the electric utility is that an application is more like a multiuse building that is coming on to the electric grid as opposed to just a toaster with a plug. Any application entering the utility must be profiled so that the optimal ensemble operating platforms can be applied to that application. In addition, a formal SLA and its associated OLA must be produced so the implications of meeting demand are understood by all parties.

## Cloud computing

Cloud computing is the delivery model because the cloud enables the RTE, since the RTE is the business architecture delivered through IT. RTI is the enabling strategy that business uses to achieve RTE. Cloud computing is the new emerging trend that is drawing IT executive attention, and many view it as a revolutionary, disruptive innovation. However, when viewed with the perspective of grids and the notion of IT utility, it is clearly a natural evolution of the digital supply chain. The concepts of cloud computing—networked infrastructure resources, available for a price and accessible via a standard interface—are quite similar to the preceding ones, with the primary differentiator being that these resources can be supplied from outside the enterprise firewall as well as internally.

Today cloud computing is widely regarded as a consumer or small-business platform,[4] but given the changing landscape of financial services, it will play an

---

[3]Bellantoni R. Fix what you have first: the ultimate green move is improving your legacy data center, *Data Center Dynamics*. <http://www.datacenterdynamics.com/ME2/Audiences/Segments/Publications/Print.asp?Module=Publications::Article&id=060B9D566E884F078A5AEBDD268D3274>; Accessed 10.09.2008

[4]Oltski J. Nebulous cloud computing, *CNET*. <http://news.cnet.com/8301-1001_3-10125537-92.html>; Accessed 17.12.2008.

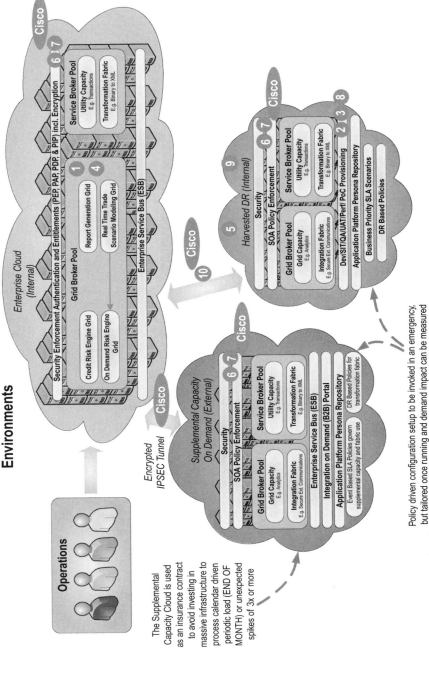

**Figure 8.3** Example cloud environment.

*Solutions:*

**①  Time of Day:** Many operations are only needed at certain parts of the day. Each grid is dynamically allocated and right sized to the demand in real time, which makes it possible to share infrastructure as desired.

**②  Resiliency:** The availability of the PoC, performance testing, UAT, and development environments is critical to meeting promised development deadlines. These environments now run within the DR harvested cloud, which self heals if a failure occurs; Environment is available except for when a full fledged disaster occurs at which point it is not needed.

**③  On Demand:** PoC and performance test environments are temporary in nature and are only needed for short periods of time, but must be able to be brought online when needed. Environments are dynamic and cost efficient / available on demand.

**④  Utilization:** There are hundreds to thousands of nodes in the grids. Each dynamically allocated grid is sized to its current processing demand; unused capacity is available for other tasks.

**⑤  DR Capacity:** A mirror of resources are allocated in case disaster strikes the Production datacenter. Since DR resources are dynamically allocated they can be tasked with other work while not needed for a disaster and quickly brought to bear when there is .

**⑥  Security:** Access to resources must be secured. Cisco Policy Manager and Policy Enforcement Points: ensures WIRE SPEED fine grained auth disallowing invalid requests before they waste resources . Business Policy Driven:
 - Policy Enforcement Points (PEPs)
 - Policy Administration Points (PAPs)
 - Policy Decision Points (PDPs)

**⑦  Security:** The development teams should have access to a standardized security model to develop against. Cisco Policy Manager and PEPs are a standardized security model.

**⑧  Environment Matching:** The test and load environment should replicate production as closely as possible. Harvested DR resources that facilitate the duplication of the production environment makes it easy to accomplish this.

**⑨  DR Assurance :** The DR environment must be tested regularly to validate its readiness. The automated provisioning and configuration of the DR environment facilitates this process; It is possible to automate this validation.

**⑩  DR synchronization:** The timely movement of data file and configurations is critical to DR success. Inter-cloud communications are optimized because Cisco QoS and CSR optimize bandwidth utilization

**Figure 8.3** Continued

increasingly important role in the datacenter of the future. Enterprises that opt to drive the efficiency of their internal IT utility to higher levels will purposely constrict the capacity available internally, perhaps shifting from engineering the utility capacity to meet 99 percent of average peak capacity demands to 95 percent. At some point, workload demand will exceed available capacity, and those enterprises will have a choice: throttle or suspend lower-priority workloads or look to supplemental capacity outside of the enterprise to meet that demand. Given the changes in the economy, new datacenters are not a viable consideration, so when that demand spike occurs due to an outage, an unforeseen demand surge, or simply because the utility operators wish to drive higher efficiencies, cloud computing is ideally suited to meet that demand. That is because the maturity of service delivery forces greater levels of abstraction and containment. In fact, as the technologies underpinning cloud computing mature, progressive organizations may wish to permanently shift a percentage of infrastructure capacity to the cloud and eventually migrate 100 percent, which is the final adoption model in Figure 8.3.

Figure 8.3 shows a mostly external cloud implementation. Assuming enterprise security concerns are addressed, such decisions will be made wholly via an economic lens rather than technology. Conversely, business may decide to offer *business as a service* for selected areas of strength such as risk management, while subscribing to business as a service for other functions such as report generation.

This is a unique paradigm shift for business to consider, as IT can actually enable business strategy, even when radical changes in the business model must be pursued. Any financial service enterprise that masters these skills early will have a distinct advantage in time to market, efficiency, and resiliency that will go directly to its bottom line.

## 8.6    Cloud delivery model decisions

Based on an organization's needs to decide how they will wish to consider service delivery in the future, this section will provide some guidance. Only Infrastructure as a Service, Platform as a Service, and Software as a Service are shown in Table 8.2, as those are the foundations required to establish Business as a Service.

- The IT Service Delivery Model needs to accommodate the rapid changes that the financial services industry continues to experience and balance user experience, cost, and efficiency.
- The IT Service Delivery Model must manage the degree of implementation volatility in the datacenter that is caused by the need to respond to changes. Traditional attempts to do so have contributed to datacenter sprawl.
- IT needs to progress through a set of infrastructure maturity phases in order to create an aligned service delivery model that enables the RTE.

### 8.6.1    Enterprise cloud design

The basic cloud is comprised of pooled resources (compute, network, and disk) that are dynamically provisioned to meet the demands requested of it. Heavy use of real-time and on-demand virtualization technologies is leveraged to facilitate the rapid deployment of resources to meet the demand. Three primary services from an internal consumption point of view are provided by the cloud infrastructure, though they are interrelated.

- *Infrastructure as a Service (IaaS)*—Raw compute, network, and disk resources on demand. Often virtualization technologies are leveraged to facilitate the real-time reconfiguration of environments.
- *Platform as a Service (PaaS)*—A complete computing platform available on demand for the design, development, testing, deployment, and hosting of applications. This includes everything provided by IaaS plus the development environment, application run-time, middleware, caching services, security services, integration services, and so on.
- *Software as a Service (SaaS)*—A server-based version of software application or content channel that a remote thin client can connect to and operate with. Management of the software is centrally controlled and preferably is managed as virtual instances available on demand and typically built upon a PaaS.

A cloud can be operated by any organization as internal or third party (external). There are various tradeoffs to creating internal or buying external cloud resources.

Many critical decisions must be made about investments that change conventional datacenter service provisioning. Deciding on the level of service (platform,

Table 8.2 Cloud Decision Model

| Problem | PaaS | IaaS | SaaS | Ensemble | Internal Cloud | External Cloud |
|---|---|---|---|---|---|---|
| Need extra CPU and memory for spikes of trading during a volatile market for a few hours at a time to run high-risk analytics. | | From an extended pool to minimize security and data transfer issues. | | Numerical Processing Ensemble | Prefer to use internal cloud providing quick (within minutes) resource allocation. | |
| Need extended platform resources available to print end-of-month statements due to increasing volume. Don't want to invest in more infrastructure and current datacenter sharing schemes cannot guarantee service window times. | Provides a tailored footprint for the kind of month-end processing required, including sufficient disk, CPU, memory, and bandwidth. Would need encryption for large bulk data transfers. | | | Numerical Processing Ensemble with heavy emphasis on large data movements. | | Operations can be run remotely by the renter. If more resources are needed to meet time windows, this would be covered under the SLA in terms of incremental cost to supply above and beyond. |

*(Continued)*

Table 8.2 Continued

| Problem | PaaS | IaaS | SaaS | Ensemble | Internal Cloud | External Cloud |
|---|---|---|---|---|---|---|
| Manage costs for general ledger and Oracle financials internally. | Create an internal PaaS that can generate allocated chargebacks for resource used in apportioning costs to process all feeds from federated LOB. | | | Information Integration Ensemble combined with Numerical Processing Ensemble | Used as a transparency measure to get LOBs to streamline their input. Too often GLs must process hundreds of input feeds every night. Internal PaaS lets IT treat the processing of GL, and so on, as a business. | |
| Stop building internal support staff to house Taleo, human resources, timesheets, and so on. | | | Get a tight contract for SLAs so that these become externally provided SaaS. | Complex Transaction Ensemble | Must resolve issues of security, possibly two-factor authentication. | |
| Reduce investments in point solutions for common services such as date/holiday service position service. | | | This should be crested with contracts in mind. | Information Integration Ensemble | This makes sense to do internally to minimize delay. | |

software, or infrastructure) will affect the level of investment in infrastructure and personnel. The strategic importance of an application, combined with its performance parameters, will dictate whether it is better to outsource an application externally or keep it internal.

The possibilities for the business to transform its operations, reduce costs, drive efficiencies, and invest in new business models is considerable when a cloud service delivery model is employed. Figure 8.3 shows a cloud delivery model that can accommodate the enterprise. A key aspect of this cloud is that there are processes and technologies that allow the cloud to do the following:

- Obtain temporary infrastructure on demand to accommodate unanticipated peaks for short durations such as a few hours or a day (bottom left IaaS cloud). This gives the organization the choice to not overprovision the infrastructure in anticipation of such a peak, avoiding considerable costs for resources that are used rarely.
- Obtain infrastructure on a regular basis to accommodate nonstrategic software that takes considerable resources, such as HR, and possibly some period reporting (bottom right SaaS cloud).

The key message to the business is that it now has choices when considering investment alternatives. The key for IT executives is that they can deliver business demand and have the option to contain their own datacenter usage.

## 8.7    Tactics that support the strategies

While strategies lay the direction for the enactment of vision, the road to strategic fulfillment is a long one when you consider that progress in financial services is measured in fiscal quarters. The growing reluctance to invest in datacenters will cause any strategy to be scrutinized quite heavily and so tactical steps that will yield value in short timeframes are the ones that have the best chance of being funded. Chapter 6 introduced playbooks that had directed missions in short timeframes. The playbooks described methods to enact change while setting the stage for process, cultural, and organizational change. The intent of any playbook can be summarized as follows:

- Change how resources are managed in order to operate more efficiently
- Change how resources are used in day-to-day operations to alleviate current pain
- Change what resources are used so more efficient technologies can be employed

These principles will be explored in this section using practical examples.

### 8.7.1   Vertical cooling in the datacenter

In the datacenter, heat dissipation has become a major concern with the proliferation of blades. The following sections explore what can be done to alleviate the heat crisis. These are examples of tactics that can be undertaken as a larger, longer-term strategy for NGDC transformation rollout.

The concept of heat rising is quite simple—something that has been accepted since the first hot-air balloons took flight. So why is it that IT equipment is designed to draw air in from the front and expel hot air out the back? Did early IT innovators think the car radiator was really extensible to IT equipment (somehow forgetting that the datacenter doesn't travel forward at 65 miles per hour)?

Early designs required discrete components (that gave off a lot of heat) to be stacked on top of one another, so to keep the upper components from over-heating, they blew lots of cold air in through the front of the components and installed equipment to draw the cold air from the rear. In a time with precious few computing resources (no space constraints) and, relatively speaking, inexpensive power, this approach worked. As time passed the design was gradu-ally improved upon but with the same basic front-to-back cooling concept. In modern datacenters the best practice design for accommodating that model is to implement aisles dedicated to either providing a flow of cold air to cool the equipment or an aisle configured to draw off the hot air (Figure 8.4).

Unfortunately this segmentation approach has been plagued by several factors in recent years: increased equipment density generating more heat in a smaller area, dramatic and seemingly unending price increases for power, and limita-tions on floor load and power budget, preventing the installation of additional CRAC units. To meet these challenges, IT has predictably come up a number of approaches to address these symptoms.

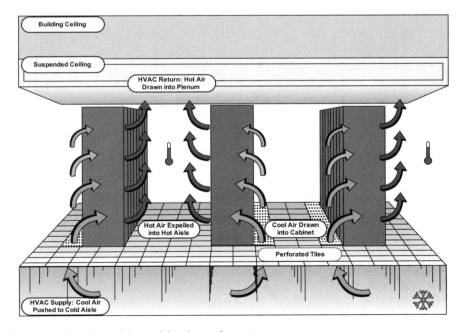

**Figure 8.4** Traditional hot/cold aisle configuration.

- *In-Row Cooling* from manufacturers such as American Power Conversion (APC) can provide a quick fix to legacy facilities struggling to figure out how to cool the next set of blades. These units are frequently referred to as fridges, as they fully contain the mounting rack, the power distribution, and the cooling for a standard 19-inch rack. They can also be configured to leverage water cooling to reduce the power consumption of the refrigeration components. The drawbacks are a high price tag and valuable datacenter floor space.
- *Ambient Air Exchange* is a relatively straightforward option for those fortunate enough to have datacenters in climates where outdoor temperature is conducive. This approach is a relatively simple concept where hot air from the datacenter floor is ducted to a chamber where a sealed heat exchange[5] takes place, leveraging the external cold air to reduce temperature before it is returned to the CRAC unit for chilling to the desired output temperature. This approach can be further improved upon by installing variable ducting to leverage hot air to heat employee work areas and to allow for the start/stop of this exchange based on outside temperatures. Drawbacks to this approach may include significant facility modifications to accommodate the ducting and air exchange, and of course it only makes sense where the internal/external temperature delta is sufficient often enough to justify the investment.
- *Water Cooling* is a derivative approach to the ambient air exchange. In this case, rather than using external air in the heat exchange chamber, you circulate water to reduce the temperature of hot air before it is returned to the CRAC units. Water is a better conductor of heat, and therefore this approach is more efficient than an air exchanger. It can also be leveraged in conjunction with an air exchanger to further reduce the hot-air temperature. The primary drawback of this approach is the requirement for facility modifications (similar to an air exchanger) and a large water supply. Innovative approaches to solving the water supply may include large underground pools/reservoirs where water is pumped through coils in the ground to leverage geothermal temperature deltas, rather than introducing heat pollution to a river or lake.
- *Pressure Gradients* are an interesting approach to ensuring maximum efficiency of facilities without any modifications to the equipment itself. In this approach the cold aisle of the datacenter is completely sealed from the rest of the datacenter by installing a ceiling connected to the top of the racks on either side of the cold aisle and installing doors on either end. Cold air is ducted exclusively to that sealed area, while the hot air is open to the rest of the datacenter where the air returns are located. This creates a pressure gradient that forces the cold air through the operating equipment and prevents any hot air from bleeding over into the cold aisle and reducing efficiency. This approach can be used in conjunction with air/water exchange techniques to dramatically improve the efficiency of cooling in a datacenter. The relatively minor drawback to this approach is the headache of doing carpentry/construction work around in-service equipment and minor complications with overhead datacenter wiring approaches.

These approaches, while innovative, do not address the core inefficiencies of traditional front-to-back cooling. One vendor, Verari Systems, pondered this

---

[5]Note that this should be a sealed air exchanger to prevent the introduction of foreign contaminants (dust, insects, etc.) in the datacenter air supply.

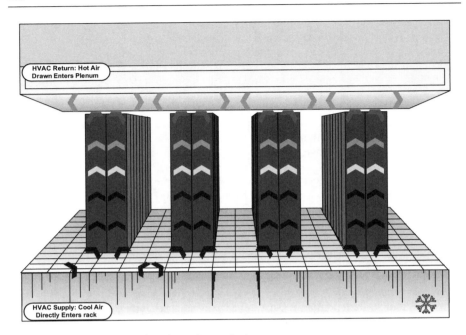

**Figure 8.5** Verari's vertical rack cooling solution.

issue years back, and rather than copying the existing approach, they set out to build a better mousetrap. And in this case the simple realization was that heat rises, so rather than trying to cool front to back, why not draw cool air into the bottom and expel it from the top of the rack? This innovative and patented approach leverages simple physics for a dramatic improvement in datacenter efficiency. The individual blades in their racks no longer require their own fans (the most common cause of blade failures) and instead rely on several large fan trays to draw air through. These large fans spin much slower and thus use less energy, while also increasing their mean time between failures (MTBF). In addition, the speed of these fans fluctuates based on the temperature of the air inside the chassis (spin faster if approaching the maximum temperature, and slower if temperature is fine). This allows for the use of their technology with much higher temperatures than a datacenter manager would typically allow for fear of failures and heat-generated safety shutdowns.

In a new datacenter this approach eliminates the need for hot air/cold air segregation, as well as allowing for much denser equipment placements. In an existing datacenter the introduction of this technology can actually significantly improve airflow and improve the efficiency of CRAC units due to Verari's ability to actually pull cold air toward hot spots in the datacenter. This can provide a tactical remedy for air dams under the datacenter floor from years of cabling changes while also providing a significant new source of computing capacity (Figure 8.5).

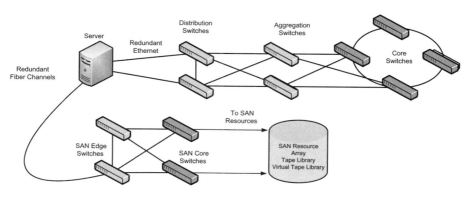

**Figure 8.6** Traditional cabling of network and SAN.

## 8.7.2 Unified fabric to reduce cabling complexity

In order to address the massive proliferation of cabling in a datacenter, new products are constantly sought. The tactics of changing how resources are managed is critical for datacenter managers. They often look to change the resources they use in order to gain efficiencies and reduce complexity.

For all the increases in networking bandwidth over the past 20 years, there have been relatively few advances that positively impacted the datacenter floor. Fortunately, with the advent of *Fiber Channel over Ethernet (FCoE)* standards that paradigm has finally changed. Cisco Systems has been a major participant and commercial sponsor of that development effort and at the time of this writing is the only vendor with a commercial switch shipping to customers.

### What is FCoE?

FCoE leverages a 10 gigabit per second Ethernet connection between the server and network switch. This connection is divided into 2 gigabit or 4 gigabit per second connectivity for fiber channel (SAN) connectivity, and roughly 5 gigabits dedicated to normal TCP/IP traffic flow. The protocol is designed to ensure that the fiber channel connectivity is "lossless," so it does not behave like normal Ethernet with buffers and flow control to manage congestion. This ensures that the host server connectivity to SAN resources performs as if it had a dedicated fiber link (Figure 8.6).

*So, you may ask, why does the datacenter manager care about a new Cisco switch?* In the current networking approach for large datacenters, you have a minimum of four networking connections for every SAN-connected server (two for Ethernet, two for SAN). You also have a tiered network topology, with Ethernet cables running from every server to a distribution switch, which then connects to a consolidating switch, which in turn is connected to a core switch. On the SAN side you have two fiber cables running from the host server to edge SAN switches, which in turn connect to core SAN switches, which then connect to the destination SAN resources (disk, tape, etc.). By leveraging FCoE

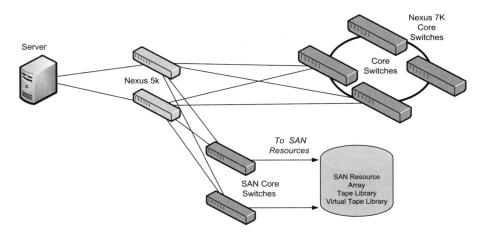

**Figure 8.7** Cisco's Unified IO (combines the network and SAN at the server).

and an integrated LAN/SAN edge switch, you cut the NIC's on the server down to two, the cables down to two, and the complete elimination of the SAN edge switch. In a large datacenter this means thousands of fewer cables (and resulting air dams), thousands of fewer power-consuming NIC's on the server, and dozens of SAN switches off the floor. The capital and operational cost reductions are very significant (Figure 8.7).

### 8.7.3  *Transformation tactics*

In Chapter 6, a Java playbook example was referenced so the anatomy of a playbook could be explored. The tactics in that playbook will be further discussed here to illustrate a transformation approach that leverages technologies that can make short-term impact that can be measured.

Figure 8.8 shows a typical arrangement of large, clustered SMP machines that are used to service a variety of client-facing applications. It is not unusual to see an arrangement that includes multiple server vendors such as Hewlett-Packard, Sun, and IBM. The reason for such diversity lay in mergers and acquisitions, or a company's purchasing strategy, that included having two vendors constantly vying for new business. The full range of hardware and network support is shown from security and proxy servers in the DMZ to web servers and large SMP application servers. Switches proliferate, and most of the servers grow at a constant rate irrespective of business growth. The reason for such uncorrelated growth was covered extensively in Chapters 2 and 4. Despite the growth, the QoE is not kept in balance, as QoS often suffers in Java applications. The following are just a few examples:

- Highly volatile memory usage causing garbage collection pauses as memory needs to be cleaned during execution time, often at the worst possible moments, during peak traffic. Despite the size of large SMP machines effective memory usage for any Java application is still limited to 2GB.

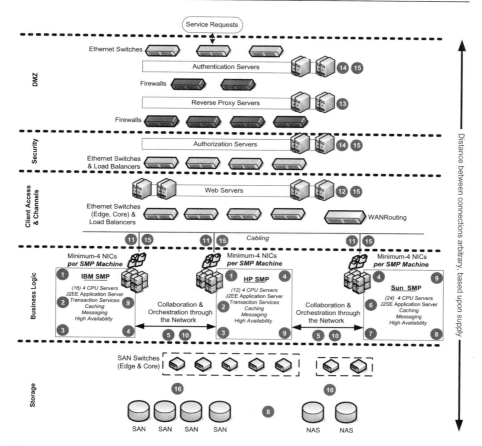

**Figure 8.8** J2EE /J2SE operational concerns in typical scale-up architectures.

- Data transformations for messages are processes by expensive servers that can consume 20–40 percent of the machines resources.
- All of the resources that an application needs are often spread across the datacenter causing unnecessary network hops and inducing unnecessary latency.

Many problems are pointed out in the diagram, and no organization can address them immediately in one big stage.

## Numerical key for Figure 8.8

## J2EE typical application concerns

1. Uncontrolled high volume of service requests during peaks that are hard to predict.
2. Response times need to be fast and predictable during peak loads. Process complex business logic with high throughput.
3. Typically, transactions require multiple data sources from legacy environments (e.g., client, product).

4. Large diverse throughput increases cache utilization, making it very volatile, which causes garbage collection pauses.
5. Collaboration between JVMs in different machines cause response time delays while increasing network traffic.

## J2SE typical problems

6. Memory-intensive processing is required, with some tight response time SLAs.
7. Multiple calculation streams are run to solve the business problem. These streams have varying workload sizes.
8. Memory usage is volatile, often involving large data sets; the data movement impedes performance.

## General operating environment problems

9. Multiple SMP vendors often require multiple skill sets.
10. Hardware dispersed across datacenter(s) forcing highly collaborative applications to communicate through extra hops.
11. Massive amounts of cabling must go to each SMP for redundant switching for each NIC.
12. Web servers that front the application servers might be numerous hops away.
13. Reverse proxies are typically servers that have operating systems on them but must be in DMZ.
14. Security is processed by different servers at different stages; fine-grained authorization is the domain of the application.
15. Message format translation is processed by the very expensive application servers.
16. Growth of unstructured data creates tiered storage that increases network utilization and delays application access.

An alternative to the big bang approach is to use the tactics laid out in a playbook, which could realize results in less than 90 days. In Figure 8.9, a transformation plan is put in place that alters the resources, changes how they are managed, and in some cases changes how resources are used. This is an evolving process.

### *Figure 8.9 numerical key*

The following legend explains the sequence of transformations that take place that drive value and make impact. The suggested sequence marked by the numbers was chosen based on ease of implementation and range of impact.

1. *Performance:* Client-facing Java applications must perform consistently. Supplement Java processing with a network attached JVM processor (Azul), which eliminates garbage collection pauses, accelerates intercommunications with less than 40 ms response time, and supplies 864 JVM cores/768GB memory. Improves response time; increases throughput.
2. *Footprint Optimization:* As functionality is transferred to the Azul appliance, the programs in the SMP become dispatcher's shells. The SMPs can be replaced by

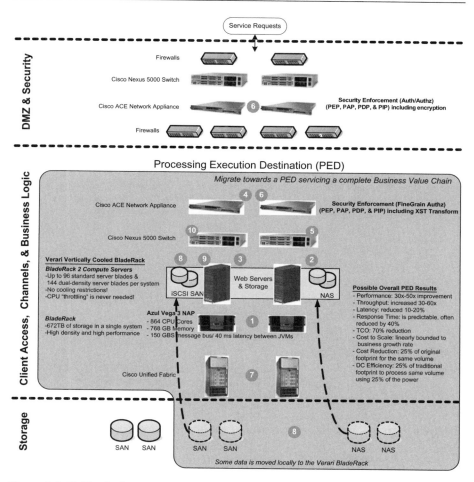

**Figure 8.9** JAVA platform remediation.

a vertically cooled Verari BladeRack, saving floor space, cooling, energy, and reducing operational complexity.

3. *Optimize Workload in Real Time:* As blades take over SMP functions and absorb web server workload, DataSynapse FabricServer™ provides real-time dynamic resource allocation based on business policies defined as parameters. As real-time thresholds are reached, resource allocations are changed.

4. *Relieve Real-Time Data Transformation Workload:* Transformations aided by ACE appliance that converts formats at wire speed. Extracts aided by 10 Ge speed ACE. Resources of expensive servers are freed, and power consumption is reduced.

5. *Large Data Movement Causes Network Congestion:* The Cisco Nexus Switch (10 Ge) reduces network congestion. It is attached to a Verari rack, which provides a dense computing platform. The combination optimizes connectivity and bandwidth needs for highly collaborative applications.

6. *Security:* Access to resources must be secured. Cisco Policy Manager and Policy Enforcement Points ensures wire speed fine-grained authorization, disallowing invalid requests before they waste resources.
   Business Policy Driven:
   - Policy Enforcement Points (PEPs)
   - Policy Administration Points (PAPs)
   - Policy Decision Points (PDPs)
7. *Physical Connectivity:* Density of servers continues to increase. Cisco Unified I/O combines network and SAN connectivity into a single converged network adapter connected to a Cisco Nexus switch to run FCoE. Quality and performance over FCoE is enabled via Cisco's Priority Flow Control (PFC), providing a lower-cost environment with higher availability that is easier to maintain.
8. *Bring Storage Closer to Compute, Including Solid-State Disks:* Verari Vertically cooled racks provide room for storage servers, Nexus switches and various appliances, including Azul. SAN and NAS traffic can be reduced by utilizing the container storage.
9. *Applications Run More Efficiently:* Run with one-third the hardware, because workload is optimized and communication is more efficient.
10. *Message Delivery QoS:* Highly important messages, such as trades and orders, must be top priority. Network traffic for trades and orders transaction types is prioritized by Cisco's QoS Policy Manager.

Figure 8.9 shows ten stages of transformation. The first step includes the introduction of a Network Attached Processor (NAP) that is specifically designed to minimize Java garbage collection, while providing over 800 CPU cores and 768 GB of shared memory. The introduction of the Azul NAP is an easy installation, and moving application workload to the Azul requires a few lines of changes in a configuration file. Application workload can be moved to the NAP, which will reduce workload on often overtaxed SMPs. The use of a few NAPs could offload enough workload to reduce the application functionality inside the SMPs to mere dispatchers. In addition, the Azul NAP makes it possible for inter-JVM communication to be much faster, making it possible to reduce response-time lags between different SMPs. The eventual result is that SMPs can be eliminated, moving the residual code that dispatches work to the Azul to a vertically cooled blade rack. This rack is denser, can run hotter, and is more compact than an SMP. The Verari blade rack can run various ensembles that make up an entire BVC. The rack can become the PED. Further transformations include network appliances that perform data transformations at line speed, offloading more work. In addition, network appliances such as Cisco's Ace can perform fine-grained authorization by inspecting requests at line speed, improving security and performance simultaneously. The sequence in the diagram builds upon each introduced capability to reduce power consumption, increase performance, return floor space, and reduce cost. In this particular case, the incremental transformations will lead to a set of ensembles that can be hardened into products internally and eventually migrated into PEDs. The core technologies table lists a range of such products and their capabilities that will enable such a sequence of transformations that are measurable.

# 8.8 Core technologies

The core technologies required to build the NGDC are varied and include software as well as various kinds of hardware, including vertically cooled racks, network attached appliances that accelerate computation for Java based applications, and network accelerators that not only translate formats at wire speed but can inspect messages for security information. Software products include service and grid brokers that dynamically allocate workload to available resources based on real-time business demand, and bare metal provisioning software that create personas of the application or service so that service brokers can allocate these applications in minutes or seconds to meet demand.

## 8.8.1 RTI technology landscape

The IT vendor industry moves in bursts, especially when a new wave is discovered (recall the internet wave of 1997–2001; product proliferation and diversity were tremendous). The technology landscape for RTI, cloud, and NGDC has reached the attention of large vendors like IBM, SUN, HP, and Microsoft, as well as niche players too numerous to mention other than a sample in this table. The rate of change, company acquisition, and product capability change is accelerating, and so will the consolidation. To that last point, how many content management vendors were there in 1998?—How many are there now?—The same is true for portal server vendors. By the time this book is published the vendor landscape will change. What will not change is the column titled **function**. Function is going to emerge as an operational requirement that must be solved in order to achieve NGDC RTI. Therefore this table is a sampling of technologies that have been shown to work together to achieve the goals of RTI.

Note that these technologies and functions are guided by the technology stack of the datacenter introduced in Chapter 4.

### Vendor culture
In Chapter 5, some time was spent on each element that involved vendor tools. An overriding theme of those elements was ensuring that there is alignment behind vendor intentions and the organization's goals. The burning question that must be continually asked in the evaluation is: Will a vendor whose vested interest is selling you hardware advise you on reducing hardware by 50 percent? When working with large vendors that have an instance of PEDs and who talk about ensembles, ensure that dynamic real-time management will work on those platforms.

### RTI technology components
Cloud Technology and Product Domain (see Table 8.3) is a list of technologies that have worked together. As mentioned in the preceding paragraph, it is not exhaustive but represents functionality that has been proven when operated together.

**Table 8.3** Cloud Technology and Product Domains

| Cloud Domain | Asset Type | Function | Vendor | Technology | Problem Addressed |
|---|---|---|---|---|---|
| Network Security | Policy Enforcement Firmware on Network Appliance | Policy Manager and Policy Enforcement Points; ensures wire speed fine-grained authorization, disallowing invalid requests before they waste resources.<br><br>Business Policy Driven: (Client and Trader Entitlements)<br><br>—Policy Enforcement Points (PEPs)<br>—Policy Administration Points (PAPs)<br>—Policy Decision Points (PDPs) | Cisco | Cisco Enterprise Policy Manager | Security policies are no longer application point solutions, fine-grained authorization performed based on roles from human resources database. Third-party authentication is possible. |
| Network Service Differentiation | Service Policy Software on Switch | QoS policy manager prioritizes traffic flow based on message type to ensure that highest-value messages get top priority during heavy network use. | Cisco | Cisco QoS Policy Manager on Switch | Optimizes traffic during network spikes, ensuring timely delivery of critical messages, limits the degree of overprovisioning required for period spikes. |
| Network Optimization | Network Compression Device | Optimize bandwidth utilization through compression of all traffic, compression occurs at wire speed. | Cisco | Cisco Compression Device | Reduces bandwidth utilization during peak traffic, avoiding excessive investment to handle periodic spikes. |
| Collaboration | Appliance | Improve collaboration and drive new business models, by adapting customizing content for different video needs while making sure that the network does not become overloaded. | Cisco | Cisco Media Experience Engine 3000® | Provides a media processing platform for user-generated content. It provides a turnkey solution for extending the reach and relevance of communication within organizations. |

| | | | | | |
|---|---|---|---|---|---|
| Collaboration | Appliance | Enable the enterprise to become more collaborative through better interaction technologies that support mobility. | Cisco | Unified Communication Manager | • Media adaptation functionality enables users to view any media content on any end-point device. Media files can be shared easily between digital signage, desktop video, mobile devices, and other applications. • Editing and production capabilities allow users to customize content with company logo overlays, transitions, file clipping, and color and video quality enhancements. Cisco Unified Communications Manager is an enterprise-class IP telephony call-processing system that provides traditional telephony features as well as advanced capabilities, such as mobility, presence, preference and rich conferencing services. |
| Mediation | Service Bus | A multiprotocol service bus that transforms formats at wire speed. | Cisco | ACE XML Gateway | Makes fast, asynchronous secure web services feasible. Offloads large XML translations from servers, saving 40% cup utilization. |
| Operating Platform | Blade Rack Storage | Dense compute and storage with vertical cooling. | Verari | Vertically Cooled Blade Racks | Floor space, power, and cooling requirements significantly reduced; exploiting the fact that heat rises. |

(*Continued*)

Table 8.3 Continued

| Cloud Domain | Asset Type | Function | Vendor | Technology | Problem Addressed |
|---|---|---|---|---|---|
| Operating Platform | Multicore CPUs | Allows multithreaded applications to run simultaneously on one chip. Can also allow multiple single threaded applications to run on one chip. | Intel | Multicore CPUs | Allows applications to run more efficiently, using less power and increasing throughput. |
| Operating Platform | Network Attached Appliance | Provides virtually transparent access to 800+ CPUs and 700+ GB memory that can be shared by multiple platforms running Java (e.g. Sun< IBM, HP SNMPS and any blade rack). Provides 140 GB/sec inter-JVM communication. | Azul | Azul Vega™ 3 Network Attached Processor | Eliminate Java application garbage collection pauses increase throughput by 10X, reduce floor space, and cooling requirements, reduce inter JVM communication, improving response time. |
| Network Dependency Awareness | Network Discovery Appliance | Automatic discovery of application relationships across a network, with detection of incremental changes. | Tideway | Tideway Foundation™ | Foundation maps business applications to their underlying physical and virtual infrastructure, making it possible to see exactly how the infrastructure supports the business. It automatically discovers configuration items across disparate technology layers (e.g., business applications to switches) capturing all dependencies. It provides the information in a single, automated view. This transparency provides the ability to slash costs, reduce risk, and manage change. |

| | | | | | |
|---|---|---|---|---|---|
| Resource Orchestration | Software | Bare-metal provision of application personas. | Scalent | Scalent VOE | Guaranteed application server deployment service levels, automation of deployments reduce error, reduce deployment time. |
| Dynamic Workload Allocation | Software | Real time dynamic demand driven resource allocation based on business policy and need. Container lifecycle is managed to provide optimal resource. | DataSynapse | Dynamic Application Service Management™ | Provide resources on demand based on business policy. Resource allocating becomes fluid so that as peak changes, resources can be reallocated. |
| Virtual Processing | Software | Provide real-time allocation of workload to optimize resources based on business policy, workload demand. | DataSynapse | GridServer® | Policy-based execution of workloads based upon real-time demand, adaptive service provisioning, and self-managed environment. |
| Virtualized Operating Platform | Software | Provide a virtualized environment that allows an application to be run on a variety of platforms. | VMware | VMWare ESX® | VMs can be allocated to run in minutes across a set of platforms and operating systems. |
| Interface | Software | Provide a facility to give Internet-based applications an immersive look and feel. | Adobe | Flex® | Creates engaging, cross-platform rich Internet applications. Flex is a framework for building and maintaining expressive web applications that deploy consistently on all major browsers, desktops, and operating systems. |
| Application Performance Management | Software | Provide a uniform view of the resources a transaction consumes across all tiers of operation. | Precise | Precise™ | Precise provides a consolidated view of resource consumption by transaction type, which helps an enterprise understand the consequences of meeting demand. |

(Continued)

Table 8.3 Continued

| Cloud Domain | Asset Type | Function | Vendor | Technology | Problem Addressed |
|---|---|---|---|---|---|
| Business Transaction Management | Software | Find out the latency of every transaction as it is processed across tiers. | Optier | CoreFirst® | Optier CoreFirst traces the latency of every single transaction in real time, providing very accurate assessments of where a transaction spans most of its time. |
| Predictive Analysis | Software | Provide predictive analysis of possible failures through real-time correlation of events. | Integrien | Alive™ | Provided predictive analysis of problems in real time, enabling operations to be proactive about upcoming failures. |
| Consumption Reporting | Software | Provide consolidated resources consumption reporting. | Evident | Evident ClearStone™ | Provides cross-domain reporting and analytics across heterogeneous infrastructure and application stacks. Evident ClearStone meters, aggregates, normalizes, correlates, and enriches usage information from multiple sources including compute grids, off-grid servers, data grids (data cache), and the enterprise network infrastructure. |
| Data Access Transparency | Software | Achieve data federation of disparate sources to provide better access for all information stakeholders in an organization without the continual massive movement and duplication of files. | Composite | Composite Discovery and Information Center™ | With Composite, you can access and combine data from disparate data sources including packaged applications such as SAP, custom applications, data warehouses, XML data stores, and more. Composite lets you deliver a greater breadth of information on demand to-business intelligence tools and a variety of composite applications, such as call center and customer self-help systems. |

**Table 8.4** Example Realized Benefits

| Scenario | Initial Environment | Environment after Fit-for-Purpose Transformation | Consequences |
|---|---|---|---|
| 300 Internet-facing applications that generated revenue or provided vital high touch services with unpredictable spikes in demand. | **Demand Profile:** 5,000 concurrent users that required transactional integrity and fast response times under 3 seconds. | **Demand Profile:** It was possible to scale to 10,000 users with an average response time of ½ second. | The business could plan for growth more effectively, with less burden on application developers to find ways to improve performance. |
| | **Supply Profile:** 300 clustered SMP servers with traditional fixed workload distribution. Average response time varied from 3–6 seconds. | **Supply Profile:** Server count was reduced to 50. Two network attached appliances were added to offload the work. | Reduced operational footprint. Reduced operating expenditures. Increased PUE. Increased response time and consumer experience. |
| A Citrix farm is used to provide fast, effective application service for overseas consumers. | **Demand Profile:** 2,000 simultaneous users expect responses in less than 5 seconds; their actions create writes that must be processed. | **Demand Profile:** Users have consistent response that allows them to do their work. | Avoided an investment in a separate system to service that user base. |
| | **Supply Profile:** 50 SMP servers using traditional workload distributions and file I/O. | **Supply Profile:** 30 SMP servers were eliminated because the problem with writing to disk was solved by the use of solid state disks, which have a transfer rate of 200 MB/sec. The disks are transparent to processing. | Reduced footprint. Cost avoidance. Improved performance and room for growth. Increased PUE. No net infrastructure change. |

(*Continued*)

Table 8.4 Continued

| Scenario | Initial Environment | Environment after Fit-for-Purpose Transformation | Consequences |
|---|---|---|---|
| Risk calculation engines running at night could not meet operational deadlines. | **Demand Profile:** Minimum of 10 GB of data needed to be transformed before calculations. 5 million rows of data had to be correlated; calculation must be completed in 6 hours.<br><br>Operational risk to the business when calculations were not finished on time. Opportunity lost due to constraints.<br><br>**Supply Profile:** 4 SMP machines were to be expanded to 8 SMP machines to meet operational requirements. Grid brokers and caching were homegrown. | **Demand Profile:** Consistent operational performance allowed more scenarios to be run in the same time.<br><br>**Supply Profile:** Transactional caching was added. A commercial transactional cache was added that radically changed the performance profile. | Business able to expand to new product lines. Operation risk eliminated.<br><br>Major cost avoidance of $3 million. Investment moved to more risk capabilities. |

### 8.8.2  Core technologies realized benefits

A handful of leading Wall Street firms[6] (including Wachovia's Corporate Investment Bank) used these tactics and technologies effectively and yielded significant improvements, which enticed senior management to continue investing so they could migrate to an RTI that was an enabler of the business. Table 8.4 depicts samples of some of these results.

[6]Source: DataSynapse Align User Conference, September 2007.

# 9 Measure for success

## Key Points

To successfully realize an NGDC, organizations must be able to measure and benchmark what they have and where they need to go. This chapter outlines best-in-class metrics and benchmarks. Moreover, it covers industry initiatives such as the Green Grid, where datacenter productivity measures are being standardized.

At the risk of belaboring the points made in earlier chapters and countless management books, we repeat the time-tested adage "You get what you measure." That is to say, if people are motivated to act in a certain way, they will begin to behave that way. Unfortunately, with unbalanced measurements, there can be a nasty side effect where all activity, whether it actually conforms to the desired/motivated behavior or not, is categorized in that fashion.

To provide a simple example closer to home, if the senior management of IT operations observes a trend of increasing severity 1 incidents, the instinctive response is to communicate to the operations teams that this trend is unacceptable to the business partners and then offer incentives if the numbers look better next month. Ideally, those teams would seek out recurring problem areas and decompose the past incidents to identify root causes around people, process, and technology and remedy them. Unfortunately, what happens more often than not (in an effort to show results quickly) is the help desk/command center begins to improperly categorize severity 1 incidents at a lower priority. Or worse yet, the service manager contacts counterparts in business units and instructs them to call directly (rather than the help desk) to get faster service. The next month's metrics for severity 1 incidents look great, but in reality the problems have likely worsened.

To avoid a similar debacle with your NGDC program, it is vital that measures of efficiency in the datacenter are balanced with metrics that are meaningful to the end user. In this chapter we explore some of the current and emerging measures for datacenters and suggest additional metrics that can form the basis of a strategic program to ensure that you achieve, and later sustain, a world-class datacenter environment.

## 9.1 Common datacenter measures

### 9.1.1 Internal metrics

Until recently, most datacenter measurements focused on internal parameters that were within the IT organization's control. Simple measures such as

doi: 10.1016/B978-0-12-374956-7.00009-7

temperature and humidity consistency were the first, and due to the sensitivity of IT equipment in decades past, those metrics were maintained at all costs because a failure to do so typically meant a failure of the IT systems. Many facilities today date back several decades, and it is not uncommon to find legacy facility-control systems largely unchanged. This is unfortunate, because even one or two degrees of temperature increase can easily be accommodated by today's IT systems, and that delta can have a dramatic impact on power consumption.

As systems have evolved, so too have many of the metrics, and today you may find any of the following attributes in place as a measure of the datacenter's performance. Many of these measures apply to other parts of the IT organization as well.

**Availability:** This metric may not be entirely fair to assign to the datacenter manager, as they typically have little to do with the upstream applications and systems design, but it is often imposed as a shared metric for the leaders of the IT organization. Of course, the datacenter can have a dramatic impact on the availability of systems (positive or negative) based on how well designed and operated it is. For instance, a robust facility with power feeds from two grids, with effective uninterruptible power supplies augmented by generators with ample fuel (and tested regularly) and dual telco entrances connected to separate central offices can sustain 10 percent availability in the worst of conditions. In contrast, a poorly run facility may require constant maintenance windows to relocate equipment due to poor planning in addition to outages caused by external conditions.

**Recoverability:** While recovery of systems is absolutely a team effort, it is common that the datacenter operations team take the lead for designing, testing, and executing disaster recovery plans. In the scenario of a complete (or significant partial) facility loss, the datacenter team plays the critical role of ensuring that the switchover to a recovery site happens as quickly and transparently as possible. In some partial failure situations, this team may be the only one that truly recognizes the severity of the failure (as application performance may be sustained by high-availability designs) and can pull the trigger and switch to a recovery site before the situation becomes critical. This measure is typically pass/fail based on the success of annual test and occasional external audits.

**Compute Density:** As more and more legacy facilities reach their saturation point, this is often measured in terms of CPU cycles per square foot and it has become popular to measure the relative effective use of physical space inside the datacenter. Of course, in many of those facilities, by increasing the compute density, you simply create another problem in supplying adequate power and cooling.

**Storage Density:** Similar to compute density, this is measured in terms of terabytes (or petabytes) per square foot to provide a view into the relative efficiency of the physical space consumed by the storage platform. Increasing that density in legacy facilities may lead to the same pooling and cooling challenges posed by compute platforms.

**Automation:** This metric is calculated by recording the number of staff per square foot of datacenter space. It is frequently overlooked, as it applies to the datacenter and is more commonly referred to gauge the activities that can replace system administrators or help desk personnel. Many routine datacenter tasks such as inventory and facility monitoring can be automated today, and doing so not only reduces labor costs but also lowers the electricity bill (the average person produces 350 BTUs per hour).[1] However, care should be taken when applying this metric, as a large but sparsely populated facility may appear "better" than a smaller one packed to the walls with high-density equipment.

**Security:** When viewed from the lens of the datacenter management, this typically relates to physical security of the facility and tends to be a subjective measurement made periodically by an external auditor.

There are emerging trends to provide internal metrics that more closely represent the actual efficiency of the datacenter, but those too can miss the mark. Consider a measure of compute density (cycles per square foot) that integrates the actual CPU utilization. It is a better measure than pure density, but who is to say that CPU is doing useful work? Perhaps a better illustration of this complexity is to apply the same utilization measure to a storage density metric. In that scenario, what if the disk used for RAID mirroring is empty rows in a database, is back-up data for DR purposes, is duplicate data, or is ten-year-old data from an acquired firm that you no longer know how to access but are afraid to remove? Your percent utilization and your density may be high, but it does not indicate you are efficient.

### 9.1.2  External metrics

Past measures focused on things within their control, on trying to quantify and manage the explosive sprawl of distributed IT systems and depict how they consumed the limited space within the datacenter. However, as systems have gotten more and more dense and electricity costs seem to rise every quarter, new metrics have emerged to quantify these challenges.

One of the leaders in generating these new metrics is a nonprofit industry organization called The Green Grid, whose mission is as follows:

> The Green Grid is a global consortium dedicated to advancing energy efficiency in datacenters and business computing ecosystems. In furtherance of its mission, The Green Grid is focused on the following: defining meaningful, user-centric models and metrics; developing standards, measurement methods, processes, and new technologies to improve datacenter performance against the defined metrics; and promoting the adoption of energy-efficient standards, processes, measurements, and technologies.[2]

---

[1] Burke J. New Datacenter Metrics that Matter, *Network World*. June 26, 2007.
[2] *www.thegreengrid.org/home*.

The Green Grid has pioneered several now-popular measures of datacenter efficiency and actively works with other organizations such as the American Society for Heating, Refrigeration, and Air Consolidation Systems (ASHRAE) to create even more effective metrics to improve performance in this space. Two of their measures are described following.

**Power Usage Effectiveness (PUE):** This measure is used to determine the efficiency of the datacenter in aggregate. It is a simple formula that divides the total amount of power entering the datacenter by the power used to run the computing infrastructure within it.

$$PUE = \frac{\text{Total Facility Power}}{\text{IT Equipment Power}}$$

Total facility power is best measured at the power utility meter, unless you have a mixed-use building, in which case you must determine what power is dedicated solely to the datacenter. Calculation of IT equipment power can be a bit more cumbersome, as you will need to calculate the load associated with all IT equipment, including servers, storage, and networking components, as well as monitors, KVM switches, workstations, and laptops used to monitor or control the facility. The closer to one (1), the more efficient your facility; as that implies, all power consumed is in use for the IT equipment. In reality, most legacy facilities today have PUE ratios above 3, with only the newest "container" approach to datacenter capacity (shipping containers retrofitted internally to house IT infrastructure) managing to eke out PUE measurements around 1.5. This metric is important to understand in your datacenter, because the implication of a PUE of 3 is that a new IT component that requires 1,000 watts to operate will actually require 3,000 watts to operate in your facility.

**Datacenter Infrastructure Efficiency (DCiE):** This metric was also introduced by The Green Grid and is simply the reciprocal of PUE as shown in the following equation:

$$DCiE = \frac{1}{PUE} = \frac{\text{IT Equipment Power}}{\text{Total Facility Power}} \times 100\%$$

Although this is simply a restatement of the PUE metric, it is effective because representing the ratio as a percentage facilitates comprehension. That is to say, a typical business executive will not grasp the meaning of a PUE ratio of 3, but she will certainly understand when you tell her that only 33 percent of the power consumed by the datacenter goes toward powering IT infrastructure, that provides some value to the enterprise.

## 9.2 The role of ITIL and service management

The IT Infrastructure Library (ITIL) is a best-practices framework for delivery of IT as a service to the business. At its core, it can help enterprises create accurate documentation, precise auditing, and automated repeatability of the processes that govern IT datacenters. It therefore serves as a useful tool to help establish the operational model to create and sustain the NGDC.

In May 2007, a new release of the ITIL framework (v3) became available that contained significant changes relevant to any transformation effort. While past versions simply addressed two core functions of *service delivery* and *service support*, the new version took a major step forward by defining a lifecycle model for definition, realization, and improvement of IT services. The new model contains the following core volumes.

*Service Strategy* focuses on identifying opportunities for services to be developed in order to meet a requirement of internal or external customers. The output is a strategy for the design, implementation, maintenance, and continual improvement of the service as an organizational capability and a strategic asset.

*Service Design* focuses on activities to develop the strategy into a design document to address all aspects of the proposed service, including the processes necessary to keep it operational.

*Service Transition* focuses on implementing the service design and the creation of a production service (or modification of an existing service).

*Service Operation* focuses on operation of the services to maintain their functionality as defined in the SLA with the customers.

*Continual Service Improvement* focuses on the ability to deliver continual improvement to the quality of the services that the IT organization delivers to the business. Key areas of this volume are service reporting, service measurement, and service level management.

This methodic approach can and should be introduced to every transformation effort to ensure that strategic vision established is realized in the production environments and, more important, produces the anticipated value.

In the context of the NGDC transformation, this lifecycle approach is vital to ensure that business users' expectations (as defined in the service level agreement) of cost, performance, and availability are delivered, and those requirements are transparent all the way down to the operational teams in the datacenter.

## 9.3    Striking the right balance

Sir Winston Churchill once remarked, "Statistics are like a drunk with a lamp-post: used more for support than illumination." When applied to datacenter metrics, this analogy, although amusing, hits close to home. A manager incented by achieving high availability will always find a way to express that statistic in a manner that shows what an outstanding job he has done; the comparison can easily be extended to other areas. For example, consider a scenario where the selection of a server is based on its energy efficiency characteristics. However, a specialized appliance with three times the power footprint offers the ability to perform that same amount of work as 20 of the servers. The rigid procurement approach in many firms would still require the purchase of the servers. Therefore, when attempting to apply metrics to the NGDC, it is vital that we have complete transparency of the business's needs down to the datacenter operations team.

### 9.3.1   The importance of architecture

In Chapter 5, we explored the architectural constructs of patterns, ensembles, and processing execution destinations (PEDs). Here is a quick review:

- Patterns are derived by decomposing the *business value chain*, the applications and systems that enable it, and subsequently abstracting common patterns of demand.
- Ensembles are the physical manifestation of these patterns, and leverage concepts like IT physics (the energy utilized to perform the totality of work) to optimize specific demand types. For financial markets firms, these ensembles can be characterized as low latency, numerical processing, information integration, and complex transaction. PEDs are the aggregation of ensembles in a discrete datacenter footprint to fulfill a business function. The PED construct provides physical containment, optimized communication, and isolation from other PEDs and helps mitigate technology risk management by simplifying disaster recovery.

Earlier we discussed internal measurements that focused on potentially misleading metrics such as storage utilization. The metric is not wrong, but the challenge is in understanding whether that storage is used in a manner that adds value to the business. Productivity experts have long embraced the saying that *efficiency* is doing things the right way, while *effectiveness* is doing the right thing. The disciplined architecture approach outlined in this text helps to ensure that IT is always doing the right thing.

### 9.3.2   The role of quality of experience

As described in Chapter 6, Quality of Experience (QoE) is a key lens to ensure that the attributes of user experience, efficiency, and cost are balanced according to the needs of the business. This balance is different for each line of business, each component in the value chain, and each application that provides a business function. In short, while an SLA specifies the business expectation for the performance of an application or system, QoE specifies the implication of that SLA in terms that are actionable to the IT organization.

The concept of QoE dovetails with architecture in promoting an efficient *and* effective realization of the NGDC that meets or exceeds the needs of the business. In accordance with ITIL and service management, every business function has an SLA. Those SLAs, in turn, generate a QoE metric. When abstracted to patterns that metric temporarily disappears, but as patterns are realized in an ensemble, QoE plays a vital role in that design to ensure that the aggregate QoE requirements of that ensemble are met. As ensembles are grouped into PEDs to deliver a business function, that QoE measure is further aggregated to ensure that the maximum requirements of the business function are delivered. In this manner the NGDC achieves top to bottom transparency of business requirements to the datacenter footprint.

## 9.4   Next generation datacenter metrics

There is a desire to reduce datacenter metrics to a simple and telling value: typically utilization. Reducing such a complex environment to a single facet will only provide limited value. Consider a chemical factory responsible for manufacturing ten different types of chemical products. If we were interested in capturing metrics about this facility, the science of operations (flow rates, queuing theory, critical paths, utilization, probability theory, etc.) would be employed to create a representative model of the infrastructure. This model would be well known by the plant manager, who is responsible for supervising the efficiency and effectiveness of the plant. Engineers may provide ideas and insight into improvements and problems, but ultimately it's the plant manager who must make the operational decision to effect change or not. The idea of reducing the metrics of this complex facility to a single key metric, such as utility of the facility, is laughable. Instead, the plant manager would require a rigorous analysis of all relevant factors affected by any suggested changes prior to making a go/no-go decision.

CIO and CTOs are often making seat-of-the-pants judgment calls. Datacenter operations' descriptions are limited to the policy and procedures of change management, which is a poor substitute for understanding the operational science of information flow. From an operations science point of view, there is little difference between the flow of chemicals in a plant and the flow of data through IT infrastructure. The biggest difference is that it's easy to see the physical materials in a chemical plant—not so in the datacenter. The consequences of failure to adequately understand the machinery is also much more apparent: a chemical spill versus a server crash. In the case of a chemical plant, even one incident can bring about disastrous consequences.

The lack of physical properties to data (and the consequence of failure) has made it easy to wave away the complexities of trying to holistically understand the datacenter environment. Until now, "good enough" has been just good enough. However, to really begin wringing the most out of an environment requires a more systematic approach to measuring performance.

Consider the chemical factory further. It's also commonplace to use the same piece of equipment (e.g., a mixer) during the creation of multiple/different products. When a piece of equipment is changed over from the manufacturing of one product to another, strict policies and procedures are enforced. In some cases, the failure to observe these procedures can lead to physical injury or even death. Being negligent in this changeover process could lead to criminal charges. Knowing how long to run before the switchover, accounting for switchover time, scheduling the use of the equipment for competing requirements, and when to purchase additional pieces of capital equipment can mean the difference between profit or loss in a fiscal quarter. Given the potentially severe consequences of an operation's failure, much effort has gone into developing this discipline. Contrast this rigorous understanding of equipment reuse and repurposing to the rigid and dedicated structures employed in most datacenters.

Trying to get metrics that span datacenter environments is also a largely futile effort. Consider two factories. One factory produces widget A and the other widget B. Does it make sense to compare the various outputs of the two factories? Yes, we might find out that 10,000 widget As may be produced for everyone one widget B. This really doesn't tell us much, especially when we find out that widget As are cans and widget Bs are car body frames. They both have raw metal as inputs, but the comparison is essentially meaningless.

Why should comparisons across datacenters be any different? If one datacenter serves a financial institution and the other a manufacturing facility, the outputs of these datacenters are meaningless when compared apples to apples. Even metric comparisons between datacenters that operate in the same industry only present limited value. Infrastructure supporting sales for one organization that uses a franchise versus another that uses branches would lead to significantly different metrics of business value. Measurements must be against the organization's goals; cross industry, organizational values only work in the broadest of terms.

All in all, datacenter operations could learn a lot from operational analysis used by the manufacturing industry to better understand and utilize their environments. One of the first lessons in operations is that how you model your environment is entirely subjective to the task at hand. Doing this is hard work, as it requires really understanding what's important about your environment and thinking about the type of measurements that will help leadership make better decisions. This contradicts conventional thinking about how we ought to measure our datacenter environments, in terms of KPIs or facility utilization. Once we accept that measuring the datacenter environment is *at least* as complicated as modeling a chemical factory's operations, we can begin applying the appropriate attention and resources to modeling our environment.

The next generation datacenter design approach has given us much of the fodder we need to develop a more holistic operational model of the datacenter environment. The BVC and DSC are clear and natural boundaries that can be leveraged in breaking down the operations process. The PEDs, and specifically the ensembles inside the PEDs, can be measured in a business context.

In our chemical factory, we may purchase a very complex piece of machinery, and it would be difficult to model its internal workings, but by understanding its inputs and outputs, we can model it within our factory. Essentially, an ensemble is analogous to a piece of capital equipment in our datacenter factory. With this point of view we can apply an operations lens to how we consider this piece of capital equipment. For example, if the ensemble is a low latency ensemble, it has key operating characteristics (bandwidth utilization and latency under load) and physical attributes (power, cooling, space, and cost) we can measure. This lends insight into the performance of this portion of the infrastructure, which may support multiple applications for the trading arm of a financial services organization. By being able to chunk the infrastructure in this way, we can control the complexity of our operational model and therefore simplify the environment into something that is understandable. The result is a holistic model that facilitates big-picture decision making.

**Table 9.1** Possible units of measure by ensemble type[1]

| Ensemble type | Units of measure |
|---|---|
| Low Latency | % Bandwidth |
|  | Latency under Specified Load |
| Complex Transaction | # Transactions/Second |
| Numerical Processing | # Scenarios/Second |
|  | (e.g., process 1,000 records with 2 MB data) |
|  | # Transactions/Second |
| Information Integration | # Events/Second |
|  | # Transactions/Second |

[1]Note: that these are just possible suggestions. Measurements of an ensemble should be driven by what's deemed important by the business.

Note that this model and operations technique can be leveraged to model how resource scheduling should occur, justify capital expenditures to increase capacity, or replace legacy ensembles. This amounts to a top-down operational model driven by business drivers and not technology drivers. Each ensemble type has specific characteristics that are most interesting to consider in terms of business ability (Table 9.1).

Furthermore, this view of operations management can also provide context for other, more traditional KPI measurements. For example, in a *complex transaction ensemble,* whose primary measure is in transactions/second, it may be tempting to give a lot of weight to CPU utilization, but it is much more interesting to focus on I/O throughput instead. Optimizing I/O throughput will have significantly more impact on increasing the cap on throughput of transactions/second.

Finally, an operational model accounts for a probabilistic view of the world rather than an average utilization. This difference can be important. If a sales PED, which is made up of a *complex transaction ensemble* and an *information integration ensemble,* is running at 50 percent average utilization, it would appear that additional capacity could be squeezed out of it. However, if you know that the standard deviation of the utilization of the load is 22 percent, you see that there is a 1.1 percent chance that the infrastructure will be running at maximum capacity and therefore slow down. Increasing the utilization higher will continue to increase the percent of time that the infrastructure is maxed, and customers are left waiting. Understanding how much additional capacity can be squeezed out is a value judgment that has to be made, which the probabilistic view provides insight into.

The introduction of ensembles and PEDs into the datacenter presents the opportunity to consider a different way of collecting datacenter metrics. How exactly these measurements are made depends on what's important to your organization (Figure 9.1).

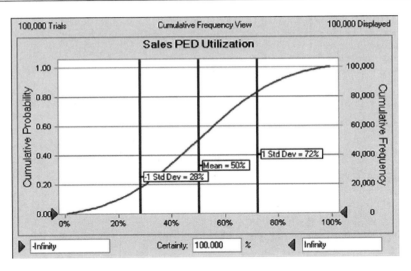

**Figure 9.1** Sales PED utilization.

## 9.5   So ... What do we measure?

The most important thing to know here is that there is no single answer, no magic formula that will guarantee your NGDC program stays on track. Certainly, there are measures that are useful to track the transformation progress, such as how many applications have been migrated to ensembles, how many ensembles have assembled into PEDs to realize a business function, and how much of your datacenter footprint has been converted to PEDs. However, the ongoing answer depends on your business, the rate of change you wish to embrace, and a myriad of other factors that will vary as you move through this transformation.

The beginning of this chapter discussed a variety of metrics that are frequently employed to measure the health of the datacenter. Any or all of those measures still hold in the NGDC with one important caveat: They must be viewed as indicative measures that are subservient to the aggregate QoE value for a PED. That is to say, the datacenter operations team cannot act to improve a particular metric isolation, it must engage with the ensemble architecture team before making any changes. For illustrative purposes, consider the storage example again: If the datacenter team observes low-storage utilization in a PED and opts to consolidate it on their own, they may be inadvertently crippling the business because in execution of that process, a large amount of transient data is required (and is cleared out at end of day). Or perhaps that PED requires extremely fast performance/response time, and by consolidating to increase utilization they've now mixed that low latency system with a numerical processing system that moves massive amounts of data during execution. Again, they will have crippled the business function. The lesson here is that if you have properly executed your architecture process, the datacenter footprint will be optimized for the business, and the traditional datacenter measures for all but total facility environment should serve solely as a sanity check.

# 10 Industry extended applicability

## Key Points

BVC-driven design works across industries.

The standardization of the IT delivery model will cause seismic shifts in IT operations.

All the principles, lessons, and strategies outlined in the previous chapters are fully extensible to other industries outside of financial services. The extreme requirements of financial services companies have mandated those in its fold to innovate to survive. Other industries leverage this effort and apply these well-tested approaches to their own operations.

## 10.1 Other industries

Many industries depend on large-scale IT infrastructures to operate, such as telecom, insurance, airlines, shipping services, energy, pharma, e-commerce, government, and so on. The fundamental components (servers, SAN, network, etc.) are the same in all these datacenters, and a limited number of data/integration patterns are repetitively used to configure components to meet the industry-specific purposes. For example, an *extract, translate, load* (ETL) process works exactly the same for a financial services organization as it does for a logistics company. As patterns are combined to meet business needs, the interaction becomes more complex but is still composed of these fundamental components.

Because of this, the attraction of delivering siloed resources is strong. However, as discussed at length in Chapter 3 and 4, this leads to a very inefficient datacenter. Financial services may have been one of the first industries to run into these challenges given its heavy reliance on IT to deliver services. Broad trends in compliance and the proliferation of unstructured data are drivers that will begin affecting all industries. In short, other industries are similarly beginning to run into the same challenges.

Thankfully, the basic approach of decomposing LOB applications by BVC into workload types to create localized and tailored ensembles of infrastructure works in any large datacenter, regardless of industry. The main difference between industries is the concentration of patterns that affect the workload characteristic types (and therefore the ensemble design) in a stage of the BVC.

Some industries will have unique needs, like financial services' trading operations, where very low latency is important. Other industry aspects share

© 2009 Elsevier Inc. All rights reserved.
doi: 10.1016/B978-0-12-374956-7.00010-3

common needs, like financial services' risk operations and pharma's research operations, that are very compute intensive. The ensemble concepts facilitate the necessary customization of the basic approach needed to meet performance as the industry measures it.

This is significant, because by restricting how the digital supply chain is constructed, any industry can take advantage of the benefits of this Next Generation Datacenter design. This will be of particular interest to industries that are thinking of adopting a real-time enterprise operating model or creating a sustainable competitive advantage through IT.

## 10.2   The datacenter as an extension of service-oriented architecture

When the first software programs were written, they started as a single, long list of instructions. The introduction of the concept of a function call introduced a new way to subdivide code. Later, the addition of the class gave a way to organize functions. Then the introduction of DLLs, followed by components with multiple interfaces, allowed for the packaging of classes. The desire to reuse components led to the development of web services, which in turn facilitated hosting of services that were easily consumable across platforms. Ultimately, this led to the development of a service-oriented architecture, where the majority of the solution is hosted as a collection of web services. The interesting thing about this innovation chain is that each time a new concept was introduced, it facilitated the abstraction of the concept that preceded it. Note that once web service technology matured, the abstraction was complete enough that the notion of *where* a service was hosted became less relevant.

Infrastructure has been slower to evolve, but it is following a similar tract. Driving factors of hardware commoditization, ultrafast specialized appliances, increasing network bandwidth, improving management tools, and virtualization technologies are enabling the abstraction of the underlying platform resources. Once the abstraction becomes sufficient such that the location of the physical becomes less relevant, the stage will be set for a great migration.

## 10.3   IT as a standard?

Industry standards facilitate the existence of marketplaces. Many standards exist today that are very much taken for granted—specific ones like SCSI and EIDE disk interfaces, to broadly applicable ones like XML and Java. Standards have enabled rich marketplaces for components and subsystems. The process of creating standards is a messy one, with winners and losers. Organizations resist standards until they have an aligned strategy in place and then try to influence the standards to meet their ends.

The roots of modern technology standards can be traced all the way back to the first integrated circuits. The packaging, pin out, power requirements, and chip functionality allowed a circuit designer to think about the chip as a black box. Over the years, standards have been moving up the stack, to the standardization of compute interfaces, personal computers, operating systems, applications, intersystem communications, protocols, and so on.

In hindsight, it's easy to see why a specific standard, or set of standards, has come about. Recent standards have largely been driven by large-company adoption, which pressures vendors to comply. Infrastructure platform standards have been somewhat slow to evolve because so many large organizations make large profits selling the resource units (servers, SAN, network, etc.). The excess overcapacity, in combination with the physical datacenter challenges of power, cooling, and space, and the overall economic outlook, have started a disruptive innovation to become more effective with existing resources.

As a cloud-based delivery model captures our collective imagination, it's going to go through the same maturation process of those technologies that are soon to be considered antiquated, like so many before. Sometime in the not-so-distant future, don't be surprised if standards around how IT as a service is delivered are commonplace.

Thankfully, not all vendors and providers will wait until industry standards emerge. If a product solution is strong enough, a de facto standard can emerge, which is a good, temporary supplement until a more holistic standard is defined. For example, Tibco was a de facto standard for years before JMS was defined as an industry standard. Those who decided to wait to adopt Tibco, or a similar nascent product, didn't have the utility of the publish and subscribe paradigm for all that time. That messaging paradigm enabled asynchronous messaging capabilities and event notification, providing a significant advantage in reacting to changing events. While market data and manufacturing were early adopters of Tibco, it took about ten years to get the JMS standard. The transformative nature of publish/subscribe was too powerful to wait for some.

Amazon and Google are examples of two early standards for cloud delivery but at present don't have the confidence of established organizations or the feature set needed. It wasn't that long ago that the industry was very skeptical of open-source initiatives, and now you'll find that many open-source solutions are the product of choice.

If the trends of separating workloads from the physical infrastructure continue (the benefits seem too large for it not to), the possibility for several new marketplaces are on the horizon.

- As organizations adopt top-down BVC-driven design approaches, sophisticated off-the-shelf ensemble designs, where numerous technologies are packaged and configured for sale as a single entity, will generate momentous commercial interest. This possibly bodes well for container-based resources, which are currently only on the fringe.
- As IT services move up the stack and underlying infrastructure platform standards emerge, it will become easier to move services out of the facility.

- Running a DR facility is exceedingly expensive and has limited utility during normal operations, making it a prime candidate for outsourcing.
- When platform supply is available dynamically and in real time from outside vendors, the *just-in-time* operation principles that have been applied in manufacturing firms can be applied to the digital supply chain.

*"Change is the only constant."*

—*Heraclitus (535 BC–475 BC)*

Heraclitus, an ancient Greek philosopher, recognized change for what it was. If history teaches us anything, it's that change is eternal. As long as the business continues to drive IT to react faster, the datacenter will continue to change and evolve—that is, until a new innovation eliminates the need for the datacenter as we know it.

# Appendix A: Wachovia CIB case study

## A.1 Business drivers/strategy

**Simplify the Delivery of IT:** The processes and complexity of deploying infrastructure and applications often takes weeks or months and directly affects business profitability.

**Agility:** Beyond reducing the time to deliver supply more quickly, the business needs to dynamically scale in real time to have resources where and when needed.

**Performance:** Resources are typically picked from what is preselected versus what is optimal, which is an inefficient use of capita.

**Environment Efficiency:** Even with the recent attention to consolidation programs, large portions of IT infrastructure are poorly utilized, which directly affects the profitability of the business.

## A.2 Key KPI improvements

**Time to Market:** Up to 50+ percent reduction.

**Total Cost of Ownership:** Up to 60+ percent less in capital and operating expense.

**Performance:** Up to 50+ percent improvement.

**Datacenter Productivity:** Up to 70 percent reduction in packaging, deploying, and changing applications and infrastructure.

## A.3 Execution strategy

**Virtual and Dynamic:** Allocate low-overhead virtual resources from physical ones dynamically and in real time.

**Fit-for-Purpose:** Creation of Processing Execution Destinations (PEDs), where the characteristics of the workload are matched with the ability of the resources.

**Robustness and Performance:** Since the resources are virtual and dynamically allocated, replacing failed resources or scaling up environments as needed becomes significantly easier.

## A.4 Key technologies

- Partner: Cisco
  - ACE XML Gateway
  - Enterprise Policy Manager
- Partner: DataSynapse
  - Dynamic Application Service Management (DASM)
- Partner: Scalent
  - Virtual Operating Environment (VOE)

- Partner: Oracle
  - Coherence
- Partner: VMWare
  - Infrastructure

## A.5  Step-by-step guide

Achieving RTI requires a journey that takes the organization through stages that mature certain processes and people skills, while introducing new enabling technology that makes RTI sustainable. A particular implementation of RTI doesn't end when a new set of technologies is introduced because the organization's business goals change and the marketplace shifts, and when RTI is established correctly, the business can engage capabilities and envision strategies that were not possible in more traditional operating environments. The major stages of this journey involve the ADIOS framework.

**Alignment** of business goals and realities with IT tactics that can properly support those goals. Activities include understanding the current demand profiles of critical applications for key lines of business, the current IT and business pain points, along with a vision for the optimal operating environment that will support business goals.

**Design** of a dynamic demand-driven platform that can optimally operate classes of applications by business function and operational characteristics. This incorporates an in-depth understanding of the types of business demand placed on applications and the constraints of current implementations.

**Implementation** of these tailored platforms, where the integration of sets of enabling technology is emphasized. These new technologies require process changes and skill augmentation and are migrated incrementally, along with better monitoring solutions that provide a more accurate depiction of how the new and old environments are operating to meet demand.

**Operation** of the new platforms that require changes in thinking about the on-boarding process for new applications, new approaches for day-to-day operations, the use of the integration lab, and the types of roles, responsibilities, and shared resource billing needed.

**Sustainment** of the platform, which is the key to long-term success. This mandates that the measurements of the environment are actively used in future planning, that investments in IT are viewed from a Portfolio Management perspective where ROI is gauged, and investments are subject to governance. This requires a shift in thinking about IT. IT transcends its cost center status and becomes a strategic enabler of the business.

The following guide to the development of a Fit-for-Purpose RTI environment is based on a case study performed at Wachovia CIB, where the preceding phases were employed and structured into actionable steps, with specific objectives and outcomes.

## A.5.1  Align

1. Define the business value chain to understand the key lines of business and the associated functions that drive revenue and IT consumption.

   At Wachovia's Corporate Investment Bank (CIB), the entire Fit-for-Purpose RTI strategy was established by first understanding the breadth of the application inventory across all business lines (capital markets, fixed income, treasury services, international, M&A, risk processing, wholesale operations, etc.). In numerous workshops, one line of business (LOB) at a time was focused on identifying the business value chain (e.g., sales, trading, operations for capital markets, etc.). These value chain components are the actual functions that the business performs to generate revenue and defray risk. Each LOB described the suites of business products they support (e.g., equities, exchange traded derivatives, OTC derivatives for capital markets). These critical business foundations provided context for the placement of all applications for an LOB. Every application could be understood in terms of its relevance to revenue, risk, reporting, and compliance, establishing relative importance for an LOB and also providing the foundation for investigating redundant functional overlaps that should be consolidated.[1,2]

2. Create a current state alignment map that indicates business-defined operating requirements for key applications.

   Once the context of aligned applications was established, the business demand that these applications must meet was established in that context (e.g., throughput volume, where low latency matters, tight operational time windows, perceived trends in peak volume). For CIB, this established clear priorities and clearly identified pain points that would be the first focus of various measurement and analysis exercises, including fixed-income trading and OTC derivatives risk analysis.[3,4]

3. Perform inventory and dependency mapping on key applications discovered through the business value chain exercise. In this step, highly collaborative application groups are defined.

   To validate management's perception of application interrelationships and the consequences of those interactions on IT supply, a mapping and discovery tool was utilized to determine the actual physical relationships of the application sets. This helped determine whether the connections between applications and services had been compromised over time due to datacenter sprawl. This enabled CIB to plan how any new initiatives

---

[1]Feig N. A new foundation: SOA implementation for business transformation. A successful services-oriented architecture, or SOA, implementation starts with making the right decisions early on in the process. *Wall Street & Technology.* April 26, 2007.

[2]Case Study: SOA delivers for Wachovia—with interest. Align Online. November 14, 2007.

[3]Tech earns interest at Wachovia. eWeek.com.

[4]Hickins M. Wachovia SOA married to the process. InternetNews.com, May 16, 2006.

would be organized in the datacenter but also identified key bottlenecks in fixed-income trading processing, which were costing the company millions of dollars per day. It also illustrated how efficiencies could be best obtained through movement of machinery, as opposed to new investments, which would not have completely solved the bottlenecks.[5]

## A.5.2 Design

4. Run consumption monitoring for definitive metrics on current environment operations.

   In order to determine how demand is actually met during peak times, various approaches to consumption monitoring had to be invoked. This included implementing a real-time transaction latency tagging tool so a transaction's latency could be tagged on each leg of its journey. That is how CIB found out the cause of a ten-second delay in fixed income trading. In addition, other tools needed to be introduced that would gauge the affects of demand on an application across all tiers that the application runs on.[6,7,8,9,10]

5. Decompose the key application workload characteristics against alignment map and monitoring results; application behaviors are targeted for one of the RTI platforms.

   CIB used results from its initial monitoring and mapping, along with focused workshops to validate why applications operate as they do. This enabled the RTI team to focus on operational bottlenecks with application teams and operations staff. It pointed out what infrastructure alignments needed to be changed, what made sense to invest in, and the best approaches for bottleneck resolution.[11,12]

6. Establish forensic analysis to determine gaps in current infrastructure.

   While the workshops were useful, the RTI team needed to distribute knowledge so operations could take responsibility for running forensics, especially when trouble arose. It was critical for CIB to have a forensic analysis process as part of its day-to-day operations given that much of the infrastructure was in flux. The analysis began to show gaps in under-utilization,

[5]Narkier S. Business process transformation with virtualization oriented architecture. *ALIGN 07—DataSynapse User Conference.*
[6]Feig.
[7]Red Hat Application Profile for Datasynapse FabricServer.
[8]DiSerio M. The serverSide.net. tangosol extends data grid support to Microsoft .NET. DIGG. March 20, 2007.
[9]Giffords B. Waters, NETWORKS, for the greater grid. Wachovia's grid network goes cross-asset and cross-business.
[10]Bishop T. Aligning business and IT through instrumentation. InfoWorld Blog, March 22, 2008.
[11]Feig.
[12]Cummings J. Virtualization hits the big time, Deploying virtualization everywhere increases benefits but creates management headaches. *NetworkWorld*, November 11, 2006.

clearly identifying that while utilization over a 24-hour period was less than 20 percent, there were obvious spikes across wide areas of the infrastructure where utilization exceeded 90 percent for an hour or more during the trading day.[13]

7. Understand the consequences of meeting demand by decomposing the supply gaps.

Some of the gaps were not easy to isolate, such as occasions where large file movements due to testing occurred and interfered with the trading network. Many of the incidents were consequences of point solutions that add network hops between collaborating systems.[14,15]

8. Create the economic model based on business demand, available supply, and importance to the business; this guides the migration process to the RTI platform.

At CIB it was important to present a model that considered driving business forces. In capital markets, latency and throughput were critical drivers, and therefore infrastructure investments were needed to accelerate them. Normal disaster recovery (DR) standards were not applicable, so special arrangements for failover had to be accounted for in the cost structure. This was compared with the potential for revenue loss.[16]

9. Instrument transactions in real time so the changes that will occur as a result of the RTI platform can be properly gauged.

CIB established a baseline for key transactions in terms of latency, response times, and peak utilization of resources so when the investments started to roll out, they could be measured to gauge the degree of effectiveness especially in key areas such as risk and trading. Early baselines established the case for a redesign of a key risk platform. The original plan was to spend $6 million, taking one year to implement. Early baseline statistics indicated that this platform could benefit from RTI and save $5 million and six months of effort.[17]

10. Define the future state alignment map, where high-value applications and infrastructure gap remediation are all placed in priority order to guide the migration to RTI.

This is the beginning of an investment strategy approach, where high-value and high-impact changes are prioritized. CIB was able to identify planned projects across capital markets, risk, and fixed income that

[13]Split-second securities trading at Wachovia. Wachovia's service-oriented architecture triples processing capacity at one-third the cost. *ComputerWorld*, May 21, 2007.
[14]BANK, systems and technology. Wachovia's global trade services group, under the command of Hong Kong–based Steve Nichols, has deployed workflow and imaging technologies in order to master the complexities of the trade finance business.
[15]Split-Second Securities.
[16]Feig.
[17]Bishop.

touched on shared services (e.g., risk, position), shared frontends (multi-asset trading frontend), server frameworks, and a host of technology initiatives (e.g., network attached processors, network appliances, solid-state disks, transactional caching). All of these were tied to specific remediations with pain points and value propositions.[18,19,20]

11. Fit-for-Purpose design is established where applications, characterized by pattern type, are defined as candidates for specific RTI operating platforms through a combination of forensic efforts and application profiling. This effort establishes what applications would benefit from service brokers, network attached processors, network accelerators, and solid-state disks.

    The design phase included a rigorous design tradeoff process that manifested in the creation of four sets of integrated ensembles and a suite of defined service layers that would use those ensembles. These ensembles covered the breadth of application families displaying the following key operating characteristics (low latency, complex transaction, information integration, and numerical processing). These four ensembles were designated to service a separately designed client access framework that would interact with the ensembles through a separate mediation framework. The ensembles would run on a set of tailored operating platforms and would access a persistence utility.[21]

12. Establish the RTI lab where the initial technologies are integrated and candidate application patterns are tested.

    The lab had two purposes: run rigorous integrations of current and new technologies, making it easier for the framework teams to deliver functionality, and provide a sandbox for development teams, many of whom were skeptical of the functionality or scared of the learning curve. This lab was also able to demonstrate how dynamic allocation of resources worked in a practical manner that spoke to developers.[22]

## A.5.3  Implement

13. Introduce applications that run on service brokers to optimize resources based on real-time demand and business policy.

[18]Feig.

[19]Crosman P. Wachovia delivers high-performance computing through a services-oriented 'Utility' in a pioneering approach. Wachovia is becoming more and more discriminating about how and to whom it provides high-performance computing. *Wall Street & Technology*, March 19, 2007.

[20]Crosman P. Wall street–style power. With high-performance computing strategic and costly, companies push efficiency. *Wall Street & Technology*, *InformationWeek*, April 14, 2007 (from the April 16, 2007, issue).

[21]Narkier S. Hands-on SOA governance practices and processes, *InformationWorld*, SOA Executive Forum, May 16, 2006.

[22]Profile: Tony Bishop. *ComputerWorld*. July 9, 2007.

One of the quickest wins for CIB was to take existing applications that ran in J2EE environments and more effectively allocate the containers to supply based on real-time demand. No code change was required when employing a service broker to better utilize existing resources and handle spikes in incoming online requests for browser-based applications in target areas across CIB's LOBs. The service broker was delivered as part of a framework offering that included caching and object relational mapping.[23,24]

14. Introduce network attached processors that accelerate Java processing: migrate candidate applications.

Even with service brokers, Java applications have inherent limitations that prevent memory sizes from growing above 2 GB. Garbage collection pauses are unpredictable for Java applications and affect highly interactive applications the most, because they have greater memory volatility. Network attached processors (NAPs) require almost no code changes but provide an operating environment with over 700 GB of memory and 800+ CPU cores, eliminating garbage collection pauses and enhancing throughput. Targeted client-facing applications in fixed-income and capital markets were migrated to an NAP.[25,26]

15. Introduce solid state disks to act as a fast caching mechanism, reducing response times.

In some cases, especially numerical processing applications that ran valuation and risk, large file sets needed to be accessed very fast in their native format. Solidstate disks let the application see the files as disk files, but the transfer rate of 200 Mbytes/second is twice as fast as the transactional cache, offering high-speed read/write access and persistence integrity. This was especially helpful for certain long-running image processing applications that consumed considerable resources and time on a regular basis.[27]

16. Introduce grid brokers for targeted applications with long-running calculation requirements.

Some applications have long-running units of work, such as transformation engines, risk calculation engines, statement generation, and PDF creation. These applications would typically benefit from a finer-grained control of resources to better enable concurrent processing and take advantage of specialized processors as needed. A grid broker enables such application type classes to run more effectively on the same resources, because it manages requests for calculation services based on a real-time view of demand and supply. In some cases the applications require some

[23]Bort J. The utility computing payoff. By virtualizing its Java application infrastructure, Wachovia Bank achieves a 300%-plus ROI. *Network World*, September 25, 2006.
[24]Feig.
[25]Crosman.
[26]Split-Second Securities.
[27]Feig.

restructuring. At Wachovia, grid brokers were used to streamline processing in PDF generation for certain international business operations, reducing the overall time to process by 50 percent on half the hardware. For
risk processing, a projected $6 million in hardware expenses was reduced
to $1 million through the use of grid brokers on commoditized blade
racks.[28,29]

17. Introduce a mediation framework, based on network attached appliances,
    that manage authorization and authentication in a strategic manner at
    wire speed, while providing a protocol converter that facilitates interap-
    plication communication through web services.
      The introduction of a specialized Network Attached Appliance (NAA)
    that performed as a protocol gateway greatly simplified security enforce-
    ment at Wachovia because it inspected each message at wire speed and
    performed appropriate security checks based on policies while converting
    formats at wire speed. NAA helped streamline the integration of online
    mortgage processing at Wachovia.[30]

18. Create the first PEDs for specific application groups based on line of busi-
    ness, operating characteristics, and degree of collaboration between target
    applications. Run them on unique vertically cooled container racks.
      The integrated frameworks and ensembles provided the first PEDs to
    run fixed-income and loan processing applications that directly affected
    revenue.[31]

## A.5.4  Operate

19. Establish an on-boarding process and SWAT team so application and
    operational teams can adjust to the new RTI paradigm, thereby ensuring
    a smooth transition.
      The new paradigm CIB engaged in broke many old operating rules, includ-
    ing ownership of infrastructure and the comfort of owning all aspects of an
    application. It was easy to misuse the new infrastructure and then claim it
    did not work (e.g., using a grid broker where a service broker would make
    more sense, using an NAP for single-threaded applications and claiming
    it did not perform). The on-boarding team profiled every candidate appli-
    cation ahead of deployment, performed an architectural analysis to pick
    the optimal platform, and helped the team migrate to the platform, help-
    ing rewrite the operational procedures. This on-boarding team was able to
    migrate 50 applications in the time it would normally have taken for 10.[32]

[28]Bort.
[29]Feig.
[30]Split-Second Securities.
[31]Waters, TRADING FLOOR, "Certoma Floors It."
[32]Giffords.

20.  Establish infrastructure services that make RTI enhancements easier to consume.

   As part of the alignment exercises, CIB management identified key services that needed to be created to end the proliferation of point solutions (e.g., risk service, position service, calendar service). Instead, these typical point solutions became Business Support Services (BSS). These services needed to be operationalized in a dynamic demand-based infrastructure that would be able to meet the anticipated service requests that this new operating paradigm would create. The infrastructure services needed to support these business services and included the ability to access more CPU, certain types of CPU, and memory in a virtualized manner. The maturity of the ensembles and its interactions with mediation services made Information as a Service (IaaS) possible, which in turn makes BSS feasible.[33]

21.  Establish IaaS by providing a federated model of key enterprise data entities that will reduce large-scale file movement for decision support and minimize the proliferation of file copies that occur to support reporting.

   IaaS was a critical CIB initiative due to the proliferation of databases and unstructured data, which resulted in excess network traffic caused by overlapping requests for data. Part of this initiative was establishing a golden record project across CIB so ownership and grouping could be properly established. It then became apparent that tools focused on structured and unstructured data identification were needed, along with a platform that enabled federated views, reducing data movement. The initial implementations in client management and for internal IT usage for MIS led to 25 percent in cost avoidance to what is normally a given in traditional environments.[34,35]

22.  Establish the self-healing operating environment by introducing tools that perform real-time event correlation on events, and then predict failures.

   As the CIB environment grew, it become more complex initially. New infrastructure mixed with old, with new applications being introduced at a prodigious rate. Failures were bound to happen as new processes were put in place to manage the dynamic infrastructure, even as the older infrastructure was maintained. Established networks were stressed and strained because they weren't designed to handle the explosive growth. Predictive tools were required that would first alert operations of upcoming problems, so that operations could have sufficient warning and make adjustments.[36,37]

---

[33]Narkier.
[34]Dealing with Technology.
[35]Waters.
[36]Walsh K. Virtualization tools balance data center loads. *TechWorld*. June 10, 2007.
[37]Waters.

### A.5.5  Sustain

23. Establish portfolio management of applications so that migrations of the business value chain can be managed and new infrastructure services can be tracked.

    CIB started this process early in the align phase where all applications by LOB were identified in terms of their business value chain metric (i.e., business functions they covered), and the products they covered. This was done to aid in the infrastructure migration plan, but it was also used to identify functional overlap and functional gaps. Portfolio management is the application of an investment discipline to all IT project decisions. It breaks siloed mentalities where only the concerns of a single project of LOBs dominate the decision-making process. CIB used this process to perform quarterly progress reviews across all LOB projects. A repository was created to capture the salient features of each application, service, and component, and the user demographics associated with them. It was used as a bottom-line assessment tool to show the business where resources were spent. Portfolio management is a key building block of the governance process that will be discussed in a later section.[38,39,40]

24. Create metrics dashboard for multistakeholder consumption so that ROI discussions about IT can be grounded in fact.

    The CIB portfolio management process needed hard numbers to assess the performance of new investments and legacy implementations. This helped guide investments for new initiatives and show how investments changed the Quality of Experience profile for key application sets. In order to do this, all performance tool outputs needed to be correlated so that trends could be shown regarding the total cost of a transaction. There were many perspectives to be captured: service level adherence, consumption by infrastructure class, chargeback projections, and so on. The purpose of the dashboard was to provide an active feedback mechanism that would augment portfolio management for executives so their strategy could be grounded in execution reality. This dashboard changed initial assumptions about priorities; in particular, the amount of upgrades to the base infrastructure that would be required was underestimated.[41,42]

25. Establish product management that will facilitate the introduction of other RTI products through an integration strategy based on established investment principles.

---

[38]SCREEN, Creating Virtualization.
[39]Wall Street Technology.
[40]Align online, Embracing Change.
[41]Waters.
[42]Tech Earns Interest at Wachovia. eWeek.com.

The reuse of design and services or components became a critical part of the CIB strategy, because there were many application types that have performance characteristics exceeding the typical COTS capabilities. Too often in CIB, specialized components could not be leveraged across other projects, LOBs, or the CIB enterprise. Product management is the discipline that ensures releases of the PEDs, and that ensembles are integrated, documented, tested, and ensured to work at certain levels of performance. Product management ensures adherence to product principles about what functionality is included and who will own the components if harvested. It is about providing an internal software vendor service for strategic choices of functionality. CIB established product strategies for the ensembles and their frameworks. CIB defined an internal product harvesting process to find and evaluate candidates to add to the service. This ensured that innovation was sustained at the infrastructure and application level.[43,44,45]

## A.5.6 Wachovia CIB experiences with IT governance

Wachovia CIB undertook multiple threads of action to restructure IT governance. The following key threads are explained.

An architecture group was reformulated to focus on enabling the design of products, aiding teams undertaking new projects, and providing objective standards that could be used to evaluate designs and systems. This architecture team set standards for component harvesting, framework design, and ensemble creation and engineering. This group also conducted strategy reviews that highlighted what services needed to be consolidated or created.

A portfolio management group was formed to facilitate the information flow between executives and asset creation staff. This group built a variety of tools that gave insight into the overall progress of the portfolio management strategy, leveraging a repository to generate monthly reports on ideal state migration and contributions to the asset base and user demographics for all applications in CIB. This group worked closely with various operations and performance measurement groups in order to build a comprehensive view of the asset base operating profiles.

A number of framework groups were created to channel investments in reusable service architectures. These groups built a client access framework, a server framework, and a mediation framework. All of these frameworks had multiple clients, harvested existing designs and programs where feasible (in addition to creating new functionality). An emphasis was placed on integrating new Fit-for-Purpose RTI technologies that would reduce cost, increase efficiency, stop data-center sprawl, and promote agility and increase throughput and performance.

---

[43]Allen P. Banks take their places on the grid. Photography by James Leynse, *Wall Street & Technology*. May 15, 2006.
[44]Walsh.
[45]Align Online.

The framework teams took direction from a technology steering committee comprised of senior members of all stakeholder groups. These members were aligned with specific LOBs and thus were able to articulate real needs. Executives were kept informed monthly of all investment. This forced a product management view of development. If the client did not ask for it or approve a feature submitted for review, no investment would be made. It created a reliable integration strategy that consistently delivered functionality in timely increments.

Quarterly strategy reviews were held by the CIO to determine progress to plan on all investment tracks. Architecture and portfolio management groups arranged the material for these reviews. These reviews fed the strategy process for the CIO and direct reports. Monthly user demographic reports were produced for all applications in all LOBs to understand changes in demand and its potential effects on the strategy. A developer university internal site was created as a repository for best practices, changes to technology, how-to guides on RTI, asset contribution, architecture reviews, and so forth. Incentives were structured from CIO directs on down to align with use of the asset base and contributions to RTI.

# Appendix B: NGDC maturity model

**Table B.1** NGDC maturity model: quality of experience

| Level | Description |
|---|---|
| Chaotic | • Enterprise cannot correlate between the three pillars of QoE (cost, user experience, and efficiency). The relationships do not exist or are largely estimated.<br>• Enterprise cannot derive costing for the majority of revenue-generating applications.<br>• Enterprise does not have a grasp on the performance of applications and how it affects user experience. |
| Rationalized | • Enterprise has an understanding of relationships between cost, user experience, and efficiency.<br>• Enterprise has taken steps in understanding all aspects of user experience and stabilized overall user experience at the expense of cost and efficiency.<br>• Enterprise has taken interim steps to stabilize user experience and developed plans to address cost and efficiency. |
| Stabilized | • Enterprise has addressed cost and efficiency in addition to user experience.<br>• Enterprise is running in a stable environment without frequent emergencies of unplanned outages.<br>• Enterprise can deal with changes within its current purview and addresses minor increases in throughput or user base without impacting the QoE balance between cost, efficiency, and user experience. |
| Optimized | • Enterprise can predict and react to standard IT demand changes quickly and rapidly without impact to cost, efficiency, or user experience.<br>• Enterprise has invested in instrumentation and is in a position to focus on the collection of information and using that information to predict and plan for changes.<br>• Enterprise concerns shift from how to implement major changes to how to simplify transition of major change.<br>• Enterprise has pervasively applied QoE. |
| Enabling | • Enterprise can predict and react to standard IT and business demand changes quickly and rapidly without impact to cost, efficiency, or user experience.<br>• Enterprise has enough information and flexibility to quickly adapt to major changes based on business demand (i.e., mergers and acquisitions, new business lines, regulatory changes) through planning and design. |

**Table B.2** NGDC maturity model: architecture

| Level | Description |
|---|---|
| Chaotic | • Architecture roles or teams do not exist or exist in an "ivory tower" context, describing what architectures should be without any understanding or emphasis on the realities of business and IT.<br>• Architectures lack documentation or are poorly documented, without any decision traceability or the reasons for those decisions.<br>• The enterprise considers architecture as too time consuming and irrelevant. |
| Rationalized | • Architecture roles or teams exist on a project-by-project basis and work in a siloed environment. An IT architect is identifiable for each project in production or in development.<br>• Some architectures and architectural decisions are documented in a manner that is traceable, including descriptions of the problem, possible solutions, and final conclusions. Occurrence is varied but encouraged and emulated. |
| Stabilized | • Architecture roles or teams exist on an LOB basis with an identifiable LOB architect. The architecture environment is a collection of silos but at the LOB layer instead of the project layer.<br>• Architecture teams have taken steps to align IT to business needs at an LOB level.<br>• Architectural gold standards in application tiers exist on an LOB level (i.e., database and application server choices). |
| Optimized | • Architecture roles and teams exist on an enterprise level. The concept of architecture is an integral part of IT strategy, with a product mentality fueling the design of shared services across LOBs that focus on maintaining or improving QoE.<br>• Contributions to architecture and the benefits of architecture are tracked across the enterprise. |
| Enabling | • Architecture teams function in an indirect model (in an "internal consultant" fashion) focused on shared services and enterprise improvements through overall architecture instead of through specific technologies and applications.<br>• Architecture teams are presented with business problems that do not have an obvious solution and work with the business in order to create solutions. |

**Table B.3** NGDC maturity model: strategy

| Level | Description |
|---|---|
| Chaotic | • IT strategy does not exist or exists but is not considered actionable, driven, or tied back to business value and business strategy.<br>• IT is viewed as a black box expense to the business due to the lack of mapping of projects to strategic initiatives. |
| Rationalized | • IT strategy exists and is considered actionable but does not tie back to business value and business strategy.<br>• Projects are mapped to strategic initiatives and visibility exists into IT expenditures.<br>• IT strategy does not reflect a holistic enterprise approach and focuses on advancing silos (i.e., grid, virtualization) without integrating all the components. |
| Stabilized | • IT strategy exists, is actionable, and ties back to business value and business strategy.<br>• Projects are mapped to strategic initiatives, and visibility exists into IT expenditures based on specific projects.<br>• IT strategy does not reflect a holistic enterprise approach and is focused on measuring progress based on silos (e.g., 40% of servers virtualized). |
| Optimized | • IT strategy includes the definition and maintenance of a service catalog for shared services.<br>• IT strategy is constantly measured and revisited in order to improve or revise components that are no longer applicable, have been completed, or reflect changes in the enterprise and/or the tech landscape.<br>• IT strategy has moved to a holistic enterprise approach and focuses on measuring progress based on overall enterprise strategy. |
| Enabling | • IT strategy is fully aligned with business strategy, and business strategies can be tied to specific IT strategies with full insight and mapping to expenditures and value added.<br>• IT strategy is regularly reviewed to ensure continual alignment with business strategy.<br>• IT is considered a strategic partner to the business, ensuring that QoE is met and is helping the business fulfill its strategy needs. |

**Table B.4** NGDC maturity model: operating model

| Level | Description |
|-------|-------------|
| Chaotic | • Operations team processes function in a reactive mode to resolve issues and problems in the environment.<br>• Enterprise has no clear understanding of pain points and has trouble determining the root cause of issues in the environment.<br>• Enterprise has a large operations and support team without much emphasis on architecture, strategy, or governance. |
| Rationalized | • Operations team processes function in a reactive mode to resolve issues and problems in the environment.<br>• Enterprise has instrumentation in place and a clear understanding of problem areas and can determine the root cause for issues in the environment.<br>• Enterprise has a large operation and support team and employs a small group of people dedicated to architecture, strategy, and governance within the operations and support teams. |
| Stabilized | • Operations team processes function in proactive and reactive modes to resolve issues and problems in the environment.<br>• Enterprise has instrumentation and monitoring in place in order to recognize issues in a more granular fashion and resolve issues prior to impact to the entire application (i.e., resolve a DB issue before application failure). A dashboard may be in place.<br>• Enterprise employs an autonomous team focused on architecture, strategy, and governance. |
| Optimized | • Operations team processes function largely in a proactive mode to preempt and diffuse problems in the environment.<br>• Enterprise has pervasively deployed instrumentation, monitoring, and dashboards throughout all environments for a complete understanding and predictive monitoring of IT environments.<br>• Enterprise employs an autonomous, large, and diversely skilled team that is focused on architecture, strategy, and governance. |
| Enabling | • Operations team processes function largely in a proactive mode in order to prepare for additional business demand.<br>• Enterprise has pervasively deployed instrumentation and business event monitoring throughout the enterprise for a complete understanding and predictive monitoring of business drivers.<br>• Enterprise employs an autonomous, large, and diversely skilled team that is focused on architecture, strategy, and governance. |

**Table B.5** NGDC maturity model: runtime execution

| Level | Description |
|---|---|
| Chaotic | • Runtime environments are in a constant state of flux due to an inability to isolate problems and are often kept running by frequent emergency-resolution calls.<br>• Applications are unable to handle current load or struggle to take on load outside the current operating range.<br>• Environments are highly fragmented and divided on an application-by-application basis, with a sense of applications owning the hardware and infrastructure on which they reside. |
| Rationalized | • Runtime environments are in a constant state of flux, with frequent emergency-resolution calls but with clear guidelines and steps to resolve issues.<br>• Applications are unable to handle current load or struggle to take on loads outside the current operating range.<br>• Environments are very fragmented and divided on an application-by-application basis, with a sense of applications owning the hardware and infrastructure on which they reside. |
| Stabilized | • Runtime environments have obtained a level of stability, leading to a sharp decrease in emergency-resolution calls.<br>• Applications are meeting SLAs and can handle fluctuations in demand that are within the defined scope.<br>• Environments are fragmented and divided on an application-by-application basis.<br>• Application teams and owners have gained a rudimentary understanding of shared infrastructure and treating hardware as a shared utility like the network. |
| Optimized | • Runtime environments are very stable and self-healing in most instances, changing repair processes from immediate failure response, to next-day servicing for low-severity failures.<br>• Applications are meeting SLAs and can handle fluctuations in demand in real time outside of the defined scope without significant impact on QoE.<br>• Environments are largely shared in a cloud computing concept, increasing stability across the board. |
| Enabling | • Runtime environments are very stable and self-healing in most instances and can quickly be reconfigured based on changes in business demand.<br>• Application changes are largely automated and fueled by business drivers and business event–monitoring data in real time.<br>• Environments are largely shared in a cloud computing concept, increasing stability across the board and enabling rapid reconfiguration based on the real-time measures of business demand. |

# Index